THE MITCHELL BEAZLEY POCKET GUIDE TO

CABERNET SAUVIGNON WINES

ROGER VOSS

MITCHELL BEAZLEY

Acknowledgments

I have received a marvellous amount of help while researching this book from wine producers around the world, from their representatives in the United Kingdom, and from the representatives of national or state wine producers' associations in London. To them all, a big thank you.

But in particular, I must mention a few generous people without whom I could never have hoped to finish this study.

For wines from Bordeaux, M. Bourdil of Ch Mouton- Rothschild; Charles Eve MW of Ch Loudenne; Christian le Sommer of Ch Latour; Yves Fourault of Ch Beychevelle; Peter Sichel of Ch Palmer.

For wines from California: Sam Folsom of the California Wine Institute in San Francisco; Gus Fertado of Fetzer Wines; Manfred Essler of Cuvaison Wines; Clarke Swanson and Chris Anstee of Swanson Vineyards; Fritz Draeger of Flora Springs.

For wines from Australia: Hazel Murphy of the Australian Wine Bureau in London; Stephen Walker of Gullin and Company, South Australia.

For wines from New Zealand: Terry Dunleavy MBE and Philip Greegan of the Wine Institute of New Zealand; Philip Atkinson of the New Zealand High Commission, London; John Hancock of Morton Estate; Rose Delegat of Delegat's Wines; Ross Spence of Matua Valley Wines; Michael Brajkovich MW of Kumeu River Wines; Bob Campbell MW of the Wine Academy, Auckland.

For South Africa: Peter Devereux, journalist; Norma and Stan Ratcliffe of Warwick Estate; Sally Simson of the Bergkelder; Gyles and Barbara Webb of Thelema Mountain Vineyard; Simon Barlow of Rustenberg; Beyers Truter of Kanonkop; John Platter, author and wine producer.

The Mitchell Beazley Pocket Guide to Cabernet Sauvignon Wines
Edited and designed by Mitchell Beazley International Limited,
Artists House, 14–15 Manette Street, London W1V 5LB

ISBN 0 85533 860 1

The author and publishers will be grateful for any information that will assist them in keeping future editions up to date. Although all reasonable care has been taken in the preparation of this book, neither the publishers nor the author can accept any liability for any consequences arising from the use thereof or from the information contained therein.

Editor	Naomi Good
Assistant Editor	Alessandra Perotto
Art Editor	Gaye Allen
Production	Barbara Hind
Map	Taurus Graphics
Co-ordinating Editor	Alison Franks
Managing Editor	Chris Foulkes
Senior Art Editor	Nigel O'Gorman

Typeset in Novarese by Servis Filmsetting Ltd., Manchester, England
Produced by Mandarin Offset
Printed and bound in Malaysia.

Contents

Introduction 4
History 5
Cabernet Sauvignon and food 11
Cabernet Sauvignon acreage around the world 12
Cabernet Sauvignon in the vineyard 14
Cabernet Sauvignon in the winery 19
Chart busting Cabernets 23
The Wine Directory 26
Bordeaux 26
Other French Cabernets 71
California 75
Washington State 100
Australia 103
New Zealand 123
Chile 132
South Africa 137
Italy 146
Spain 153
Portugal 155
Bulgaria 156
Other countries 157
Index 158

Foreword

This book is the study of a grape as it is grown and turned into wine around the world. It is arranged in two sections: the first a general survey of the history of the Cabernet from its earliest recorded days, how it is treated in the vineyard and in the winery, and what styles of wine it makes. The second section is a directory of the best producers of Cabernet, or of Cabernet-blend wines in each area of the world in which it is planted. Each directory section is preceded by a short introduction to that country or wine region.

Cabernet producers in the directory section are rated, according to the general quality of the wine they produce. I should emphasize that the rating is based on Cabernets alone: some producers with low ratings in this book make star wines from other grape varieties – and vice versa. The rating system works as follows:

* Below average quality   *** Good in their class
** Average quality   **** Supreme examples
→ Represents finer gradations within this framework.

I have referred in the text to the following books: Charles Albert Arnoux: *La Vigne, Voyage autour des Vins de France*. Paris, Plon, 1878; Michael Cooper: *The Wines and Vineyards of New Zealand*. Auckland, Hodder & Stoughton, 1984; Hugh Johnson: *The Story of Wine*. London, Mitchell Beazley, 1989; André Jullien: *Topographie de Tous Les Vignobles Connus*. Paris, 1816; James Laube: *California's Great Cabernets*. San Francisco, Wine Spectator Press, 1989; Robert Parker: *Bordeaux, the Definitive Guide to the wines of Bordeaux*. London, Dorling Kindersley, 1986; Jan Read: *Chilean Wines*. London, Sotheby's Publications, 1988; Jancis Robinson: *Vines, Grapes and Wines*. London, Mitchell Beazley, 1986; Olivier de Serres: *Théâtre d'Agriculture*. Paris, 1804 edition

Introduction

The Cabernet Sauvignon is not the world's most widely planted red-wine grape variety; that honour belongs to the Carignan. But in terms of the sheer quality of the wine it produces virtually wherever it is planted, it is quite simply the best.

Before further upsetting the supporters of Pinot Noir, that other contender for top place, let me explain. In its home in Burgundy Pinot Noir produces wines as fine as any that come from the home of Cabernet Sauvignon in Bordeaux. It can produce great wines in other parts of the world but it cannot be relied on to do so, whereas Cabernet Sauvignon performs with effortless ease; it makes fine red wines, whether it is planted in hot climate Australia, cool climate New Zealand, or somewhere in between in Napa Valley, California.

Does that explain the popularity of the Cabernet Sauvignon as the most sought after red-wine grape variety in the world? Only partly. The favourite of a wine producer – a vine that causes few problems, and which, given certain simple conditions, can be relied upon to make good wine almost every year – is not necessarily the favourite of the consumer. That Cabernet Sauvignon is the favourite of both producer and consumer is a matter of taste and of history.

In its role as principal grape variety in the world's most familiar red wine – claret or red Bordeaux – the Cabernet Sauvignon was familiar to wine producers long before varietal labelling brought it before a wider public; it was known as the principal component of Lafite, Latour, Margaux, and the other great Bordeaux châteaux.

Where better for New World wine producers to go than to Bordeaux for the model of a great red wine? And what better grape than Cabernet Sauvignon? Merlot, the other Bordeaux choice, was less familiar then because its home ground, St-Emilion and Pomerol, was less well known than the Médoc and Graves.

For the world public Bordeaux was also a much more familiar model than its obvious rival, Burgundy. Sheer quantities of wine (large in Bordeaux, small in Burgundy) saw to that, as did the dominance of British tastes in the way the world viewed fine wines even after World War II.

This is where taste comes in. Claret, the British name for red Bordeaux, has long been regarded as the epitome of great red wine. Historically Bordeaux was the source of England's red wines from the Middle Ages when the English flag flew over Aquitaine. In the 19th century claret dominated the British red-wine drinking consciousness in a way that Burgundy never did. To this day, when vintages are discussed by wine connoisseurs, it is in terms of Bordeaux that they speak, rarely of Burgundy.

So, to the British at least, great red wine was claret; and claret from the Médoc and the Graves at that. That attitude influenced producers in the newer English-speaking wine countries – Australia, California, later New Zealand. The world had become firmly used to the taste of claret, and that taste was dominated by Cabernet Sauvignon.

What is that taste? The vine is hard wooded, very resilient, producing clusters of tiny berries, with a high proportion of pip and skin to flesh. The wines it produces are, therefore, naturally tannic (from the pips and skins) and deep coloured (from the skins). Tasted young they are almost undrinkable, very mouth-puckering, with considerable acidity. Sometimes the words "green" or "stalky" are used for Cabernet wines from cooler climates. The most predominant fruit character is the taste of cassis or blackcurrant.

Given this very intense set of tastes, and with the addition of wood flavours from the oak-ageing with which the Cabernet is usually associated, it is small wonder that great Cabernet Sauvignon wines, particularly in Bordeaux, need years – decades – in which to reach maturity.

It is also small wonder that in the home of Cabernet Sauvignon no wines are actually made solely from that grape. Every claret is a blend, with, in the Médoc and the Graves, anything from 60 to 80 percent of Cabernet Sauvignon, but always with the addition of other varieties such as Merlot, Cabernet Franc, Malbec, Petit Verdot. In these cool climate vineyards, affected by the ocean, the Cabernet is just too tough, too hard by itself.

It is something of a puzzle that outside Bordeaux, the Cabernet Sauvignon has so often been used almost alone. While claret may have been the role model for the New World reds, the copyists seem to have left out the element of blending. Certainly, the warmer conditions mean greater ripeness and softness for the Cabernet, but it still seems to give its best as a major component in a blend, rather than entirely by itself. Look, for example, at the Cabernet/Shiraz blends of Australia – so much better, I would argue, than most Australian 100 percent Cabernet wines.

That this lesson is now being learnt is evident from a new generation of great Bordeaux-style blends coming out of New World vineyards. In these the harsh and sometimes bitter tannins of Cabernet Sauvignon and its very dry taste are softened by the juiciness of the Merlot, or the raspberry fruit flavours of the Cabernet Franc. However, in these blends it is always the Cabernet Sauvignon which provides the backbone, the structure of the wine, its ability to age, and its class and elegance. These are the characteristics that have made Cabernet Sauvignon supreme among red-wine grapes.

History

The Cabernet Sauvignon is a mystery vine. You might think that, as the source of so many famous wines, its origins would be carefully documented. Instead, like virtually all vine varieties, it was used in winemaking long before there was any systematic naming of specific varieties in vineyards. Growers just had a number of vines in their area and planted them because they had certain known qualities.

But even allowing for this lack of documentation, Cabernet Sauvignon seems to have been a late arrival in the role of top quality black-grape variety in the Bordeaux vineyards. It seems to have sprung into prominence within a very few years. In his *Topographie de Tous les Vignobles Connus* (1816), André Jullien lists the black-grape varieties harvested in the Gironde departement around Bordeaux as "Muscat Noir, Malaga Noir, Malaga Gris, Grande and Petite Vidure, Carmenet, Carmanère, Malbek (sic), Gros and Petit Verdot, Petouille, Alicante, Mancin, Balouzat, Tarnex, Cioutai, Chasselas".

The three major varieties that now dominate Bordeaux, Merlot,

Cabernet Franc and Cabernet Sauvignon, are not mentioned – at least by those names. However, there is pleasantly learned discussion about the origin of at least one set of names in that list. For the start of that discussion we have to go back to the sixteenth century, to Olivier de Serres and his *Théâtre d'Agriculture*. In the notes to the edition of that work published in 1804, there is talk of a grape variety called Beruieres, or Biturica. According to the editor of that edition, it was a name given by a Roman geographer, Columella, to a vine variety grown in Aquitaine, and recorded by Pliny. It is not an impossible leap from Biturica to the variety which Jullien calls Vidure. That name was taken to describe the toughness of its wood. Cabernet Sauvignon has hard wood, and, the speculation follows, it is possible that this was the original name of the Cabernet. According to Jancis Robinson in *Vines, Grapes and Wines*, the Cabernet is still called Vidure in parts of the Graves in Bordeaux, so the link is there, if a little tenuous.

Even if the Vidure is the Cabernet, we are still left with the name change during the first half of the nineteenth century, and with the addition of the name Sauvignon, and its links with the white Sauvignon grape.

In *The Story of Wine*, Hugh Johnson postulates that the Carmenet variety, mentioned by Jullien as growing in the Médoc, is another name for the Vidure and hence the Cabernet Sauvignon. It sounds logical until you read Jullien's description of the wines the Carmenet produces: "the Carmenet and the Carmanère give lightly-coloured wines, delicate, light, with a pleasing taste and full of aromas." That lightness, especially of colour, hardly accords with what we know of the Cabernet Sauvignon.

The link with the Sauvignon is easier. The word itself means grassy, as in the sense of green tasting. Anybody who has tasted wines from either the Sauvignon Blanc or the Cabernet Sauvignon will know that they can produce, especially in cooler climates, wines which are essentially green, even mean, lacking the rounded voluptuousness of, say, Pinot Noir and Chardonnay. The rapport in taste is hardly surprising: they both come from the same sub-species of vine. The connection with Cabernet Franc is also relatively straightforward. In fact, until well into the nineteenth century, the two vines were known as the Petit Cabernet (the Cabernet Sauvignon) and the Gros Cabernet (Cabernet Franc), in reference to the size of the grape bunches, and possibly also the yields. If we accept the link with the Vidure, it is not difficult to see that the Petite Vidure mentioned by Jullien is the Cabernet Sauvignon, while the Grande Vidure is the Cabernet Franc.

If we return to Jullien's survey of the Bordeaux vineyards early in the nineteenth century, we get to the section on what he calls Le Palus, but which we now call Entre-deux-Mers. And here it seems – certainly at the beginning of the nineteenth century – is where the Vidure vine came into its own.

It appears that the wines from Entre-deux-Mers were used to give body to the lighter wines then being made in the Médoc. As Jullien writes: "the top quality wines of the Palus and the Côtes [what is now the Premières Côtes de Bordeaux on the north bank of the Garonne] are often used to give weight to the wines from the Médoc." This may have been the reason why the Cabernet migrated across the river to the Graves and up to the Médoc.

Certainly it seems that the work of Baron Hector de Branne in developing the estates of the Médoc in the late eighteenth century brought about a change in taste and greatly increased the search for quality. It is, after all, surprising to learn that until almost the end of the eighteenth century the wines of the Médoc were a random blend of black and white grapes, were low in alcohol, and of varying quality. It is small wonder that beefier wines from Entre-deux-Mers, brimming with Vidure, were needed to bolster the wines for the export market, particularly for the English, used as they were to the big red wines and ports from Portugal. *Le travail anglais* it was called, and the process of blending wines from across the Bordelais region became the work of a growing class of wine merchants in Bordeaux rather than of the estate owners.

It was the appearance on the scene of the first named managers of the big estates of the Médoc at the time of the Revolution which spearheaded the rapid development of the Médoc into an exclusively red-wine producing area, and the planting of Cabernet Sauvignon.

Why the Cabernet Sauvignon never achieved total dominance in Bordeaux is an inevitable mix of historical accident and practicality. As a late arrival, it was taking its place among many varieties, all of which were able to bring some quality to the final wines. Few growers were able to afford – or were prepared – to replant all their vineyards with Cabernet, and so it prospered alongside the other established varieties. With true French pragmatism the Bordelais also reckoned that, with their somewhat marginal climate, they should hedge their bets against damage to a particular variety in any year. That this caution is necessary even today is illustrated by the 1984 vintage when the Merlot failed to flower.

By the time the Cabernet Sauvignon began to come into its own in Bordeaux, the vineyards were entering their first golden age. From the Restoration in 1815 until the arrival of phylloxera in the late 1870s, the Bordeaux vineyard reached its greatest extent. Most of the expansion was in the relatively ''new'' area of the Médoc, now becoming the land of the Cabernet Sauvignon. On the right bank of the Gironde, the vineyards of St-Emilion and Pomerol were still comparatively neglected.

Despite its acknowledged qualities though, the Cabernet Sauvignon was still slow to spread out of a fairly tight circle of top estates in the Médoc and Graves. On the right bank of the Gironde, in St-Emilion and Pomerol and even in its home territory of Entre-deux-Mers, it was firmly in second or even third place behind Merlot and Cabernet Franc. The reasons are not hard to find. St-Emilion and Pomerol have slightly harsher and longer winters than the Médoc, while the heavier soils are less conducive to Cabernet Sauvignon than to Merlot; but I suspect that the real reason why the Cabernet was slow to take off was its low yield. The French farmer has always aimed for quantity as well as quality: with Cabernet Sauvignon he found the quality, with Merlot he found both.

Even today, Cabernet Sauvignon occupies only half the area of Merlot in Bordeaux. Its increase has been rapid over a very short period of time, and has taken place against a background of decline and neglect in the Bordeaux vineyard throughout much of the early part of the twentieth century . In the latter part of the nineteenth century the twin disasters of oidium and phylloxera devastated much of the vineyard, and for nearly twenty years, from the 1870s to the 1890s, total production was well down. Equally devastating was drastic economic decline in the first half of the twentieth century, coupled with two World Wars which, by 1945, had left the vineyards in a state of disrepair. It is the replanting since then, and especially in the late 1950s and 1960s, that has brought about the rapid increase in area of Cabernet Sauvignon in Bordeaux.

THE CABERNET TRAVELS

By this time the Cabernet Sauvignon was well settled abroad. Like the white Chardonnay of Burgundy, the Cabernet has proved a most successful and intrepid voyager.

It has probably helped that, like Chardonnay, the Cabernet Sauvignon is a very flexible variety. It suffers from few diseases, it ripens reliably and regularly, it seems relatively unaffected by the climate. In addition, it commands high prices. Which comes first – the high prices, or the quality of the wines – is difficult to determine. But lurking behind its popularity outside France is the all-important model of the great Bordeaux estates, Lafite, Margaux, Latour, Mouton. Until very recently growers in California or Australia were always making comparisons with the French wines. Now that they have gained greater confidence, they still like to taste their own against Bordeaux wines, even if only to point up the differences.

California In his book *California's Great Cabernets* James Laube says that a native of Bordeaux named Jean-Louis Vignes made his first wine in 1837 in the unlikely area of Los Angeles. But gradually it was realized that further north would produce better conditions for Cabernet; so the next major series of plantings, in the 1850s, by Charles Le Franc, another Bordelais, were in the Santa Clara Valley; and by the 1860s in southern Sonoma, with the plantings at Buena Vista by that rogue and visionary, the Hungarian Count Agoston Haraszthy.

Early California Cabernets went by the name of clarets, and were modelled as closely as possible on the Bordeaux model. It is most likely, therefore, that these early Cabernet-based wines were in fact blends much as the French originals. They certainly travelled back to the Old World to win numerous prizes at wine shows and exhibitions; and, again according to Laube, they aged well, with wines of the 1890s tasting good in the 1980s.

The curse of Prohibition put a temporary stop to all development in the California wine industry. From 1919 to 1933 only wines for sacramental purposes and grapes for home winemaking could be produced. By 1933 there was little Cabernet Sauvignon left in the vineyards. Demand anyway was for cheap, sweet wines, and not for the serious, dry red styles. But a few wineries, such as Charles Krug, Louis Martini, Inglenook, Beringer and Beaulieu made some top-rate Cabernets in the late 1940s, many of which are still showing extraordinary freshness and life.

The real expansion in Cabernet plantings began in the late 1950s. Ridge Vineyards in the Santa Cruz mountains was one of the earliest, but it was soon followed by two other great names in California Cabernet – Robert Mondavi and Joe Heitz.

By the 1970s, the floor and sides of the Napa Valley became carpeted with Cabernet and it spread widely in Sonoma Valley, Alexander Valley, and Dry Creek Valley. Smaller plantings took place further south in Monterey, but the surprisingly cool climate of that county has, on the whole, militated against widespread Cabernet plantings.

The northwest states of Oregon and Washington received their Cabernets at about the time of the great California plantings. On the whole, despite being further north, Washington has had more success with Cabernet, while Oregon has shown greater aptitude with the cooler climate varieties such as Pinot Noir and Chardonnay.

Australia Australia was another early entrant in the Cabernet stakes. It is quite possible that cuttings of Cabernet Sauvignon were among the vines thoughtfully included by Captain Arthur Phillip in the cargo inventory of the First Fleet, although it is much more likely that those vines came from the Cape and Brazil rather than from France. However, Cabernet was almost certainly planted in the early part of the nineteenth century by those other pioneers John Macarthur and James Busby. Moving inland from Sydney, neither found the ideal conditions for Cabernet. Busby, who discovered the Hunter Valley as a viticultural area, was not slow to realize that the region was better suited to Shiraz and, strangely, to Pinot Noir and Chardonnay, than to Cabernet.

The Cabernet came into its own further south with the development of vineyards in South Australia, Victoria and Tasmania. While the most famous plantings around Adelaide were of southern French varieties like Grenache and Shiraz at, for instance, Dr Penfold's vineyard at The Grange, Cabernet was being planted further north in Clare and the Barossa Valley and further south in Coonawarra and the Southern Vales, where Château Reynella now stands on one of the very first South Australian vineyard sites.

Victoria was slower to receive Cabernet, simply because the first major vineyard plantings were in the cool Yarra Valley east of Melbourne, which was then considered more suitable for white wines. However, the establishment in 1860 of Château Tahbilk on the Goulburn River, north of Melbourne, found an ideal site for strong, full-flavoured Cabernets, still produced there to this day.

Plantings of Cabernet also took place in 1888 and 1889 as part of the great irrigation scheme on the Murray River.

But while small plantings of Cabernet were taking place, it was only after World War II, with the growth of the table-wine industry, that Cabernet Sauvignon took a major place in Australian viticulture. Now it is planted in every vineyard region, and for many vignerons produces their best wines.

New Zealand The Cabernet is as old as viticulture itself in New Zealand. The first vines brought by that Australian pioneer, James Busby, when he was transferred to New Zealand as Resident, included Cabernet. By the late nineteenth century it was well regarded by the small wine industry, then centred just north of Auckland. But, like Australia, New Zealand turned to making cheap wine and fortified wines, and Cabernet did not fit the bill. Plantings all but disappeared, and did not begin again until the 1970s. Now it is the most widely planted red-wine variety in New Zealand, constituting around 10 percent of the total vineyard.

Chile The Cabernet arrived in Chile in 1851, as part of the radical reorganization of the vineyards begun by a French oenologist, M. Bertrand, under the auspices of Silvestre Ochagavia Errazuriz, a wealthy landowner, whose name survives today in one of the country's bodegas. The idea was to replace the ubiquitous Pais (the grape that went to California as the Mission) with some noble European varieties.

It was lucky that this development took place when it did. Twenty years later, because of phylloxera the only vines available for export would have been grafted on American rootstocks. As it was, the plants that reached Chile from France were the original, ungrafted pre-phylloxera vines.

Chile is lucky that phylloxera has never reached it – the only major wineproducing country in the world of which this is true. The geographical isolation of Chile probably helped prevent the arrival of the beetle. In Chile we find descendants of the original Cabernet from France, still planted on its original rootstocks.

Cabernet is now by far the most important noble red variety in Chile, covering 12 percent of the vineyard area.

South Africa The Cabernet Sauvignon was introduced into South Africa probably at the turn of the century. By the 1920s it was recognized as an important producer of quality wines. Interestingly, it was often blended with Cinsaut, although nowadays it is more often seen with the other Bordeaux varieties, Merlot and Cabernet Franc.

Major quality producer though it may be, it still accounts for only 2.5 percent of South African vineyard plantings, probably because much of the vineyard area is too hot for successful Cabernet production. Most plantings are in the southern Stellenbosch area.

Rest of Europe Two European countries outside France now account for large-scale plantings of Cabernet – one is Italy, the other Bulgaria.

In typical Italian fashion, there has been and still is immense confusion in the vineyards between Cabernet Sauvignon and Cabernet Franc. Wines are indeterminately labelled just "Cabernet". In practice, much of the wine so labelled is Cabernet Franc, which is far more widely spread than Cabernet Sauvignon, especially in the northeast of the country, in Friuli and the Veneto.

The history of Cabernet Sauvignon in Italy, however, is actually more exact than it is in France. In *Vines Grapes and Wines*, Jancis Robinson records how it was introduced into Piedmont in vineyards owned by the Count of Sambuy near Alessandria in 1820. Although it never took off in the Italian northwest (due to the major influence of the Nebbiolo and Barbaresco grapes in that region), it became widespread in the northeast where it began to take a major part in the wines of Friuli.

Over the Apennines, in Tuscany, Cabernet was already established by the middle of the nineteenth century. Once Barone Ricasoli had perfected the recipe for Chianti in the 1840s and 1850s, there was instant tinkering with the formula. More serious wine producers took to adding 10-15 percent of Cabernet or Malbec to the Sangiovese, to enable the wines to age better.

Certainly today while the bulk of wines made from Cabernet (of whatever sort) comes from Italy's northeastern regions or from the Alto Adige, the most exciting innovations have taken place in Tuscany and more recently in Piedmont. In Tuscany, besides continuing the tradition of adding Cabernet to make Chianti, a new generation of super-wines such as Sassicaia and Tignanello has been made with 100 percent Cabernet: and the same thing has happened in Piedmont. While a resurgence of Italian vinous pride has prevented Cabernet Sauvignon replacing the traditional varieties, the grape still has an important place in lending an extra element of ageability to the local varieties.

Unlike Italy, the Bulgarian experience with Cabernet Sauvignon is both more recent and planned. The development of the wine industry after World War II as a means of gaining exports and hard currency is well known; and the success of Bulgarian Cabernet Sauvignon – by 1989 the biggest-selling red wine in the UK market – is a matter of record.

But the fact that the first Cabernet was not planted until 1962 is less well known. Its subsequent spread through nearly all the Bulgarian wineproducing regions has been as rapid as it has been successful and, while not wholly replacing the local varieties, it has certainly come to dominate them in reputation as well as quantity with its phenomenal growth.

In other European countries, Cabernet has moved more slowly, and more recently. Its only major success has been Spain, where it forms the base for some of the top Penedés red wines from a handful of bodegas.

Cabernet and food

The generally accepted rule is that Cabernet wines are best with red meat. While this is broadly true, there are other occasions when a Cabernet-based wine would make an excellent partner. It is certainly worth exploring the less obvious combinations.

	Light and fruity Cabernet	Elegant Bordeaux style wine	Australian Cabernet/Shiraz wines and Rich Californians
Soups and Starters	Smoked ham Salamis Corn on the cob Snails	Meat pate Ham Soup	
Fish and Shellfish	Paella Poached salmon		
Poultry, Meat, and Game	Cold meats Roast rabbit Roast chicken	Plain roasts Beef Wellington Kidney and liver Plain steak Roast game	Boeuf Bourgignon Rich stews Moussaka Tandoori dishes Steak with sauce Coq au Vin Game pie Dishes with peppers Meat barbecues
Cheeses		Mild hard cheese Dolcelatte Goat's cheese Roquefort	Camembert

World-wide distribution of Cabernet Sauvignon vineyards

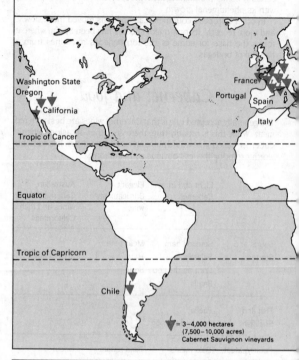

Washington State
Oregon
California
France
Portugal
Spain
Italy
Tropic of Cancer
Equator
Tropic of Capricorn
Chile

= 3–4,000 hectares
(7,500–10,000 acres)
Cabernet Sauvignon vineyards

Areas under Cabernet Sauvignon in major

		hectares	acres
France	1979:	22,962	56,740
Italy	1982:	1,540	3,805
California	1979:	6,735	16,643
Washington State	1979:	184	455
Australia	1980:	4,089	10,000
New Zealand	1980:	290	717
Chile	1980:	5,257	12,990
South Africa	1979:	2,786	6,884
Bulgaria	1979:	1,843	4,554

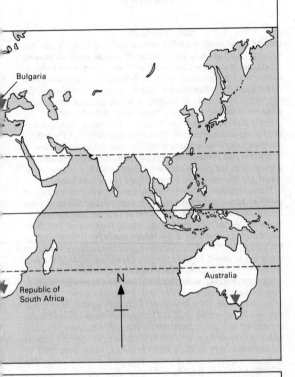

producing countries			* estimate
	hectares	acres	% increase
1988:	36,468	90,114	58.8
1989:	4,500	11,120	192
1988:	10,667	26,359	58.4
1989:	412	1,018	123.9
1988:	3,622	8,950	− 11.4
1989:	351	867	21
1985:	8,000*	19,768	52
1989:	2,928	7,235	5.1
1989:	2,792	6,899	51

Cabernet Sauvignon in the Vineyard

SOIL AND CLIMATE

Like its great white travelling companion, the Chardonnay, the Cabernet Sauvignon is very tolerant of a wide range of growing conditions. It seems to be equally at home in the Napa Valley in California, Hawke's Bay in New Zealand, or Coonawarra in Australia, as it is in Bordeaux, France. It seems to be able to adapt to different climatic and soil conditions, and to produce wines that – while never tasting the same – have equal intrinsic quality.

Yet in its home vineyard of Bordeaux it is seen as having a very precise set of requirements. It likes the gravelly soil of the Médoc and the Graves – the left bank of the Gironde – to the heavier clays of St-Emilion and Pomerol on the right bank. It is said to prefer the slightly more temperate climate of the left bank – nearer to the ocean – to the marginally cooler climate of the right bank.

The importance of the relationship between a high percentage of gravel in the soil and the quality of the wine was borne in on me very forcibly by a tasting organized for me at Château Loudenne at St-Yzans de Médoc. For their lesser wines, they buy in fruit from neighbouring communes in the Médoc *appellation*. This far north in the Médoc (apart from the outcrop of gravel in Loudenne itself), the soil is low in gravel, high in clay. Just a few miles south, the gravel increases as you approach the village of St-Estèphe.

We compared two wines, both 100 percent Cabernet Sauvignon, from the same vintage – 1989 – and from grapes grown only a few miles apart. One, from the estate of Loudenne itself, from gravel soil, was full of colour, fruit and tannin, very deep, potentially the constituent of a great claret from a fine year. The other, from the village of Couqueques, with soil heavy in clay, fermented in exactly the same way, was so much lighter in colour, much more rustic to taste, having much less tannin: altogether a lesser wine. The influence of the soil leapt from the glass.

Of course, soil is not the only influence on a fine wine. The great châteaux of the Médoc have old vines with low yields, employ rigorous selection when making their top wine, and spend millions of francs on equipment and new wooden barrels. But they could not – and would not – do this without first having the potential from the raw material in the vineyard. That is why the extensive gravel banks stretching all the way down the left bank of the Gironde from St-Estèphe, and which go beyond the city of Bordeaux into the Graves, are the sites of the finest Cabernet Sauvignon wines.

Why should this gravel soil be so important? Drainage is the principal reason. Few vines like their roots in too much water: the Cabernet is particularly demanding in this respect. The gravel soil allows the water to drain quickly and easily. In aspect, also, the gravel ridge which contains the best Médoc vineyards contains useful slopes, which again improve drainage.

Good drainage limits the yield of the vine. High water content in the soil can, given the right climatic conditions, increase the yield of the vines. High yields, in turn, can mean a diminution in the quality of the wine. It is no coincidence that the best estates in Bordeaux limit their yields well below the officially permitted figures.

Finally, good drainage reduces the risk of damp-associated diseases, such as mildew, which are common in Bordeaux and to which Cabernet Sauvignon is prone. You have only to remember that the commonest chemical used against mildew – copper sulphate – is also known as Bordeaux Mixture, to realize what a problem this fungus has been in Bordeaux.

The climate in Bordeaux is heavily influenced by the ocean. The spring is earlier than in the interior of France – for example, Burgundy – and the heat of the summer is normally tempered by the cooling influence of the water. The growing season is longer, extending into October, and this suits the Cabernet Sauvignon which is notorious as a late-ripening variety.

Being near to the ocean, the risk of serious frost is low compared with Burgundy. However, for the same reason, the incidence of wet springs is high. For the Merlot, an early flowering vine, this is a serious problem, and is the regular cause of *coulure*, the dropping of the blossom during flowering. The Cabernet Sauvignon, flowering later, rarely experiences the same problems.

Despite being quite far south in France, Bordeaux is still a comparatively marginal red-wine area. The example of the neighbouring Charentes region, home of the thin white-wine base of Cognac, shows that the influence of the ocean, tempered though it is by the Gulf Stream, does hold summer temperatures down.

In terms of climate, the nearest comparable viticultural areas around the world are Coonawarra in Australia, southern and central Napa and Sonoma in California, Hawke's Bay in New Zealand, and the central vineyards of Chile. All, it seems, are influenced in one way or another by the ocean. All are sources for the best Cabernet Sauvignon wines outside Bordeaux.

For many, Coonawarra is without question the best place to grow Cabernet in Australia. Its minty, eucalypt flavours stand out for their elegance in any tasting of Australian Cabernets. Here, as in the gravel vineyards of Bordeaux, the soil is the key. The famous red loam soil, the terra rossa, a strip 15km (9 miles) long and about 1.5km (1 mile) wide is now seen as the best land for growing Cabernet. It is well drained – shades of Bordeaux – and the high water table (important in dry Australia) means that irrigation is natural rather than artificial. Climatically, although only at 37 degrees south (compared with Bordeaux' 45 degrees north), the weather is cooled by the cold southern seas less than 100 km (62 miles) away. The long, not too hot, often cloudy, growing season (again back to Bordeaux) allows the Cabernet Sauvignon to makes its leisurely way to ripeness.

While world-class Cabernet Sauvignon is only just emerging from New Zealand, it is now recognized that one of the best sources of top-quality fruit is Hawke's Bay on the east coast of North Island, the home of estates like Te Mata, Vidal, Esk Valley, and many of the Auckland wineries buy their fruit from here. The city of Napier, the main town of the region, has sunshine hours and temperatures similar to Bordeaux. The margins of the coastal Heretaunga Plain are the home of many of the best vineyards: and here the alluvial soil is mixed with well-drained shingle and gravel. Further inland, new plantings west of Fernhill, are on gravel terraces by the beds of the rivers Tuki Tuki and Ngaruroro.

Crossing the Pacific Ocean to California, we arrive in Napa. The stretch of vineyards on the western side of the valley between Oakville and St Helena, the so-called Rutherford Bench, is seen as a major source of top-quality Cabernet Sauvignon. From here comes the fruit for the great Heitz wines, Martha's Vineyard and Bella Oaks, for the great Cabernets from Robert Mondavi, Inglenook and Beaulieu. And here also is the Cabernet Sauvignon for the American-French collaboration, Opus One.

The central vineyards of Chile, north and south of Santiago, produce the vast majority of the country's red wines. The Maipo Valley, south of Santiago, is regarded as the best for Cabernet Sauvignon. Although in latitude terms (at 35 degrees south) this is Mediterranean country, the cooling effect of the Humboldt current in the Pacific Ocean to the west, and the Andes to the east combine to keep temperatures down. The best soil has good drainage from small stones which combine with limestone and clay. Many vineyards indeed are in the alluvial sands along the river banks.

YIELDS

It is generally agreed that too high yields from vines lead to a general diminution in the quality of the wine. Small quantities of fruit can concentrate the energy of the vine into the production of sugar – and later ripeness and alcohol.

For many vines, controlling yields is a problem. They naturally want to give more and more fruit, unless firmly restrained by the vigneron. Not so the Cabernet Sauvignon. It yields meanly and sparingly. While that may be good for quality, for many growers who are after high quantities, it represents a pretty poor deal.

In French *appellation contrôlée* laws, the yields are laid down in great detail, even though there is considerable flexibility in amounts between different years, different *appellations* in Bordeaux and different vineyards within those *appellations*. The permitted yields are always pitched at a higher level in the right bank, Merlot and Cabernet Franc vineyards, than in the left bank, Cabernet Sauvignon estates – a recognition both of the higher quantities produced by the first two vines, and also the smaller overall production of each estate.

Yields from the Cabernet Sauvignon are similarly comparatively low in other parts of the world. In Australia, for example, it is by far the lowest yielding of all the major grape varieties planted. Even in Italy, where it is often confused with Cabernet Franc, it is recognized as a low-yielding variety – a probable explanation for the much greater spread of the Cabernet Franc except in very special estates such as Sassicaia in Tuscany.

As a partial compensation for its low yields, the Cabernet Sauvignon is a highly reliable vine variety. It has few tantrums and few diseases which seriously affect its regular cropping.

DISEASES

In Bordeaux the most serious problems that affect Cabernet Sauvignon are fungal in origin. Oidium, which first appeared in 1852, attacks the young wood on the vine, the young leaves and unripe grapes, leaving whitish spots which dry up the young shoots and fruit. A disaster at the time, it is now easily controlled using traditional sulphur sprays or more modern chemicals. The other main fungal problem is mildew, which is endemic in the Médoc and Graves and to which Cabernet Sauvignon is especially prone. However, regular spraying with the blue copper sulphate Bordeaux Mixture is quite sufficient to keep the mildew under control.

Grey rot is also prevalent in Bordeaux. In fact, in another guise –

MITCHELL BEAZLEY
PUBLISHERS OF FINE BOOKS ON WINE

As a wine lover, you can help us to create new and interesting books on wine by answering the questions on this card. Simply fill in the details below (block letters please) and post the reply-paid card back to Mitchell Beazley.

In return, we will send you a handy **MITCHELL BEAZLEY WAITER'S FRIEND** comprising a corkscrew, foil cutter and bottle opener.

Offer closes 31st August 1991
(One gift per household)

Title of this book...

Was it a gift? Yes/No....................................

Do you own any of the following books?

Please tick where appropriate

THE STORY OF WINE ☐

VINTAGE TIMECHARTS ☐

THE WORLD ATLAS OF WINE ☐

UNDERSTANDING WINE ☐

HUGH JOHNSON'S POCKET WINE BOOK
1990 ☐   '89 ☐   '88 ☐

WEBSTER'S WINE PRICE GUIDE
1990 ☐   '89 ☐   '88 ☐

Other wine books..
....
....

Are there any other wine book subjects that would interest you?..
....
....
....

Name...

Address..
....
.........................Postcode............................

BUSINESS REPLY SERVICE
Licence No WD 4234

Caroline Proud
MITCHELL BEAZLEY LONDON LTD.
Artists House
14-15 Manette Street
LONDON
W1E 6QZ

as noble rot – it is positively welcomed in Sauternes. But when it attacks the Cabernet Sauvignon, as it can do when the pre-harvest weather in September is wet and humid, it is a menace, and necessitates spraying, always a problem in itself so near to harvest time.

A new problem in Bordeaux is eutypiose. This is a fungal disease which attacks the vine where it has been pruned, spreading through the wood and into the trunk of the vine. It is becoming a serious problem in the region, where it is estimated that three to four percent of Cabernet Sauvignon vines are now dying each year. At present, with no known cure, the only advice that is being offered to vignerons in southwest France (where it is particularly prevalent because it likes wet conditions) is to prune when it is dry, to disinfect secateurs, to seal up the wound in the vine, and to burn all prunings.

In drier areas, such as most of Australia, and in California, Chile, and South Africa, these particular fungal problems are much less relevant. Also, most of these diseases – apart from the newly-recognized eutypiose – are absolutely controllable.

THE GROWING SEASON

The growing season for the Cabernet Sauvignon is long and starts late. While, in Bordeaux, the Merlot may start flowering at the end of May, the Cabernet will start at least two weeks later. This gives it an advantage over the Merlot because it is more likely to miss any late spring frosts. Also, unlike the Merlot, it is resistant to *coulure*, the failure of the flowers to develop.

Late flowering also means late ripening. While, in most years, this ensures a long ripening season, and therefore greater flavours in the fruit, in some poor years it can actually mean problems in ripening the fruit at all. This was true in Bordeaux in 1988, where a cool, dry summer meant that the Cabernet did not really ripen until the end of October. In parts of New Zealand, in Oregon, even in parts of California such as Monterey, underripe green Cabernet wines are a perpetual problem. On the other hand, with its leisurely ripening and thick skins, the Cabernet Sauvignon can cope well with sudden weather problems.

GROWING FOR QUALITY

During its growing season, the Cabernet Sauvignon needs less in the way of quality management than many other varieties. Research at the University of Calfornia Davis has shown, however, that, like most vines, Cabernet Sauvignon fruit can suffer if it is too well shaded during the ripening season. Too many leaves shading the fruit from the sun will reduce the size of the berries, reduce the sugar and raise the acidity. The research also found that the shading of one bunch by another bunch could affect the colour in the skins of the grapes, and consequently the colour of the wine.

New techniques to give the ripening bunches just the right exposure to the sun have been developed. Canopy management has been systemized in New Zealand, by an Australian agriculturalist, Dr Richard Smart. New Zealand, even more than Bordeaux, experiences the problems of luxuriant growth in its vines, due to the moist, humid climate and rainfall well into the ripening season. This technique involves training the vines to ensure maximum exposure, and spacing the rows of vines so that one row does not shade another too much. It also means that instead of wasting its resources on producing leaves and new growth, a vine can concentrate on ripening the fruit.

The relatively moderate vigour of the Cabernet Sauvignon vine means that control of leaf growth is easier than it is with very vigorous varieties such as Chardonnay.

The standard trellising in the Médoc and Graves is known as the Guyot method, and consists of three wires running between upright posts. The rows are normally one metre (3.3 feet) apart, and the vines will also be planted one metre apart. This gives a density of 10,000 vines per hectare (2.5 acres) in the Médoc and Graves. Two branches from the vine are trained on to the lowest wire, with two or three buds on either side of the main root. During the season, these buds will produce the shoots which will be trained on to the upper wires.

There are variations on this system even in Bordeaux. Some growers, in lesser *appellations*, are planting to take advantage of mechanical harvesting, with widely spaced rows, more buds per vine and high training to allow more bunches to develop. While officially frowned upon, it has spread in areas like Entre-deux-Mers.

Another system, found experimentally in the Premières Côtes de Bordeaux, is to train the vine on wires which viewed from the end of the row look like a "U" or a lyre. This divides the growth of the vine, and allows air and sun to get down into the middle of the plant. It is also used in New World countries, such as New Zealand.

There has also been research on trellising in California at the Robert Mondavi Winery. The standard Napa Valley trellis, a high-trained two-wire system, is planted 3.7 metres (12 feet) between rows to allow for mechanical harvesting. The Mondavi experiment has created a modified "U" or lyre system, by dividing the vine on three crossbeams, again to allow the sun to get into the centre of the plant.

The equation that any viticulturalist has to face today – certainly in New World vineyards where mechanization is more and more important as labour costs rise – is that wider spacing to allow machines between the vines also reduces the yield per hectare. Therefore there is pressure to push up yields to compensate.

HARVESTING

In Bordeaux Cabernet Sauvignon is normally picked in early to mid October, while in California and Italy it is picked at the beginning of October. In the southern hemisphere, Cabernet is picked in most of Australia during March, but in cooler areas like Coonawarra and Margaret River, harvesting will go into April; the same applies in Chile, but in South Africa the hotter conditions mean an early March harvest. In cool New Zealand, the harvest for Cabernet starts in mid-April and can run into early May.

Its thick skin and relative toughness as a grape mean that Cabernet Sauvignon is easy to harvest mechanically. However, many estates, especially those producing premium wines, set great store by the virtues of hand picking, despite often horrendous labour costs. I find the difference in taste negligible.

CLONAL SELECTION

Clonal selection is the buzz word in the wine industry of the 1990s. Clones of particular vines are developed for a variety of reasons: to get rid of endemic diseases, to increase yields, and to improve quality. However, compared with the two Burgundian grapes, Pinot Noir and Chardonnay, relatively little work has been done on different clones of Cabernet Sauvignon.

The most significant work was started in Bordeaux in 1989. The five premier cru châteaux of the Médoc and Graves, along with two estates in St-Emilion (Ch Cheval Blanc and Ausone) and one in Pomerol (Ch Petrus) are cooperating on field research in Cabernet Sauvignon, Cabernet Franc and Merlot clones, with the University of Bordeaux.

These eight estates have decided to rationalize the clones they plant. There are 50 different possible clones, most with particular advantages and disadvantages (although one clone, compulsorily recommended during the 1960s, proved a disaster). These châteaux have been allocated five clones of each variety. Each estate is concentrating on a different set of clones. The aim is to strike a balance between the health of the vine and the quality of the fruit.

Although this experiment has only just started, one of the participants, Château Haut-Brion began clonal experiments in its vineyard as long ago as 1977, with the first wines being made in 1981. They used specially selected plants from INRA, the official French agricultural research body. But, to give some idea of the length of time these experiments take in Bordeaux, they are still waiting for the first test wines to reach full maturity before they can decide on which clones are most suitable.

A shorter experiment in Victoria, Australia, compared clones developed in France, in Australia and in California, and, over six years, managed to isolate four clones which could be planted to give reasonable yields and remain virus free. It was however significant that the highest-yielding clone also produced the grapes with the lowest sugar content, further proof, if it was needed, that high yields do not necessarily go with ripe grapes.

Cabernet Sauvignon in the Winery

The revolution in winemaking has had much less of an impact on red wines than on whites. The risks of oxidation, the need for careful extraction of the juice from the grapes, and the general delicacy of the juice, all problems with white wines, are hardly present with red wines. It is still possible – as is still done in parts of Portugal, for example – to tread the red grapes by foot and yet make fine wine.

Of course, technology has affected the way red wines are produced. Stainless steel fermenting tanks can now be found even in some of the first-growth châteaux of Bordeaux – Haut-Brion and Latour, both of which introduced stainless steel in the 1970s, much to the shock and horror of their competitors. Stainless steel gives the same advantages to producing Cabernet Sauvignon wines as it does to any white wine: the control of the fermentation temperature, the complete exclusion of air (which means less need for sulphur), the ease with which the equipment can be cleaned.

As with white wines, you have to go to the New World to see high technology really in action in red-wine making. At Wirra Wirra Wines in the Southern Vales in South Australia, in a gesture worthy of modern architecture, the winery is designed so that all the services are on the outside – for easy cleaning; and, like many other Australian wineries, they use Potter fermenters, designed to extract maximum colour by gently rotating the grape must. While all the fermentation takes place in modern conditions behind the old winery building, inside there is an instant slowing of pace as it matures in barrels; for Cabernet Sauvignon wines, the instant slowing down of tempo once the wine is made is essential.

Of all wines, Cabernet Sauvignon needs ageing – in barrel and in bottle. While great clarets are the longest-lived table wines, any Cabernet Sauvignon-based wine can expect to live a good, useful life, and mature to a lively old age. The reason is the high tannin content, derived from the fact that the skins themselves are tough and the grapes are small.

The considerable quantity of tannin in a Cabernet Sauvignon grape is one reason why it is normally found in Bordeaux as the main constituent in a blended wine, rather than as the sole variety in a 100 percent wine. However, the thick skins of the grape do mean that colour extraction is much less of a problem with Cabernet Sauvignon than it is with some other red-wine grape varieties.

THE BORDEAUX WAY

The traditional treatment of the grapes is still widely carried out in Bordeaux. The grapes arrive at the cellars normally in small buckets to avoid damage from undue weight of fruit. Their stalks are then removed, the skins gently broken, and they are transferred into fermentation vats. In Bordeaux, many of even the top châteaux still use wooden vats, either freestanding as at Château Lafite, or set into a two-level room, so that it is possible to empty the grapes into the top and remove the juice from the bottom.

As the fermentation progresses, the skins and pips of the grapes rise to the top of the vat, threatening to form a solid, hard cap. This would have the effect of slowing down the fermentation and restricting the amount of colour and tannin which can be taken from the grape skins. To avoid this, the traditional practice is to pump juice from the bottom of the vat on to the top of the cap, a procedure known as *remontage*.

It is also at this point that the grape must may be encouraged to produce a little extra alcohol by the addition of some sugar. It is not widely known that wines in Bordeaux are often given a lift by the addition of sugar which turns into alcohol during fermentation. It is a process known as chaptalization, after Jean-Antoine Chaptal, noted chemist and one of Napoleon's Ministers, and it is more often associated with wicked practices in Burgundy. It was not permitted in Bordeaux until 1938, after a run of spectacularly bad vintages, and – unlike Burgundy – is not allowed every year, although it has, since 1962, been used more often than not. The aim with chaptalization in Bordeaux is to raise the alcohol level by 1 to 1.5 degrees, in years such as, most recently, 1987 in which the grapes are particularly underripe.

Temperature control during fermentation is much more difficult with wooden vats than it is with more modern stainless steel. However, the top Bordeaux châteaux keep a watchful eye on the fermentation, taking constant temperature readings. While the normal fermentation temperature is between 28° and 30° C (82° and 86° F), some of the finest Bordeaux estates – Mouton-Rothschild for example – push the temperature right up to 34° C (93° F), just below the point at which the heat is too much for fermentation to continue. They do this, they say, in order to extract as much colour as possible from the skins.

Fermentation by this traditional method runs for about one week. However, in order to extract further colour and tannin, the skins are left in the vats in the top estates for another two weeks or so (depending on the year, the quality of the fruit and the château). In lesser estates, a rapid heating of the must for a few hours is used to give more colour without the extra tannin.

The naturally high acidity of Cabernet Sauvignon grapes in Bordeaux means that a second fermentation, known as the malolactic fermentation, is necessary. This converts the sharp malic acid into softer lactic acid. While it can be done in the large vats, the normal practice is to rack the wine off the skins (by pumping it out of the vats leaving the solid matter behind), and transfer it into *barriques*. These are 225-litre (49.5 gallons) wooden barrels in which the wine will mature. Even in hot years in Bordeaux, when the grapes are very ripe, malolactic is encouraged to start straight after the first, alcoholic, fermentation: normally it starts by itself, but if the weather is cold, the cellars will be heated to encourage it to start.

The wine is then left in the *barriques* for maturing. Normally, the wine will be transferred from its first barrels after a year into another set of barrels. This is done for a number of reasons: if the first-year barrels are of new wood, it may be felt that more than one year's contact with new wood is too much for the wine, so older barrels will be used for second-year wine. It is also used to clean up the wine, removing any solid matter left from the malolactic fermentation, and generally ensure that it is clean. It will also be done so that for example, the same cellar is always devoted to first-year wines.

Wooden barrels were once used simply as containers which, by virtue of their age, gave very little character to the wines. Now, with the almost universal use of new or one-year-old barrels for some part of the maturing process, the wine can easily take on too much wood taste; so the tendency is to bottle early, after a traditional filtration using egg whites, and to continue the maturing of the wine for another few months in bottle, before it is labelled and released for sale.

THE NEW WAY

To call it a ''new way'' is perhaps a misnomer, because, apart from the use of stainless steel, there is a much greater convergence of methods in making red wines between the traditionalists and the modernists, than there is with white wines. Stainless steel fermentation tanks are used, but it is equally possible to see open fermentation tanks, cement tanks, wooden vats, anywhere in the world.

There is also general agreement that red wines need relatively high fermentation temperatures. Few producers ferment red wines under 20° C (68° F), while that is normally considered a maximum for white wines. During fermentation, the traditional techniques of preventing the cap from drying out – pumping the juice over, plunging by ramming down the cap into the fermenting must, or submerging the cap by means of a grid placed in the vat – are all used.

In some countries – Australia is the best example – a system known as autovinification is used. The wine ferments in a stainless steel tank which acts rather like a coffee percolator, pumping the fermenting must over the cap simply by the pressure of carbon dioxide in the closed vessel. Known in Australia as Potter fermenters, these can extract maximum colour in the shortest time, and thus avoid excessive tannins from the Cabernet Sauvignon grapes. With another system, called rotofermentation, used in California as well as Australia, the must is placed in a horizontal tank which rotates at given intervals, thus mixing the skins and pips into the fermenting wine: again this system extracts colour quickly.

After the first fermentation, it is quite common in New World countries to drain the wine off the skins, and then to press the skins, adding the extracted juice back into the wine. This increases colour and extract in the wine.

CABERNET AND WOOD

There are Cabernet Sauvignon wines made in stainless steel or cement tanks which never see the inside of wooden barrels. These are the ones made to be drunk young, light in colour and extract. But with these few exceptions, virtually all Cabernet Sauvignon goes into wood for maturing.

The wine from the Cabernet Sauvignon has a great affinity to wood. The taste of wood seems to enhance the quality of the wine, giving it complexity, richness, and, above all, a long life. The wine benefits from the gentle oxidation that a barrel gives, combining wood tannins with the fruit tannins that are natural to the grape.

Where the idea of using quantities of new barrels each year came from, is difficult to pinpoint exactly. Go to Bordeaux, and they will tell you that with increased income in the 1970s and since, they were able to afford the huge investment in new wood, and then the idea spread to California. Go to California, and you will be told that the idea of using new wood was developed there, and then spread back to France. All of which means that a new generation of wine producers decided simultaneously to experiment with the effect of new wood on Cabernet Sauvignon wines.

Nowadays, no top producer will be seen dead without some new barrels in the cellar. Not only that, but for Cabernet Sauvignon wines, they will almost certainly be using the Bordeaux-sized 225-litre (49.5 gallons) casks. In the high flying estates, they may use 100 percent new wood for first-year maturing, but the proportion will vary according to the income of that estate, and how well the wine itself can take the very strong tastes of new wood.

Since a new barrel can now cost anything up to £400, careful research has to go into what sort of wood it should be made from. Round the world it seems French oak is the preferred wood for Cabernet Sauvignon over its rival American oak. It is considered that American oak gives rather too obvious tastes, while French oak gives greater subtlety – and also costs more.

Once the decision has fallen to France, the winemaker has next to decide on which type of French oak to use. There are five main oak-forest areas in France, all with definite differences in style of wood and hence taste: Limousin, Allier, Nevers, Tronçais and Vosges.

Limousin is the nearest forest to Bordeaux, and although it is found in Bordeaux cellars, its strong-flavoured wood is considered too much for table wines, and is more often found in the maturing of Cognac in the nearby Charentes. Nevers, a finer-grained wood, has been the traditional choice in Bordeaux. But Allier, with its dense, close grained texture, which gives up its flavour slowly, is increasingly popular. In other Cabernet Sauvignon vineyards, a combination of Nevers, Limousin, and, more recently, Allier are all used. The modern wine producer then has to decide on how he wants his new barrels toasted by the coopers. Barrels in France are still made in the traditional way, over a fire, and the skilled coopers can vary the length of time the heat chars the inside of the barrel – from a matter of a few minutes just to give time for the wood to bend, to up to 45 minutes for heavily charred, or toasted, barrels.

The very idea of calling for a particular toast would seem ludicrous to producers of a generation ago. Even today, if you talk to some Bordelais, they will sneer at the concept as a new-fangled, New World idea. Certainly some of the pioneering work was done in California in the Robert Mondavi Winery in Napa Valley: here they found that lightly-toasted barrels were more suitable for Cabernet Sauvignon, while heavier toasts were better for Chardonnay and Pinot Noir. But, in fact, less than two years after these experiments, the most famous Bordeaux cooper, Demptos, was carrying out just the same experiments with the same results.

The degree of toasting in the barrels and the percentage of new barrels will determine how long a Cabernet Sauvignon wine is aged in wood. The top Bordelais châteaux seem to age their wines longer than most Cabernet Sauvignon producers. This probably relates to the fact that red Bordeaux is designed for very long ageing in bottle. Long barrel-ageing needs longer bottle-maturation to restore the balance of the wine. Most New World producers are making wines which can be drunk sooner. In Australia and in California the extra ripeness of the grapes (compared with Bordeaux) means that the very direct fruit flavours can be spoilt by too much barrel-ageing.

Whatever the length of time in barrel, a Cabernet Sauvignon wine will normally have a period of time – a few months or even a year – in bottle in the producer's cellars before it is released. This brings the wine back to balance after wood-ageing and bottling, and gives it a start on the longest period in a great Cabernet Sauvignon's life – bottle-maturation.

The Chart Busting Cabernets

While researching this book, I have tasted innumerable Cabernets from round the world, some great, some highly enjoyable, some which I would prefer to forget. As I tasted, I decided to work out a league table to try and place them in some kind of order. The results are in the lists below. They are not to be taken as tablets of stone: for a start they are my personal taste, and everybody with an interest in wine has different tastes, and, equally to the point, one producer's terrific wine one year maybe the same producer's disaster next year. So read the lists and see if you agree – or disagree.

The 20 Greatest Cabernets in the World

These are the finest wines that I have tasted while researching this book and which are from vintages currently available, or at least still accessible. The order is alphabetical, by producer, within country.

Australia

Cape Mentelle 1988, Margaret River, Western Australia
Lindemans St George 1985,

Coonawarra, South Australia
Ch Tahbilk 1985, Goulburn, Victoria

France – Bordeaux
Cos d'Estournel 1985,
  St-Estèphe
Ch Gruaud-Larose 1989,
  St-Julien
Ch la Gurgue 1989, Margaux
Ch Lafite-Rothschild 1986,
  Pauillac
Ch Lynch-Bages 1986, Pauillac
Ch Margaux 1986, Margaux
Ch Mouton-Rothschild 1989,
  Pauillac

France – other
Mas de Daumas Gassac 1982,
  Vin de Pays de l'Hérault

Italy
Sammarco 1985, Castello dei
  Rampolla, Tuscany

New Zealand
Stonyridge Larose 1987,
  Waiheke Island
Vidal Cabernet Sauvignon 1987,
  Hawkes Bay

Spain
Gran Coronas Black Label Mas
  la Plana 1983, Torres, Penedés

USA – California
Carmenet Vineyard 1985,
  Sonoma
Diamond Creek Red Rock
  Terrace 1985, Napa
Heitz Martha's Vineyard 1985,
  Napa
Joseph Phelps Insignia 1986,
  Napa
Ridge Vineyards Monte Bello
  1985, Santa Clara

The 20 Most Famous Cabernets in the World

Here are the Cabernets that have made the greatest waves, hit the
most headlines. Some are the same as in the list of the greatest. I
have not included vintages: the wine's name is important here.

Australia
Cape Mentelle, Margaret River,
  Western Australia

France – Bordeaux
Ch Haut-Brion, Pessac-Léognan
Ch Lafite-Rothschild, Pauillac
Ch Latour, Pauillac
Ch Léoville-las-Cases, St-Julien
Ch Margaux, Margaux
Ch Mouton-Rothschild, Pauillac
Ch Palmer, Margaux
Ch Pichon-Longueville Comtesse
  de Lalande, Pauillac

Italy
Sassicaia, Marchese Incisa della
  Rochetta, Tuscany

New Zealand
Te Mata Coleraine, Hawkes Bay

Spain
Gran Coronas Black Label Mas
  la Plana, Torres, Penedés

USA – California
Beaulieu Vineyards, Georges de
  Latour Private Reserve, Napa
Caymus Special Selection, Napa
John Daniel Society, Dominus,
  Napa
Heitz Cellars, Martha's Vineyard,
  Napa
Robert Mondavi Reserve, Napa
Opus One, Napa
Ridge Vineyards, Monte Bello,
  Napa
Stag's Leap Wine Cellars, Cask
  23, Santa Clara

The 20 Top Old World Cabernet Producers

These are the producers who seem, consistently, to be able to make
fine Cabernets of world-class standard.

France – Bordeaux
Cos d'Estournel, St-Estèphe
Domaine de Chevalier,
  Pessac-Léognan
Ch Ducru-Beaucaillou, St-Julien
Ch Gruaud-Larose, St-Julien
Ch Haut-Brion, Pessac-Léognan

Ch Lafite-Rothschild, Pauillac
Ch la Lagune, Haut-Médoc
Ch Latour, Pauillac
Ch Léoville-Barton, St-Julien
Ch Léoville-las-Cases, St-Julien
Ch Lynch-Bages, Pauillac

Ch Margaux, Margaux
Ch La Mission-Haut-Brion, Pessac-Léognan
Ch Montrose, St-Estèphe
Ch Mouton-Rothschild, Pauillac
Ch Palmer, Margaux
Ch Pichon-Longueville Comtesse de Lalande, Pauillac

France – other
Mas de Daumas Gassac, Vin de Pays de l'Hérault

Italy
Marchese Incisa della Rochetta (Sassicaia), Tuscany
Castello dei Rampolla (Sammarco), Tuscany

The 20 Top New World Cabernet Producers

Again, this list is based on current track record.

Australia
Cape Mentelle, Margaret River, Western Australia
Leeuwin Estate, Margaret River, Western Australia
Lindemans, South Australia
Orlando, South Australia

New Zealand
Villa Maria, Auckland, North Island
Vidal, Hawkes Bay, North Island

South Africa
Kanonkop, Stellenbosch
Warwick Estate, Stellenbosch

USA – California
Beaulieu Vineyards, Napa
Carmenet Vineyard, Sonoma
Caymus Vineyard, Napa
Diamond Creek Vineyards, Napa
Heitz Wine Cellars, Napa
Mayacamas Vineyards, Napa
Robert Mondavi Winery, Napa
Opus One, Napa
Joseph Phelps Vineyards, Napa
Ridge Vineyards, Santa Clara
Stags Leap Wine Cellars, Napa

USA – Washington State
Columbia Winery

The 20 Best Value Cabernets

This is the hard one. The list below is different from all the rest – many of the names are different: the greatest wines don't come cheap, nor do their producers normally underestimate the price they can charge. But some producers manage to balance the magic equation of quality and value with at least one of their wines.

Australia
Brown Brothers Koombahla, Victoria
Orlando St Hugo, Coonawarra, South Australia
Penfolds Bin 707, South Australia

Bulgaria
Svishtov Cabernet Sauvignon

Chile
Concha y Toro, Casillero del Diablo
Santa Rita, Medalla Real

France – Bordeaux
Ch Fonbadet, Pauillac
Ch Gruaud-Larose, St-Julien
Ch Haut-Bages-Averous, Pauillac (2nd wine of Ch Lynch- Bages)
Ch Labégorce-Zédé, Margaux
Ch Larose-Trintaudon, Haut-Médoc
Ch Léoville-Barton, St-Julien
Ch la Louvière, Pessac-Léognan
Ch Tronquoy-Lalande, St-Estèphe

South Africa
Backsberg, Klein Babylonstoren
Delheim Cabernet Sauvignon

USA – California
The Christian Brothers Napa Valley Cabernet, Napa
Fetzer, Barrel Select, Mendocino
Inglenook Napa Valley Cabernet, Napa
Robert Mondavi Woodbridge Winery, Napa

THE WINE DIRECTORY

Bordeaux

The cult of the Cabernet comes from Bordeaux. Here the grape is the principal constituent of some of the world's greatest red wines; and it is this model which has inspired its use around the world. In California, Australia, South Africa, producers wished initially to make a wine that was like red Bordeaux – claret, the British call it. The name claret was used on a thousand bottles that had never seen a Cabernet Sauvignon grape, let alone Bordeaux: but the emotive effect of the name was enough.

Bordeaux is described as the largest quality wineproducing area in the world. This means that, under European law, it produces more wine that has quality status (that is, recognized as meeting the requirements of the French *appellation contrôlée* system) than anywhere else. Real quality, though, is in the mouth of the wine drinker not the pen of the lawyer, and there is plenty of so-called quality wine in Bordeaux that is pretty mediocre stuff.

But among the vast quantity of wine produced in the Bordeaux region (6,500 million bottles of red wine in 1989, for example), there is also a far greater quantity of good quality wine than from any other wine region in France. And, as a contrast with Burgundy, where top wines may be made only in hundreds of bottles, many of the finest wines are made in tens of thousands of bottles.

The role of the Cabernet Sauvignon in Bordeaux wine production is crucial, but surprisingly limited. It is not by any means the most widely planted grape in Bordeaux – that description goes to Merlot. Nor are there any 100 percent Cabernet Sauvignon wines in Bordeaux, whereas there are some which are 100 percent Merlot. In some parts of the Bordeaux vineyard, it is virtually non-existent. So why should it have been Cabernet Sauvignon, rather than Merlot, which inspired the Bordeaux look-alikes round the world?

I believe it was partly a question of timing. At the time when quality wines were beginning to emerge from California and Australia, the great Merlot-based wines of Pomerol and the Cabernet Franc wines of St-Emilion were relatively unknown. But Ch Lafite, Ch Latour, the great Cabernet Sauvignon wines, were known and recognized round the world. They had to be the role models, because they were the only ones that were available.

That, of course, is not the only reason. Cabernet Sauvignon is a pretty hardy, adaptable grape variety. In Bordeaux, though, the Cabernet seems at its most finicky. It takes centre stage in the Médoc and in the Graves, the western side of the region. But across to the east, in St-Emilion and Pomerol and associated villages, it gets only a minor walk-on part. It seems happy in areas of the wine world where Merlot just does not flourish. So if there was a choice the decision was bound to go in favour of Cabernet.

Soil and climate are partial explanations, as we shall see under the section on vineyards. But there is also the question of tradition, a matter of great importance in France.

Tradition is important in other ways in Bordeaux. The greatest tradition of them all is the arranging of wines in categories. The classification of the wines of the Médoc in 1855, which created five tiers of "growths", from the top first-growth level down to the fifth, has been, apart from one adjustment in 1973, the most important reference point in Bordeaux for 140 years. The fact that it was originally based on the price the wines fetched, not necessarily their quality, has been conveniently overlooked. Châteaux on the list lead a relatively charmed existence, however their winemaking quality may have slipped. Those outside, while often making better wine, have to fight hard to claim their rightful place in terms of both quality and price. Any attempts to change the classification are met with such fierce resistance that they are abandoned – the only change (the promotion of Ch Mouton-Rothschild from second to first-growth) took nearly 50 years of hard pressure to achieve.

The classification in the Médoc has spawned a veritable industry in Bordeaux. There are classifications in St-Emilion, in Sauternes, in the Graves, and of the *crus bourgeois* of the Médoc. Apart from the Sauternes classification, which was also arranged in 1855, the other listings at least have the merit of being based on quality and of being, officially at least, changeable. Indeed, the most recent reclassification in St-Emilion actually had the temerity to demote a wine and promote others.

From the point of view of the directory of producers which follows, the two classifications which matter (apart from the 1855 Médoc classification) are the Graves and the *crus bourgeois*.

The Graves classification was simple. Those châteaux that were recognized by the French national appellation body, INAO, as having a good track record, were given *cru classé* status. The range of quality in the wines included was enormous – from Haut-Brion at one end to a tiny 4ha (10 acre) vineyard at the other. Today all those Graves *crus classés* are actually in a new *appellation* of Pessac-Léognan, but still retain their Graves status.

The listing of *crus bourgeois* was originally compiled in 1920, but was revised in 1978 simply because many estates had disappeared while others had improved in quality and status over the years. *Crus bourgeois* are regarded as the next best thing to the 1855 classed growths – in theory some *crus bourgeois* should move into the league of classed growths, while some classed growths should move down.

There are three categories of *crus bourgeois*. The basic level is Cru Bourgeois, which must come from a property with at least 7ha (17 acres) of vineyard and must be made at the property. There are 68 of these. A number of estates which had been classified as Cru Bourgeois before 1978 decided not to be involved in the new listing. These now describe themselves as Cru Bourgeois Superieur.

The next category is Cru Grand Bourgeois. In addition to the rules for the basic category the wines must be matured in oak. There are 41. The top category is Cru Grand Bourgeois Exceptionnel. All the other conditions apply, and in addition the wine must be made in a commune of the Haut-Médoc, and must be château-bottled. There are 18.

All this information is listed in the directory which follows. However, all that will appear on the wine label is the phrase "Cru Bourgeois". The European Commission does not recognize the other terms, and its labelling regulations forbid their use.

Another term which appears in the directory is "second wine". A château's second wine is useful both for the producer and for the consumer. For the producer it is a way of utilizing wines that are not quite good enough to go into the château's first wine, or is from vines that are still too young. For the consumer, it gives a foretaste of the first wine without requiring a loan from the bank manager.

There is of course the *appellation* itself. There are three major *appellations* in the area under study: Médoc, Haut-Médoc and Graves. There are also more tightly restricted village *appellations*, which recognize the particular qualities of certain villages within the Haut-Médoc and Graves. In the Haut-Médoc, those villages are: St-Estèphe, Pauillac, St-Julien, Margaux, Moulis and Listrac. In the Graves there is one village *appellation* of Pessac-Léognan.

THE CABERNET VINEYARD

The home of the Cabernet in Bordeaux is the wider region of the Médoc and the Graves. The reasons for this lie in the soil and in the climate. While all the Bordeaux region has the well-drained soil essential for good wine production, there is a distinct division between two soil types that corresponds with the predominance of either Cabernet Sauvignon or Merlot.

Both the Médoc and the Graves vineyards are based upon ridges of gravel soil that rise and fall in low lying hillocks in the Médoc and in small ridges in the Graves. A vineyard with a high proportion of gravel is likely to have a high proportion of Cabernet. You can almost work out the soil type of a given vineyard by seeing how much Cabernet is planted.

While the gravel soil predominates in many parts of the Médoc and Graves, it is also mingled with the other soil type of Bordeaux – a clay which dominates St-Emilion and Pomerol, and which also occurs in parts of the Médoc. The northern Médoc is mainly clay soil, with localized outcroppings of gravel. This is a region with no classed growths and a preponderance of lesser (though often very enjoyable) wines with a high percentage of Merlot. The southern Médoc – called the Haut-Médoc – is mainly gravel soils, and it is here that all the great wines are produced.

The Graves, as its name suggests, is mainly gravel. But again there is a division. The northern Graves, under the Pessac-Léognan *appellation* is more gravelly than the south, and it is in the north that the Cabernet Sauvignon-dominated wines are produced. In the southern Graves, with more sand and clay in the soil, it is the Merlot which takes over, although never as completely as in Pomerol.

Elsewhere in the Bordeaux region, Cabernet Sauvignon takes second place to Merlot. In St-Emilion it only rarely (as at Ch Figeac) reaches 35 percent of the total vineyard – the normal figure varies between 10 and 25 percent. In Pomerol it is never more than 20 percent, and sometimes is completely absent. In the smaller *appellations* it can vary from 10 to 30 percent.

The size of the Bordeaux region (148 km (92 miles) from northwest to southeast) means that there are considerable climatic variations. As a general rule, the regions of the Médoc and the Graves, which are closer to the Atlantic Ocean but protected from the full force of the sea by the pine forest of Les Landes, have a more temperate climate than the more inland areas of St-Emilion and Pomerol. Spring arrives a little earlier, and there is a longer growing season in the Médoc and Graves which is essential for the late-ripening Cabernet Sauvignon.

Climatic conditions are very important to the Bordeaux vintage. Where Cabernet is concerned, the vines need a ripening season that can extend into October, with a dry September and early October to allow the grapes to attain maximum ripeness. The succession of memorable vintages in the 1980s should not obscure the fact that two years – 84 and 87 – were of lesser quality because of the weather. However, disasters on a massive scale can now be avoided both by the use of chemical sprays in the vineyard and modern technology in the cellar.

MAKING CABERNET

As with any great wine, the quantity of grapes on a vine is a factor in the quality. Too high yields can lead to a dilution of the quality. With low-yielding Cabernet, this is less of a problem than with the abundant Merlot, but conscientious producers will still cut out bunches of grapes during the growing season if there appears to be too plentiful a potential harvest.

More recently, the top estates have made a strict selection of grapes before they reach the *chai* or cellar. Any doubtful bunches are eliminated before they can contaminate or affect the wine must in any way.

Traditional methods run alongside high technology in the Bordeaux *chai*. One château may be using the most modern high-tech equipment, while next door the producer may still be using wooden fermentation vats. It is not just a question of money: Ch Mouton-Rothschild uses wooden vats, while Ch Latour uses stainless steel. Both do it because they believe it is right for their wines.

While most estates ferment the Cabernet grapes (which are normally completely destemmed to reduce the natural tannins) at a temperature around 25° C to 30° C (77-86° F), a few châteaux go higher in order to obtain maximum colour and tannin from the skins. Doing this involves risks and constant attention to prevent the wine going over 35° C (95° F), at which point the fermentation sticks and acetic bacteria can turn it into vinegar.

After fermentation, every Bordeaux château puts its wines through the malolactic fermentation; the natural acidity of Cabernet would otherwise produce wines which have a strongly grassy, tart and stalky quality, which producers wish to avoid. In most years, the malolactic starts and stops naturally, occasionally in cooler years (the last time was 87) it has to be assisted by inoculating the wine to convert the malic, to the softer lactic, acid.

In the early spring after the vintage, the château will make up its blend from the different lots of wine. At this point it will determine the final percentage of different grape varieties in that year's wine, and will decide which wines are to be included in the Grand Vin, the first wine, and which are to be made into a second wine or sold off to a merchant house.

Wooden *barriques* of 225 litres (49.5 gallons) are widely used in Bordeaux for maturing the wine. Until 15 years ago these barrels were simply containers. They were generally old, and imparted no taste of wood to the wine, although their gentle oxidizing effect was beneficial. Today there is a greater awareness of the taste quality of new wood in Bordeaux. Allier is generally regarded as the best wood for maturing wines. Most châteaux use a percentage of new wood every year: a few top estates which have rich enough fruit use 100 percent new wood for the first year of maturation. As the *régisseur* at a leading château told me: "the use of new wood has not necessarily made the wines better, but it has made them different, with greater complexity."

With the greater use of new wood, the time a wine spends in barrel has been shortened. While most wines might have spent two years to 30 months in barrel, now it can be as little as 12 months, with 18 months as an average, except in the top growths. This allows more fruit tastes in the wine, less oxidation and dryness.

Before bottling, the wines are fined, traditionally with egg whites (the preferred choice of top estates), or in a more modern way with bentonite and gelatin. Filtering is also done at some châteaux to make the wine clear, but there is argument about whether this also strips some taste from the wine.

Bottling of all the classed growths and the *crus bourgeois* now takes place at the châteaux. It may take place in a travelling bottling line (a large van that turns up for the day) or it may take place on a permanent bottling line. This is a new development: until well into the 1970s, some of these châteaux were still having their wine bottled by merchants in Bordeaux. Now the words "mise en bouteille au château" are an essential phrase on a label.

After bottling, the wine is stored for a few months before release. And then, for most red Bordeaux, there comes the waiting – for the wine to mature slowly into the superb products that have spurred the emulation of the rest of the wine world.

Since this is a study of Cabernet Sauvignon, and not just of Bordeaux, I have restricted the directory to good producers in the region whose vineyard and wine contains more than 50 percent Cabernet Sauvignon. That is why it is confined to the Médoc and the Graves, and why some châteaux even in those two areas are conspicuous by their absence.

Médoc AC

The northernmost *appellation* in Bordeaux, the Médoc, was until recently almost ignored apart from a few outposts, such as Ch Loudenne. It is far from the main centres of Bordeaux, it is still divided among many landowners, only a few of whom actually bottle their own wine, and it is where the gravel soil, the magic ingredient in great Cabernet Sauvignon wines of the left bank of the Gironde, finally runs out.

However, there are a few outcrops of gravel soil, and these produce the best Cabernet Sauvignon-based wines of the *appellation*. Elsewhere, on the heavier, clay soils, the Merlot predominates for the only time on the left bank. Some excellent estates, such as Ch La Tour-St-Bonnet, are excluded from this guide for that reason.

The style of wines from the Médoc *appellation* is light in colour and in body. They are not, on the whole, wines for long ageing. This style is emphasized by a greater reliance on tank or stainless steel fermentation and less use of new wood for ageing. The producers aim rather to emphasize the fruity nature of the wines.

PRODUCERS

CH BLAIGNAN　　　　　　　　　　　　　　　　　　　　　　*→
33340 *Lesparre-Médoc*

Appellation and classification: Médoc, Cru Bourgeois
Total v'yds owned: 55ha (136 acres)

Owned by the merchant house of Mestrezat, Ch Blaignan was formerly known as Ch Taffard-de-Blaignan. Its vineyards sit at a high point in the commune of Blaignan. The wines are never very exciting: an 83 (tasted in 1988) showed rather green, high acid tastes, with a dominance of Merlot rather than the greater intensity of Cabernet.

CH LA CARDONNE →**

Blaignan, 33340 Lesparre-Médoc

Appellation and classification: Médoc, Cru Grand Bourgeois
Total v'yds owned: 85ha (210 acres)
Cabernet area: 61ha (151 acres)
Average production: 420,000 bottle.

Now owned by the Domaines Rothschild, part of the same group as Ch Lafite-Rothschild, Ch la Cardonne is the largest in Blaignan. The vineyard is on the highest point of the commune, and has been extensively replanted. Cabernet forms 72 percent of the normal blend. The wine is vinified in large vats rather than small wood to maintain its essential fruit nature. A wine like the 85 Cardonne, was drinkable by 89, and offered a pleasantly fruity wine, with some tannin, but essentially a smooth, supple taste.

CH DU CASTÉRA →**

St-Germain-d'Esteuil, 33340 Lesparre-Médoc

Appellation and classification: Médoc, Cru Bourgeois
Total v'yds owned: 45ha (111 acres)
Cabernet area: 23ha (57 acres)
Average production: 180,000 bottles

One of the oldest buildings in the Médoc, the tower of which dates back to the Middle Ages. More recently, it has belonged to the négociant firm of Alexis Lichine, who have modernized the *chai* and enlarged the vineyard. The wines have undergone a similar change, from rather clumsy wines of the 1970s to more vibrant, juicy wines, which benefit from some wood ageing. They are soft and fruity, the 86 (tasted in 1990) showing very forward fruit, some mellowness and ripeness, and are ready to drink.

CH LA CLARE *→

Bégadan, 33340 Lesparre-Médoc

Appellation and classification: Médoc, Cru Bourgeois
Total v'yds owned: 20ha (49 acres)
Cabernet area: 12ha (30 acres)

Owner Paul de Rozières has a vineyard on the gravel outcrop at By, which is planted with 60 percent Cabernet Sauvignon, 30 percent Merlot and 10 percent Cabernet Franc. Wines are matured both in large casks and in *barriques*. The style is light, the 83 showing some sweetness, freshness, even if spoilt by a slightly harsh aftertaste.

CH GREYSAC **→

Bégadan, 33340 Lesparre-Médoc

Appellation and classification: Médoc, Cru Grand Bourgeois
Total v'yds owned: 60ha (148 acres)
Cabernet area: 30ha (74 acres)
Average production: 420,000 bottles

Owned by Baron François de Gunzburg, Ch Greysac has made a big impression in recent years, especially in the USA, for its smooth, elegant style, quite rich, not particularly aggressive but sufficiently complex to be more than just another Médoc wine. Half the estate is planted with Cabernet Sauvignon. The wines mature over a period of 5 to 6 years, so that the 85 (tasted in 1989) had a smooth, velvety palate, with attractive cigar-box flavours, some acidity and plenty of cassis fruit. The 89 (tasted in 1990) was less exciting despite the vintage, perhaps lacking intensity and tannins.

CH HAUT-CANTELOUP   * → **
Couqueques and St-Christoly-Médoc, 33340 Lesparre-Médoc

Appellation and classification: Médoc, Cru Bourgeois

A classic case of confusion here, in that there are two proprietors of Ch Haut-Canteloup, both making wine under the château name: so look for wines from both M. Vilas-Samiac and Mme Jacqueline Sarrazy. They are the son and daughter of the previous owners, who divided the estate on their death. The vineyards, too, are split between gravel bank running between St-Christoly and St-Bonnet and the clay soils of Couqueques. There is little to choose between the wines of the two proprietors; both very straightforward styles.

CH LOUDENNE   ** →
St-Yzans-de-Médoc, 33340 Lesparre-Médoc

Appellation and classification: Médoc, Cru Grand Bourgeois
Total v'yds owned: 50ha (124 acres)
Cabernet area: 26.5ha (65 acres)
Average production: 180,000 bottles

One of the most famous Médoc estates, and currently with a reputation for producing some of the best wines of the *appellation*, Loudenne's wines, under the control of the British firm Grand Metropolitan (the Gilbey family had owned the estate since 1875), are supple, light and very elegant. The style is derived from the gravel soils which make up much of the vineyard, in sight of the river. The average blend has 53 percent Cabernet Sauvignon. The wines are not designed for long ageing – so the 82 (tasted in 1989) was already very mature and mellow, but when young they exhibit good fruit: the 88 (tasted in 1990) showed fine balance, some new wood tastes and attractive acids, but was already a wine that could be drunk.

CH LES ORMES-SORBET   * →
Couqueques, 33340 Lesparre-Médoc

Appellation and classification: Médoc, Cru Grand Bourgeois
Total v'yds owned: 20ha (49 acres)
Cabernet area: 13ha (32 acres)
Average production: 120,000 bottles

Jean Boivert's family has owned this estate since 1764. While half the crop is sold in bulk to négociants, the other half is bottled at the estate. The blend is normally around 65 percent Cabernet Sauvignon, with the remainder being Merlot. The style, typical of the Médoc, is light, fruity and easy-to-drink. Good vintages, such as the excellent 78 or the more powerful 82, are exceptions to the rule. The 83 (tasted in 1988) was more in the house style: light, softly fruity, rather one-dimensional but perfectly enjoyable to drink.

CH PATACHE D'AUX   ** → ***
Bégadan, 33340 Lesparre-Médoc

Appellation and classification: Médoc, Cru Grand Bourgeois
Total v'yds owned: 38ha (94 acres)
Cabernet area: 27ha (67 acres)
Average production: 260,000 bottles

This estate, property of the Lapalu family, has been very popular in the past decade, a popularity not always justified by results. Wines from the late 1970s and early 1980s were rather herbaceous but since an excellent 82, things have looked up: the 83 (tasted in 1988) was a ripe, minty wine with a touch of oak. 85 and 86 were even better, the 86 (tasted in 1990) is full and concentrated, with considerable rich tannins, a wine to keep until the late 1990s. The estate has a mix of grapes – 70 percent Cabernet Sauvignon, 20 percent Merlot and 10 percent Cabernet Franc.

CH POTENSAC   → ***
Ordonnac, 33340 Lesparre-Médoc

Appellation and classification: Médoc, Cru Grand Bourgeois
Total v'yds owned: 40ha (99 acres)
Cabernet area: 22ha (54 acres)
Average production: 240,000 cases

The vineyards, planted to 55 percent Cabernet Sauvignon, are on a gravel outcrop between St-Yzans and St-Germain-d'Esteuil. The Delon family which owns this estate (as well as Léoville-Las-Cases in Pauillac) also owns two other nearby properties, Ch Gallais-Bellevue and Ch Lassalle. Wines from all three are made in the *chai* at Potensac. Equipped with stainless steel for fermentation and *barriques* for maturation (20 percent renewal each year), the *chai* is home to some of the Médoc's best wines. Bottles are stored before release in the village church, now part of the estate. The vintages of the mid and late 1980s, particularly, show a depth and quality that is unusual for many Médoc estates. The 85 showed excellent cassis fruit and elegance, while the 86 (tasted in 1989) was more tannic, bigger, chewier. Of older vintages, the 78 was still youthful, full of colour and vibrancy, the equal of many wines from the Haut-Médoc.

CH ST-BONNET   * →
St-Christoly-Médoc, 33340 Lesparre-Médoc

Appellation and classification: Médoc, Cru Bourgeois
Total v'yds owned: 35ha (86 acres)
Cabernet area; 17.5ha (43 acres)
Average production: 216,000 bottles

Ch St-Bonnet is often described as a traditional Médoc, and its rustic, earthy tastes mark it apart from some of the more sophisticated offerings now being made in the northern Bordeaux vineyards. For some, including me, the earthiness has become a little too much in vintages of the mid to late 1980s, but that the château can make fine Médocain wines is shown by a vintage like 83, which (tasted in 1988) was rich, spicy and quite powerful. The vineyard has 50 percent Cabernet Sauvignon, 50 percent Merlot.

CH LA TOUR-DE-BY   **
Bégadan, 33340 Lesparre-Médoc

Appellation and classification: Médoc, Cru Grand Bourgeois
Total v'yds owned: 61ha (151 acres)
Cabernet area: 40ha (99 acres)
Average production: 470,000 bottles

Situated on a high gravel ridge, Ch La Tour-de-By is sufficiently close to the river to boast a former lighthouse as one of its buildings. The estate, under the control of Marc Pages, now has some stainless steel in the *chai*, and matures its wine in *barriques*, a small proportion of which are new each year. The wines, with 65 percent Cabernet Sauvignon, can mature slowly and well, for better vintages at least 10 years. Among the best recent vintages are a warm, meaty 85 and a tannic, medium-bodied 86 (tasted in 1989).

Haut-Médoc AC

The Haut-Médoc *appellation* covers a diverse range of châteaux, from classified growths like La Lagune to simple, small unclassified properties. But it is in the middle range of properties, the bourgeois growths, that we find the typical, best value, Haut-Médoc wine.

Until the late 1960s, this was an area in decline, with poor returns on wine production leading to the abandonment of many vineyards, and the neglect of others. A revival of prices from the early 1970s onwards (despite the occasional hiccough) has meant a massive replanting – over 3,000ha (7413 acres) between 1970 and 1988. The opportunity has been taken to increase the proportion of Cabernet Sauvignon in the vineyards, which had been dominated by Merlot. Most of the better estates now have at least 50 percent Cabernet Sauvignon, while many go up to 60 or 70 percent.

The Haut-Médoc *appellation* runs from the outskirts of Blanquefort in the south to the border with the Médoc AC area in the north, and takes in all the vineyard area not covered by the village *appellations* (Margaux, Pauillac, St-Julien, St-Estèphe, Moulis and Listrac). Much of this Haut-Médoc land is in the central belt of vineyards between Margaux and St-Julien, in villages such as Arcins, Lamarque and Cussac-Fort-Médoc. Other important Haut-Médoc villages are located further away from the River Gironde: St-Laurent-et-Benon, St-Sauveur, Cissac-Médoc. North of St-Estèphe, just before the northern edge of Haut-Médoc, is the village of St-Seurin-de-Cadourne, which is currently home to some of the best of the bourgeois growths.

All the better estates take advantage of the gravel outcroppings which are still dominant in the Haut-Médoc, and in which Cabernet Sauvignon prefers to grow. Those estates with more clay in the soil are more likely to have a higher proportion of Merlot.

As these estates have charged higher prices for their wines, so they have been able to invest in new equipment. More and more, stainless steel is in evidence for fermentation, while an increasingly high proportion of new wood is used for maturation in the better estates. In the opinion of many observers, some estates classified as Grand Cru Bourgeois in 1978, are the equal of many fourth or fifth classified growths. Whether consumers would be happy to pay the extra price that would inevitably be charged if the wines were to be reclassified is another matter – and somewhat academic, since no formal reclassification is likely in the near future.

PRODUCERS

CH D'AGASSAC   *→
Ludon-Médoc, 33290 Blanquefort

Appellation and classification: Haut-Médoc, Cru Grand Bourgeois Exceptionnel
Total v'yds owned: 30ha (74 acres)
Cabernet area: 18ha (44 acres)
Average production: 108,000 bottles

Under the same ownership as Ch du Tertre in Margaux and Ch
Calon-Ségur in St-Estèphe, Ch d'Agassac is showing distinct signs
of improvement. The 82 was a rich, fruity wine, but not one that will
last; the 85 showed warm, forward flavours, again not a wine for
keeping.

CH BEAUMONT   →***
Cussac-Fort-Médoc, 33460 Margaux

Appellation and classification: Haut-Médoc, Cru Grand Bourgeois
Total v'yds owned: 85ha (210 acres)
Cabernet area: 48ha (119 acres)
Average production: 360,000 bottles

Now part of the same group as Ch Beychevelle in St-Julien, Ch
Beaumont is enjoying something of a renaissance. The quality of
wines from the 85 and 86 vintages at this exquisite château
southwest of St-Julien, has shown a marked improvement. The 86
(tasted in 1989) showed deep, rich fruit, good tannins and an
intense, balanced taste that suggested long ageing. The 88 (tasted
in 1990) was perhaps less exciting, but still showed potential behind
very firm tannins. Of older wines, the 82 (tasted in 1988) had
concentrated cassis fruit, tobacco flavours and a ripe, sweet taste.
There is a second wine at this estate, Ch Moulin d'Arvigny.

CH BELGRAVE   →**
33112, St-Laurent-et-Benon

Appellation and classification: Haut-Médoc, Fifth Growth
Total v'yds owned: 55ha (136 acres)
Cabernet area: 33ha (82 acres)
Average production: 250,000 bottles

This must have been one of the least known and most neglected
classified growths until its purchase in 1979 by Dourthe-Kressman.
The vineyard, planted with 60 percent Cabernet Sauvignon, is on
gravelly soil behind Ch Lagrange, on the border with St-Julien-
Beychevelle, and should certainly be producing better wines than it
has. Vintages of the mid-1980s show the potential: the 86 (tasted in
1989) big, rich, full-bodied and with some ripe tannins, giving an
ageing ability of some 10 years or more.

CH DE CAMENSAC   →***
33112 St-Laurent-et-Benon

Appellation and classification: Haut-Médoc, Fifth Growth
Total v'yds owned: 60ha (148 acres)
Cabernet area: 36ha (89 acres)
Average production: 240,000 bottles

Until its takeover in 1965 by the Forner family, Ch de Camensac had been badly neglected. But since then, it has shown a great improvement with modern vinification and an emphasis on fruit rather than wood. Tastings show that in vintages like 82, there is good, forward fruit, good intensity with some spicy, vanilla flavours from new wood, all well held together and structured. The 86 (tasted in 1988) showed ripe, cassis flavours and piles of fruit, while the 85 (also tasted in 1988) had hints of classic tobacco and cigar-box smells over big, warm tannins.

CH CANTEMERLE   ***
Macau, 33460 Margaux

Appellation and classification: Haut-Médoc, Fifth Growth
Total v'yds owned: 55ha (136 acres)
Cabernet area: 25ha (62 acres)
Average production: 250,000 bottles

The splendidly-restored château at Cantemerle, glistening in its pale yellow stone, is matched by the modernized *chai*, which is now full of new oak *barriques*, as well as stainless steel fermentation vats. The wines have similarly shown a marked improvement, from a low point in the mid-to-late-1970s. The proportion of Cabernet Sauvignon planting in the vineyard, at 45 percent, has been increased, and is likely to go higher at the expense of Merlot, which forms about 40 percent of planting. The wines are never going to be heavyweights coming from this far south in the Médoc, but the 89 (tasted in 1990) was full of new wood and big, chewy, spicy fruit. The 88 (tasted in 1990) showed delightful soft, ripe fruit and considerable richness, with a balance that means it could almost be drunk. The 85 (tasted in 1989) had a lovely smooth, rich taste, very warm and welcoming.

CH CISSAC   ** → ***
Cissac-Médoc, 33250 Pauillac

Appellation and classification: Haut-Médoc, Cru Grand Bourgeois Exceptionnel
Total v'yds owned: 30ha (74 acres)
Cabernet area: 22.5ha (56 acres)
Average production: 165,000 bottles

Under owner Louis Vialard, whose family has been at Ch Cissac since 1885, many traditional methods have been retained, including the use of wooden fermentation vats. But new wood – up to 50 percent each year – is a massive investment for a bourgeois growth and shows that this is no neglected estate, but a model of care and attention. The wines have a considerable following in the UK, where consumers are willing to wait for the tannins, and dark, often austere taste to mellow. Some vintages of the 1970s were too lean, but wines like the 86 (tasted in 1989) show much more cassis-like fruit, while the powerful 82 (tasted in 1988) showed strong new oak tastes temporarily dominating ripe fruit.

CH HANTEILLAN   ** →
Cissac-Médoc, 33250 Pauillac

Appellation and classification: Haut-Médoc, Cru Grand Bourgeois
Total v'yds owned: 83ha (205 acres)
Cabernet area: 40ha (99 acres)
Average production: 420,000 bottles

Under the watchful eye of Mme Blasco, the proprietor, Ch Hanteillan has been extensively renovated, since its purchase in 1972, with new plantings. The high proportion of Merlot is a result of areas of clay soil in the vineyard. The wines tend to be big and chewy, rather forbidding when young, but evolve well and surely. The 85 (tasted in 1989) has a good, solid taste, with forward spicy perfume, and some intensity of fruit. The 86 (tasted in 1989) seems lighter, and has a pleasing tobacco and tar taste, with good spicy flavour. Both wines will mature over about ten years.

CH LA LAGUNE   *** →
Ludon-Médoc, 33290 Blanquefort

Appellation and classification: **Haut-Médoc, Third Growth**
Total v'yds owned: 55ha (136 acres)
Cabernet area: 30ha (74 acres)
Average production: 300,000 bottles

The simple *appellation*, Haut-Médoc, belies the importance of this château, the first that a visitor to the Médoc sees coming north along the road out of Bordeaux. A series of committed owners has upgraded the *chai* to one of the most revolutionary in Bordeaux (with stainless steel pipes taking the wine straight from fermentation vat to ageing barrel) and replanted the vineyard. Wines from any vintages after the mid-to-late-1960s, and especially from 78 onwards, are outstanding. The wine is often dominated by new wood when young (100 percent new wood in most years), as with the 86 (tasted in 1987) which was tasting strongly of new wood, indeed almost suggested a New World wine, not only with wood but with underlying weighty, ripe fruit. However, older vintages such as the 78 (tasted in 1988) show huge fruit on tannins that are beginning to soften, and a long period before maturity finally arrives.

CH DE LAMARQUE   **
Lamarque, 33460 Margaux

Appellation and classification: **Haut-Médoc, Cru Grand Bourgeois**
Total v'yds owned: 47ha (116 acres)
Cabernet area: 23.5ha (58 acres)
Average production: 300,000 bottles

The fortress of Lamarque dominates the small village and the ferry-boat crossing point to Blaye on the opposite bank of the Gironde. The estate produces a good middle-range wine, aged in wood, 25 percent new each year. The wines became even better in the 1980s, showing depth as well as fruit. The 82 (tasted in 1989) was just mature, with attractive berry fruit and muted tannin. The 86, a bigger wine altogether, had spicy, herby fruit and some weight.

CH LANESSAN   → ***
Cussac-Fort-Médoc, 33460 Margaux

Appellation and classification: **Haut-Médoc, Cru Bourgeois Superieur**
Total v'yds owned: 40ha (99 acres)
Cabernet area: 30ha (74 acres)
Average production: 150,000 bottles

From early in the 19th century, Lanessan has been regarded as one of the better estates of the Médoc, and would, according to André Jullien, have been classified as a fourth growth in 1855, if the then-owner had not been so uninterested. Today it still makes wine above its classification of Cru Bourgeois. The style of the wine is rich and powerful, with a capacity for long ageing which can be impressive. Of recent vintages, the 78, the 82 and the 83 were all of high quality. Even the 87 from a leaner year, showed big, raisiny, chewy fruit.

CH LAROSE-TRINTAUDON **
33112 St-Laurent-et-Benon

Appellation and classification: Haut-Médoc, Cru Grand Bourgeois
Total v'yds owned: 172ha (425 acres)
Cabernet area: 103ha (255 acres)
Average production: 970,000 bottles

One of the largest estates in Bordeaux, Ch Larose-Trintaudon is owned by the Forner family, who also own Ch de Camensac as well as Marqués de Cáceres, Rioja. Despite the location and the reasonably high proportion of Cabernet Sauvignon, Larose-Trintaudon makes a surprisingly light wine. There appears to be a deliberate policy to make soft wines that mature quickly and in this the Forners succeed admirably. The 86 (tasted in 1988) from a big vintage, was a smooth, supple wine, with pleasing spicy flavours, ready to drink by 1990.

CH LIVERSAN **→
St-Sauveur, 33250 Pauillac

Appellation and classification: Haut-Médoc, Cru Grand Bourgeois
Total vineyard owned: 48ha (119 acres)
Cabernet area: 23.5ha (58 acres)
Average production: 240,000 bottles

A change of ownership in 1983 has heralded a new era. A new *cuverie* has been installed, with stainless steel fermentation, and the wines are now aged in *barriques*, a large proportion of which are of new wood. The results are apparent in two recent vintages: the 85 (tasted in 1989) was definitely showing new wood plus attractive ripe fruit. The 86 (tasted in 1989) was firm, tannic and chewy, but with considerable fruit underneath.

CH MALESCASSE **→
Lamarque, 33460 Margaux

Appellation and classification: Haut-Médoc, Cru Bourgeois
Total v'yds owned: 35ha (86 acres)
Cabernet area: 28ha (69 acres)

This château is owned by the same family which owns Ch Pontet-Canet in Pauillac and Ch Lafon-Rochet in St-Estèphe. The vineyard is at the highest point of the commune of Lamarque and is of good gravel soil. Recent vintages have shown considerable quality: the 85 (tasted in 1989) medium-bodied but with plenty of rich, now quite forward fruit; the 86 (tasted in 1989) bigger yet also more elegant, with excellent fruit and tannin balance.

CH DU MOULIN-ROUGE **→
Cussac-Fort-Médoc, 33460 Margaux

Appellation and classification: Haut-Médoc, Cru Bourgeois
Total v'yds owned: 15ha (37 acres)

Forget any association with Paris nightclubs: this is a well-made bourgeois growth from a vineyard that lies just south of St-Julien on a ridge of gravel. I have tasted some good wines from this château, particularly from the mid-1980s onwards. The 85 (tasted in 1989) was rich, balanced, oozing with ripe fruit; the 86 (tasted in 1989) is also dominated by good fruit, quite a soft style for the year, but there is enough rich fruit to give it the chance to age well. The 87 (tasted in 1990) was naturally lighter, but even this had excellent fresh-flavoured fruit.

CH RAMAGE-LA-BATISSE   *→**
St-Sauveur, 33250 Pauillac

Appellation and classification: Haut-Médoc, Cru Bourgeois
Total v'yds owned: 52ha (128 acres)
Cabernet area: 31ha (76 acres)
Average production: 300,000 bottles

This château has had a patchy period during the 1980s. Some vintages stood out: 83 (tasted in 1988) showed jammy fruit and plenty of oak tastes. But 82, which should have been better, was lighter and disappointing, as was 86; while the 87 (tasted in 1989) was a properly balanced wine, better than many properties in a difficult year.

This is an interesting property, reconstituted since 1961 from a number of patches of vineyard into one unit. With 60 percent Cabernet Sauvignon in the vineyard, and gravel soil, it should be able to make good wines on a more reliable basis.

CH SÉGUR   →**
Parempuyre, 33290 Blanquefort

Appellation and classification: Haut-Médoc, Cru Grand Bourgeois
Total v'yds owned: 35ha (86 acres)

A relic of the ancient estate of the Marquis de Ségur, which covered much of the Médoc in the 18th century. The estate today is on a mix of clay and gravel soils, much of the land on a high gravel ridge. With the 85 vintage, the château has been producing two cuvées, one made entirely in new oak, which has complete superiority in taste and excitement over the regular cuvée.

CH SOCIANDO-MALLET   ***
St-Seurin-de-Cadourne, 33250 Pauillac

Appellation and classification: Haut-Médoc, Cru Grand Bourgeois
Total v'yds owned: 30ha (74 acres)
Cabernet area: 18ha (44 acres)
Average production: 230,000 bottles

This château makes a wine that is built to last in a traditional way, with long skin contact to get maximum colour and tannin, and long barrel-maturation. The result of Jean Gautreau's policy is superb wines that are quite undrinkable for the first 10 – 15 years of their life. The 78 (tasted in 1988) was still quite inky black and impenetrable. The massive 82 (tasted in 1989) was the equal of many classed growths, big, chunky, full of fruit and tannin – not to be touched before the late 90s. Even the 87 (tasted in 1989) was big, with a smoky bouquet and excellent strawberry fruit flavours under some tannins. There is a second wine, Ch Lartigue-de-Brochon.

CH TOUR-DU-HAUT-MOULIN   **
Cussac-Fort-Médoc, 33460 Margaux

Appellation and classification: Haut-Médoc, Cru Grand Bourgeois
Total v'yds owned: 32ha (79 acres)
Cabernet area: 16ha (39 acres)
Average production: 144,000 bottles

A traditional style still operates here, with Laurent Poitou, the fourth-generation owner, making big, chewy wines, aged in 25 percent new wood, which last well for 10 years before maturity. The 87 (tasted in 1989) showed what could be made in that year: a firm, closed medium-bodied wine, that revealed fruit and potential, but which should not be drunk until the mid-90s. The 82 (tasted in 1989) needs even longer, still firm and closed, but with some blackcurrant.

CH VERDIGNAN   →**
St-Seurin-de-Cadourne, 33250 Pauillac

Appellation and classification: Haut-Médoc, Cru Grand Bourgeois
Total v'yds owned: 47ha (116 acres)
Cabernet area: 26ha (64 acres)
Average production: 360,000 bottles

The château produces good, solid wines. It is run by Jean Miailhe, who also runs Ch Coufran. The vineyards are grouped in one plot around the château, but the actual *chai* is in the village of St-Seurin a couple of kilometres away. They are not complex wines, but the cassis taste of Cabernet Sauvignon is never far away: the 87 (tasted in 1989) was enjoyable and fruity with some spicy flavours.

St-Estèphe

Of all the great communes of the Médoc, St-Estèphe is probably the least known. That is partly because it is the furthest from Bordeaux, but also because the style of its wines is the most difficult to appreciate when young. They have a bigger, heavier style, with more tannin and less fruit, which can be initially off-putting.

The stylistic difference has a lot to do with the soil. There is gravel soil in St-Estèphe, but the depth of gravel is less than in Pauillac to the south, and there is more clay around as well. Until comparatively recently, certainly in the 1960s and early 1970s, wines made on these soils and using the high percentages of Cabernet Sauvignon (80 percent plus) prevalent in Pauillac, turned out to have too much acidity and tannin and not enough fruit. They needed just a little more Merlot – and that is what is happening in St-Estèphe now.

It is most apparent in one of the village's top wines, Ch Montrose, whose more traditional efforts were blockbusters, but which is now making somewhat lighter wines. It is also apparent in Ch Haut-Marbuzet, which I have not included in the directory, because the vineyard has less than 50 percent Cabernet Sauvignon: this is one of the stars of St-Estèphe, precisely because of its high (50 percent) Merlot content. As a contrast is the redeveloped vineyard of Ch Lafon-Rochet, with 80 percent Cabernet Sauvignon, making wines that are weighty and tannic, slow to develop and rather austere.

The heavy style of traditional St-Estèphe may have had something to do with the relatively poor showing the village made in the

1855 classification: two second-growths, one third, one fourth and one fifth. But that lack of classified recognition is more than compensated for today by the wealth of bourgeois growths which are making wines often as good as the classified growths, but at lower prices. It does mean that, for the consumer, prices of St-Estèphe wines are relatively good value, certainly if compared with other Médoc village *appellations*.

PRODUCERS

CH BEAU-SITE * → **
St-Estèphe, 33250 Pauillac

Appellation and classification: St-Estèphe, Cru Grand Bourgeois Exceptionnel
Total v'yds owned: 27ha (67 acres)
Cabernet area: 16ha (39 acres)
Average production: 180,000 bottles

Beau-Site, owned by the Castéja-Borie family (who also own Batailley in Pauillac and other estates), is in the small hamlet of St-Corbain, inland from St-Estèphe, and next to Calon-Ségur. The intention has been to make wines which are drinkable early, and little new wood is used for maturing. This was apparent in wines from the early 1980s, but the policy must be changing, because the 86 (tasted in 1989) seemed firmer, with firm tannins on most attractive fruit, while the 89 (tasted in 1990) was very rich and tannic, a wine for 10-15 years ageing.

CH CALON-SÉGUR **
St-Estèphe, 33250 Pauillac

Appellation and classification: St-Estèphe, Third Growth
Total v'yds owned: 48ha (119 acres)
Cabernet area: 29ha (72 acres)
Average production: 180,000 bottles

Originally on the site of a Roman villa, Calon-Ségur was most likely the first place at which vines were planted in St-Estèphe. It was part of the vast estates of the Marquis de Ségur in the 18th century (when he also owned most of Pauillac). The present owner, Philippe Gasqueton, lives at nearby Ch Capbern-Gasqueton. The wines have an uneven reputation: some commentators feel they are very patchy, and do not live up to their classification. Others praise their consistency, if not immense flair and excitement. Some recent tastings suggest some quality: the 88 (tasted in 1990) was smoky, rich, almost sweet, certainly well made, if not designed for long ageing. The 86, with 90 percent Cabernet Sauvignon (tasted in 1989) was deep in colour, very firm and tannic. But 89 (tasted in 1990) was a disappointment, rather light and fruity rather than rich and tannic. The second wine is Marquis de Ségur.

CH CHAMBERT-MARBUZET → **
St-Estèphe, 33250 Pauillac

Appellation and classification: St-Estèphe, Cru Bourgeois
Total v'yds owned: 8ha (20 acres)
Cabernet area: 5.6ha (14 acres)
Average production: 46,000 bottles

This small estate, the property of the Duboscq firm, produces some good, solid, wines, tannic when young, but with reasonable ageing potential. The best wine from the château in recent years has been the 86 (tasted in 1989) a smoky, strawberry flavoured, very fruity wine, with plenty of new oak tastes. The 85 (tasted in 1989) was certainly lighter and more forward. The 89 (tasted in 1990) was also light, a wine that will mature comparatively quickly.

COS D'ESTOURNEL →****
St-Estèphe, 33250 Pauillac

Appellation and classification: St-Estèphe, Second Growth
Total v'yds owned: 54ha (133 acres)
Cabernet area: 32ha (79 acres)
Average production: 220,000 bottles

There is no château at Cos d'Estournel, but every visitor to St-Estèphe admires the oriental design of the magnificent *chai*, recently restored to all its former glory. Its splendour reflects the quality of the wine, which almost certainly is the best in St-Estèphe at the moment. Of all the classified growths in the Médoc, Cos d'Estournel can have the highest proportion (40 percent) of Merlot in the blend, depending on the year, which accounts for the jammy, very forward fruit character in the wines when young. But the 60 percent Cabernet Sauvignon is plenty to give them excellent ageing ability. Recent vintages, such as the 85 (tasted in 1989) showed very rich fruit, opulent and juicy, but some good tannins as well. The 88 (tasted in 1990) was bursting with new wood taste, big and chewy, but again with immediate fruit quality. The 89 (tasted in 1990) was superb, one of the best wines of the vintage, with immense quantities of fruit underneath tannins. The second wine here is Ch Marbuzet.

CH LE CROCK →**
St-Estèphe, 33250 Pauillac

Appellation and classification: St-Estèphe, Cru Grand Bourgeois Exceptionnel
Total v'yds owned: 31ha (77 acres)
Cabernet area: 20ha (49 acres)
Average production: 190,000 bottles

Owned by the Cuvelier family since 1903 (they also own Léoville-Poyferré), Ch le Crock is set in a beautiful, faintly English park. The wines have been getting better from the mid-1980s onwards: the 86 (tasted in 1989) showed a big, chunky, fruity wine, still covered with tannin. The 87 (tasted in 1990) was an average wine for the vintage, with some spicy fruit, but lacking great weight. Of older vintages, 78 is still very much alive and developing.

CH LAFON-ROCHET **
St-Estèphe, 33250 Pauillac

Appellation and classification: St-Estèphe, Fourth Growth
Total v'yds owned: 45ha (111 acres)
Cabernet area: 36ha (89 acres)
Average production: 145,000 bottles

There have been big changes at Ch Lafon-Rochet since Guy Tesseron bought the estate in 1960. There have been big improvements in the *chai*, but more important has been the change in the vineyard from a high proportion of Merlot grapes to 80 percent Cabernet Sauvignon. Whether this has had the desired effect of improving quality is debated among commentators. There is the argument that St-Estèphe's soil conditions demand a relatively high percentage of Merlot: too much Cabernet here means wines that are too austere (although other estates get away with 70 percent Cabernet). Others see a high percentage of Cabernet as the means of improving the reputation of the estate. The wines themselves provide a mixed answer: the 86 (tasted in 1989) starting out very tannic, is now showing an excellent raisiny, smoky character, with the ability to age well. But the 82 was rather too unyielding for the vintage and certainly needs years to soften.

CH MEYNEY →***
St-Estèphe, 33250 Pauillac

Appellation and classification: St-Estèphe, Cru Grand Bourgeois Exceptionnel
Total v'yds owned: 50ha (124 acres)
Cabernet area: 35ha (86 acres)
Average production: 330,000 bottles

Meyney has a high reputation in St-Estèphe for its reliable and high quality and among consumers for its good value. The wines are big and fruity, with good tannins when young, and as they age they can have austerity and a little acidity, but also, as with the 78 (tasted in 1988) have good cassis and jammy fruit. Recent vintages, like the 86 (tasted in 1989) show very good fruit, considerable intensity and ripe tannins. There is a second wine, Prieur de Meyney.

CH MONTROSE ***→
St-Estèphe, 33250 Pauillac

Appellation and classification: St-Estèphe, Second Growth
Total v'yds owned: 67ha (166 acres)
Cabernet area: 43ha (106 acres)
Average production: 280,000 bottles

The name Montrose comes from the pink colour of the wild flowers that used to flourish on the hill before the vineyard was first planted back in the 18th century. Today the château still commands fine views of the river – a sign of a good wine, according to Médoc tradition. Montrose always had a reputation for hugely tannic wines that took years to mature: the relatively high percentage of Cabernet Sauvignon saw to that. Since then, the amount of Merlot in the blend has sometimes been increased – in 85 it was 40 percent – and in some years the wine has become lighter. However, recent vintages, such as the 88 (tasted in 1990) very tough and firm, or the 86 (tasted in 1987) very hard and chewy but with immense fruit underneath, show a return to the old style. The second wine is La Dame de Montrose.

CH LES ORMES-DE-PEZ ***
St-Estèphe, 33250 Pauillac

Appellation and classification: St-Estèphe, Cru Grand Bourgeois
Total v'yds owned: 30ha (74 acres)
Cabernet area: 15ha (37 acres)
Average production: 150,000 bottles

The style of the Cazes family, who own Les Ormes-de-Pez as well as Ch Lynch-Bages in Pauillac, is evident in the attention to detail both in the vineyard and the *chai*. Vines are planted unusually close together so that they have specially low yields, always reckoned a sign of quality. Casks for maturing come from Lynch-Bages and Latour; there is little filtering of the finished wine. It all adds up to some impressive wines which, with their fruit quality, always attract. The 86 (tasted in 1989) had a lovely smoky, cassis taste; the 85 (tasted in 1988) was lighter but still well made; the 87 (tasted in 1989) was exceptionally weighty and tannic for the year.

CH DE PEZ   **→
St-Estèphe, 33250 Pauillac

Appellation and classification: St-Estèphe, Cru Bourgeois Superieur
Total v'yds owned: 23ha (57 acres)
Cabernet area: 16ha (39 acres)
Average production: 175,000 bottles

One of a group of châteaux in the hamlet of Pez, Ch de Pez is housed in buildings which date back to 1450. Owned today by Robert Dousson, it makes an elegant wine that makes up in balance and charm what it sometimes lacks in weight. Good vintages include the 83 (tasted in 1988) very tannic and dense at that time, but with balanced fruit underneath; the 82 (tasted in 1988) peppery and cassis flavours, with a good balance between oak and fruit; and 78 with a higher proportion than usual of Merlot, rich, jammy and fruity.

CH PHÉLAN-SÉGUR   →**
St-Estèphe, 33250 Pauillac

Appellation and classification: St-Estèphe, Cru Grand Bourgeois Exceptionnel
Total v'yds owned: 52ha (128 acres)
Cabernet area: 31ha (76 acres)
Average production: 264,000 bottles

Next door to Montrose, Ch Phélan-Ségur is yet another of the estates that recalls the ownership of the Ségur family in the eighteenth century. Phélan comes from the name of a nineteenth century owner. The wines made at the estate today tend towards a soft style, with good colour and a modest bouquet. The 87 (tasted in 1989) was a pleasing wine, already maturing well, with slightly light fruit. The 89 (tasted in 1990) showed much greater style and richness, with huge dollops of fruit underneath impressive tannin.

CH TRONQUOY-LALANDE   **
St-Estèphe, 33250 Pauillac

Appellation and classification: St-Estèphe, Cru Grand Bourgeois
Total v'yds owned: 16.5ha (41 acres)
Cabernet area: 10ha (25 acres)
Average production: 85,000 bottles

Arlette Castéja produces one of the weightiest of the *cru bourgeois* St-Estèphe wines here, using expertise from the family firm of Dourthe Frères as well as her own skills acquired since taking over the property in 1973. The wines are matured partly in second-year casks from Dourthe and partly in tanks, and this allows the fruit free rein. The 86 (tasted in 1989) was huge, deep purple/black in colour, very weighty, almost too much, but probably with enough fruit to keep it going. The 89 (tasted in 1990) was a similar massive effort, but there is some structure to it as well to allow it to age well.

Pauillac

Pauillac is where the Cabernet Sauvignon reaches its apogee in the Médoc. Its châteaux have the highest percentage of Cabernet in their blends, which lends to the wines their distinctive cigar-box and opulent fruit character when mature, and the need to age them for years. The fact that it is also home for three of the five first-growths means that the wines of Pauillac are often seen – wrongly – as a model for the rest of the Médoc; and they have been the model for all those other Cabernet producers round the world who want to emulate the style of great Bordeaux.

Pauillac's fame comes from its soil. This is where there is the highest concentration of the famous gravel of the Médoc, the soil on which Cabernet Sauvignon thrives. The ground is higher here – up to 30 metres (98 feet) above the river (high for the predominantly flat Médoc) in the vineyards of Mouton-Rothschild and Pontet-Canet, and drainage on the slopes is better than it is in the flatter vineyards of a village like Margaux.

Pauillac does not produce a homogeneous style of wine. You only have to compare the difference in style between the first-growths to understand that. There is the gorgeous opulence of Mouton-Rothschild, the chunky, powerful Latour and the elegant Lafite. The Cabernet predominates to a greater extent at the first two, situated at opposite ends of the commune. There are soil differences: Mouton has sandstone as its soil base, while Latour has deeper, finer gravel. Lafite, the stylish elegant wine of the three, has more Merlot in the blend, and limestone in the soil.

It is possible to relate other châteaux to these three – in *Bordeaux, The Definitive Guide* Robert Parker partners Lafite with Haut-Batailley, Mouton with Lynch-Bages and Haut-Bages-Libéral, but admits there is no stylistic partner for Latour. The best of the non-first-growths, Pichon Lalande, with the highest percentage of Merlot among all the classed growths in the commune, has as much of the character of a silky wine of St-Julien as of a sterner wine of Pauillac.

Outside the 17 classified growths of Pauillac, there is little room for *cru bourgeois*. Most of the vineyard near the river and on the high ground just inland is classed growth, a higher concentration than anywhere in the Médoc.

PRODUCERS

CH BATAILLEY
33250 Pauillac

** →

Appellation and classification: Pauillac, *Fifth Growth*
Total v'yds owned: 50ha (124 acres)
Cabernet area: 36.5ha (90 acres)
Average production: 265,000 bottles

This château produces good solid wines which are generally seen as offering fair, rather than exciting value. The style on this estate, centred on the large 18th century château, is very reliable, with firm fruit when young, and a slow evolution. The 82 (tasted in 1987) showed good open fruit flavours, combined with some ripe oakiness. The 86 (tasted in 1989) had heavy tannins over chunky fruit and considerable concentration. The 89 (tasted in 1990) showed more potential elegance and style than previous vintages, and this did not suggest a long ageing.

CH CLERC-MILON   ** →
33250 Pauillac

Appellation and classification: Pauillac, Fifth Growth
Total v'yds owned: 30ha (74 acres)
Cabernet area: 21ha (52 acres)
Average production: 105,000 bottles

This is the smallest of the properties owned by Baronne Philippine de Rothschild. The west-facing vineyards border both Lafite and Mouton, and certainly since it was bought by the Rothschilds in 1970, the quality has improved. There was an excellent, quite full 81, still with some life when tasted in 1990; a big, firm, tannic, well structured 86 (tasted in 1990) and a rather medium-weight 82 (tasted in 1988). The 89 (tasted in 1990) was light, but its fruit quality and spicy oak flavours are outstanding.

CH DUHART-MILON-ROTHSCHILD   ***
33250 Pauillac

Appellation and classification: Pauillac, Fourth Growth
Total v'yds owned: 65ha (161 acres)
Cabernet area: 41ha (101 acres)
Average production: 250,000 bottles

Bought by the Rothschilds of Ch Lafite in 1962, Duhart-Milon-Rothschild is now producing wines worthy of its status after extensive replanting of the vineyard (which lies on the Carruades plateau just inland from Lafite) and re-equipping of the *chai*. The wine tends to be fleshier than neighbouring Lafite, generally bigger but less elegant and refined. The reason comes from the greater amount of clay in the subsoil at Duhart, and the consequent planting of a greater proportion of Merlot than at Lafite. But the wines have great style: the 86 (tasted in 1987) had an inky black colour, with piles of concentrated fruit; the 85 (tasted in 1987) had a cedary bouquet, with opulent attractive fruit, not at all complex; the 82 (tasted in 1987) was a seriously concentrated wine, very big, very tannic, the sort of wine that will be best drunk in the next century. The second wine is Ch Moulin-Duhart.

CH FONBADET   ** →
33250 Pauillac

Appellation and classification: Pauillac, Cru Bourgeois Superieur
Total v'yds owned: 15ha (37 acres)
Cabernet area: 9ha (22 acres)
Average production: 78,000 bottles

The small Fonbadet estate is based on an 18th century château set in its own park away from the main road. Vines up to 40 years old allow owner Pierre Peyronie to make wines which are classic Pauillac – tannic when young, with excellent blackcurrant flavours which mature into complex full-bodied tastes. The 82 (tasted in 1984) was a rich, opulent wine, brimming with fruit, if lacking the complexity of greater estates. The 86 (tasted in 1988) was still firmly tannic, but there was definite intensity of flavour. Both wines will mature well.

CH GRAND-PUY-DUCASSE ** → ***
33250 Pauillac

Appellation and classification: **Pauillac, Fifth Growth**
Total v'yds owned: 36ha (89 acres)
Cabernet area: 25.2ha (62 acres)
Average production: 210,000 bottles

The château at Grand-Puy-Ducasse is nowhere near the vineyards but on the quayside beside the river in the centre of Pauillac. Until recently it also housed the town's Maison du Vin. The vineyards are in three separate parcels within Pauillac. The château is run by the Bordeaux merchant house of Mestrezat. They make excellent wines, very much in a classic Pauillac style, perhaps fruity rather than tannic, but with a definite ability to age: a 70 (tasted in 1989) was still fresh and youthful, with good tannins, and a long life ahead. More recent tastings include a lovely smoky, spicy, elegant 85 (tasted in 1988) and a firm, strongly tannic 86 (tasted in 1988). The second wine is Ch Artigues-Arnaud.

CH GRAND-PUY-LACOSTE ***
33250 Pauillac

Appellation and classification: **Pauillac, Fifth Growth**
Total v'yds owned: 45ha (111 acres)
Cabernet area: 31.5ha (78 acres)
Average production: 145,000 bottles

The vineyard of Grand-Puy-Lacoste consists of one large parcel on the plateau by the hamlet of Bages on the edge of Pauillac. Now owned by the Borie family of Ducru-Beaucaillou in St-Julien, it is making very fine wines, with tannin and chewy fruit in their youth: it is still too early in the new regime (which took over in 1978) to say how the wines will mature, but that they will take a long time is in no doubt. The 86 (tasted in 1987) was very much in this mould – firm and tannic with excellent (and typical) Cabernet Sauvignon acidity. The 82 (tasted in 1988) was an enormous wine, revelling in its huge fruit and tannin. The 89 (tasted in 1990) was still dominated by wood. The second wine is Lacoste-Borie.

CH HAUT-BAGES-LIBÉRAL → ***
33250 Pauillac

Appellation and classification: **Pauillac, Fifth Growth**
Total v'yds owned: 26ha (64 acres)
Cabernet area: 18.2ha (45 acres)
Average production: 120,000 bottles

The mid-1980s saw a renaissance at this château. Now run by Bernadette Villars, who has made such a success of Ch Chasse-Spleen in Moulis, it is well placed to leap in general estimation. The run of good wines under her control started with the 85 (tasted in 1988) a very powerful wine, very concentrated. The 86 was even better, with even greater concentration, tannins and powerful fruit. Both are likely to need long ageing, as will the 89 (tasted in 1990) which had an unusual almost Australian minty tone, and a fine potential balance of fruit and tannin.

CH HAUT-BATAILLEY ***
33250 Pauillac

Appellation and classification: Pauillac, *Fifth Growth*
Total v'yds owned: 20 h (49 acres)
Cabernet area: 13ha (32 acres)
Average production: 90,000 bottles

Owned by the Borie family of Grand-Puy-Lacoste, Haut-Batailley was part of Batailley until 1942. The style here has normally been quite light and elegant, normally with a comparatively rapid maturation period. However, there seems to have been a change with the 86 vintage (tasted in 1987) which was as hard, tough and tannic as any Pauillac. And the 89 (tasted in 1990) seemed likely to combine the elegance of the former style with the power and weight of the new. If it works – say at the turn of the century – it should be very fine wine indeed.

CH LAFITE-ROTHSCHILD   ****
33250 *Pauillac*

Appellation and classification: Pauillac, *First Growth*
Total v'yds owned: 90ha (222 acres)
Cabernet area: 63ha (156 acres)
Average production: 300,000 bottles

Arguments can rage happily about which first-growth is the best. To me, they are all as good as each other, only different. At various times one may edge ahead of the others, or go through a comparatively lean patch, but a year or so will see a readjustment. The character of the wines is much more important – as well as elusive – to capture. Lafite, for many writers, is the elegant wine par excellence, perhaps lighter than its peers, but none the less just as long-lasting. Compared with the other first-growths of Pauillac, Lafite has a lower percentage of Cabernet Sauvignon, a higher of Merlot and this may account for its lightness of touch and also what Edmund Penning-Rowsell has described as its "elegant and supple" style. Tasted in 1987, the 86 was rich, with huge fruit and tannin balanced with a lovely poise and style; the 85 showed some perfumed fruit, plenty (but not an overwhelming amount) of smoky wood and a deft touch of acidity; the 82 had a perfect soft wood and herb nose, sweet fruit and that suppleness, with a bite of tannin at the end. The 89 (tasted in 1990) showed more weight and rich fruit quality than Lafite's style used to suggest. The second wine is Les Carruades de Lafite.

CH LATOUR   ****
33250 *Pauillac*

Appellation and classification: Pauillac, *First Growth*
Total v'yds owned: 60ha (148 acres)
Cabernet area: 48ha (119 acres)
Average production: 192,000 bottles

Latour's reputation among the first-growths is of a big, tough wine, loaded with tannins when young and taking many, many years to mature. The high proportion of Cabernet Sauvignon will have something to do with it (although Mouton has more). The wine is left in contact with the skins after fermentation for anything up to two weeks, to get extra colour and tannin. Like other first-growths, the wine is matured for anything up to 30 months in Allier wood, which for the first year at least is 100 percent new. When I tasted the 88, in

1990, it was still in wood, showing considerable acidity as well as spicy wood: the grapes, I was told, were very concentrated and mature when picked and certainly the wine is very dense. The 89 (tasted in 1990) was very tannic and without quite the weight of fruit underneath, but maybe that was a stage in the wine. Of older vintages (tasted in 1987) 85 was more of an elegant wine than a blockbuster; 82 was superb, almost black in colour, full of ripe, opulent, dense fruit, very closed, likely to last almost for ever; 78 was a perfectly balanced wine, still full of tannins, but showing a poise and style to set against the concentration. The second wine, Les Forts de Latour, is made from vineyards not used for the Grand Vin and from young vines: it is a fine wine in its own right, the equal of some classed growths.

CH LYNCH-BAGES   *** →
33250 Pauillac

Appellation and classification: Pauillac, Fifth Growth
Total v'yds owned: 80ha (198 acres)
Cabernet area: 56ha (138 acres)
Average production: 340,000 bottles

Owner Jean-Michel Cazes is a well-known figure in Pauillac, both as an ambassador for his wines and for those of Pauillac, and as hotelier (he owns the nearby Ch Cordeillan-Bages). At Lynch-Bages, he has organized a massive renovation and improvement programme, which has resulted in an enlarged and modernized *cuverie* and *chai*, and almost certainly has contributed to the very high quality of the wine being made at the moment. Since 1982, there has been a run of terrific wines: the 83 (tasted in 1986) has much more fruit than many wines from the vintage, great cassis and rich flavour; the 85 will mature relatively quickly, but has excellent fruit and spicy wood flavours; the 86 (tasted in 1987) had almost inky black fruit, and big, overpowering tannins. Wines like this certainly suggest Lynch-Bages is well above its current classification. The second wine is Ch Haut-Bages-Averous.

CH MOUTON-BARONNE-PHILIPPE   → ***
33250 Pauillac

Appellation and classification: Pauillac, Fifth Growth
Total v'yds owned: 50ha (124 acres)
Cabernet area: 32.5ha (80 acres)
Average production: 180,000 bottles

The next-door neighbour to Ch Mouton-Rothschild was originally part of the same estate. It was reunited under the ownership of Baron Philippe de Rothschild in 1933, but its wines are treated absolutely separately, although it would have been possible to put the two vineyards together again. The style, despite its proximity to Mouton-Rothschild, is very different. A higher percentage of Merlot (20 percent) means that the wines are softer and mature more quickly. They are aged in two and three-year old casks from Mouton, which means they get a lower amount of wood tastes. Of vintages of the 1980s (tasted in 1990) the best were the 86, a powerful dense wine with big, chewy tannins; the 83, fine, firm with attractive cigar-box flavours; and the 89, showing at that stage a delightful floral bouquet, and just beginning to take on wood tannins.

CH MOUTON-ROTHSCHILD   ****
33250 *Pauillac*

Appellation and classification: Pauillac, First Growth
Total v'yds owned: 72ha (178 acres)
Cabernet area: 61.2ha (151 acres)
Average production: 240,000 bottles

Of all the first-growths, Mouton-Rothschild has the highest proportion of Cabernet Sauvignon in the blend. Its characteristic opulence, generosity and impeccable style show how Cabernet Sauvignon can make just as gorgeous wines as can Merlot in different circumstances. But then most Merlot wines would not age so long: I have been lucky enough to drink more old vintages of Mouton-Rothschild than any other first-growth, and they hold up superbly well. More recent vintages, from the outstanding 82 onwards, show that Mouton is on a winning streak at the moment. Tasted in 1990, the great vintages since then have been the 82, perhaps the finest wine from what will be a very great vintage, layers of fruit and spicy, cigar-box flavours, gorgeously complex; and the 89, again one of the very best wines from the vintage, without too many wood tannins at that stage to overlay the fruit, it had marvellous perfume, a rich, sweet wine with huge dense flavours. As for any Mouton, wait for 20 years at least.

CH PICHON-LONGUEVILLE-BARON   →***
33250 *Pauillac*

Appellation and classification: Pauillac, Second Growth
Total v'yds owned: 30ha (74 acres)
Cabernet area: 24ha (59 acres)
Average production: 170,000 bottles

That vast sums of money were being invested in new cellars and *chai* at the château were very apparent during 1989/90 to any drivers on the road from the south into Pauillac. Huge cranes dominated the skyline beside the fairy-tale turreted château, traffic lights controlled the flow. What the neighbours across the road at Ch Pichon-Longueville Comtesse de Lalande, and at Ch Latour made of the disruption to their lives is not recorded. One hopes that they welcome the work of Jean-Michel Cazes of Ch Lynch-Bages who is the new administrator of Ch Pichon-Baron (as it is called for short). His first year was 1987, and it is to be hoped that he will show a move away from the light, rather forward style that has characterized the wines during the 1970s and early 1980s. The 89, certainly, is an outstanding wine, with its concentrated fruit, dense flavours and outstanding potential balance between oak and fruit. If this is the new style, this is a château to be watched – and not just for the building works.

CH PICHON-LONGUEVILLE COMTESSE DE LALANDE   ****
33250 *Pauillac*

Appellation and classification: Pauillac, Second Growth
Total v'yds owned: 60ha (148 acres)
Cabernet area: 28ha (69 acres)
Average production: 300,000 bottles

If there were to be any further revision of the 1855 classification, it would have to be to move Ch Pichon-Longueville Comtesse de

Lalande (known as Ch Pichon-Lalande) from second-growth to first. Its wines are consistently as good (and, come to that, as expensive) as the first-growths, sometimes even better. The owner, Mme de Lencquesaing, is a formidably charming figure on the Bordeaux scene. The wines she and her daughter make derive much of their lush softness from the highest proportion of Merlot in any Pauillac classed growth. They are certainly among the most attractive Pauillacs when tasted young: the 88 (tasted in 1990) while huge and rich, showed so much fruit that it would have been (almost) a pleasure to drink. The 89 (tasted in 1990) showed equal fruit, even if the tannins are heavier and firmer. All three vintages of the early 80s are outstanding, and the 81 is probably the best wine made by any château that year. The 86 (tasted in 1988) is right up with the top two or three, with its huge power, richness and beautiful fruit. The second wine is Réserve de la Comtesse.

CH PONTET-CANET   ** →
33250 Pauillac

Appellation and classification: Pauillac, Fifth Growth
Total v'yds owned: 75ha (185 acres)
Cabernet area: 51ha (126 acres)
Average production: 360,000 bottles.

This is the largest classed-growth estate in Pauillac, on the high ground north of the town, opposite Mouton-Rothschild. Its fortunes have been mixed, with some of the wine being sold in the past as a non-vintage brand to French railways. Now that it is owned by Guy Tesseron, improvements are being made, and the quality of the last three or four vintages shows a marked change of style. The high proportion of Cabernet Sauvignon is showing up as well: as in the 86 (tasted in 1988) very Pauillac in its tight, rich tannins, which will need years to mature. The 88 (tasted in 1990) had excellent fruit, good colour and a big, chewy, spicy flavour.

St Julien

St-Julien's perfumed, soft style (soft, that is, by comparison with Pauillac) makes its wines some of the most immediately attractive of the great wine villages of the Médoc. A sign of its traditional quality is that it has the highest proportion of *crus classés* to other vineyards of any commune. That is partly because its vineyards are compact, relatively near the river, and all on the gravel bank that rises up just south of the village on the edge of the vineyards of Beychevelle.

But despite being comparatively small, St-Julien's wines are happily very contrasted. There are three main concentrations. One is at the southern end, where Beychevelle and Branaire-Ducru face each other, both producing wines that mature relatively quickly (although they can also age well) and with delicious fruit and perfume. Nearby is the vineyard of Ducru-Beaucaillou, one of the two best châteaux in the commune, making elegant wines that always have a strong backbone.

At the far northern end of the commune is the divided estate of Léoville, united until the beginning of the 19th century, and then split into three. Léoville-las-Cases, in its walled vineyard, the rival to

Ducru- Beaucaillou for top wine in the commune, but in complete contrast – rich and tannic, built to last, nearer in some ways to Pauillac (whose vineyards are right next door) than to southern St-Julien. Close by Léoville-las-Cases are Léoville-Barton and Léoville-Poyferré, the other vineyards derived from the Léoville estate: they, too, have a similar firmness and tannic quality.

The third area of classed-growth vineyards is further inland, to the west of the hamlet of Beychevelle. Here the two Cordier estates of Talbot and Gruaud-Larose produce wines which are fleshier, fruitier than the wines that come from the riverside vineyards.

The soil in St-Julien varies from the very gravelly land in the north of the village to more clayey land away from the river, which obviously affects the style,. with less overtly elegant wines coming from the inland vineyards.

The percentage of Cabernet Sauvignon in all the classed-growth vineyards hovers between 60 and 70 percent. A small increase in percentage can make quite a difference to neighbouring wines as in the example of the very fruity Gruaud-Larose with 65 percent Cabernet and 25 percent Merlot, and the more austere Talbot with 71 percent Cabernet and 20 percent Merlot.

PRODUCERS

CH BEYCHEVELLE   ***
St-Julien Beychevelle, 33250 Pauillac

Appellation and classification: St-Julien, Fourth Growth
Total v'yds owned: 72ha (178 acres)
Cabernet area: 43ha (106 acres)
Average production: 300,000 bottles

New owners and management in 1984 have meant that Beychevelle quality and, equally importantly, reliability have improved immeasurably. Extensive renovations to the château are now taking place, and the vineyard is being improved, with a greater emphasis on Cabernet Sauvignon. The intention is to make wines that, while keeping the St-Julien softness and smoothness, also have greater ageing ability than Beychevelle's wines have in the past. The 87 (tasted in 1990) from a light vintage, showed perfumed fruit, a dry style and colour on the light side; 88, too, showed this perfumed character, supple and rounded; but 86 (tasted in 1990) while it kept the fruit, was also big and chewy, with a colour that was still deeply purple. The 89 was more elegant than powerful.

CH BRANAIRE-DUCRU   →***
St-Julien Beychevelle, 33250 Pauillac

Appellation and classification: St-Julien, Fourth Growth
Total v'yds owned: 48ha (119 acres)
Cabernet area: 29ha (71 acres)
Average production: 240,000 bottles

The weighty, traditional style of Branaire-Ducru derives from long skin contact with the grapes, and a high proportion of new wood, which gives an especially spicy character to the wine. Over the years the owner M. Tapie has made wines which are fat, chocolaty and full of fruit. Although they are heavier than some St-Julien wines, they have the same forward fruit character, and can be drunk young with enjoyment. The 88 (tasted in 1990) had good, spicy fruit, with some acidity and plenty of wood, weightier than the other St-Julien wines in the same tasting. The 85 (tasted in 1988) was very advanced , with jammy fruit, very ripe, highly enjoyable, perhaps not destined to be long-lived. The 89 (tasted in 1990) had a lovely toasty character, balancing acidity, fruit and tannin, one of the top from this vintage.

CH DUCRU-BEAUCAILLOU   ****
St-Julien Beychevelle, 33250 Pauillac

Appellation and classification: St-Julien, Second Growth
Total v'yds owned: 49ha (121 acres)
Cabernet area: 32ha (79 acres)
Average production: 204,000 bottles

"Beau caillou" means fine gravel, and that's just what the soil at this château is. The château itself sits on the top of a rise looking down on to the Gironde, one of the best settings in the Médoc. Jean-Eugène Borie, who owns the château and lives there, has been making one of the very best St-Juliens for at least two decades. Since 1978, the wines have certainly outclassed the vintage: the 82 (tasted in 1984) was a hugely rich, concentrated wine with a silky, velvety backdrop to tannins and fruit. The 86 (tasted in 1988) has considerable tannin, but also equal volumes of fruit, and will obviously live a long time. The 89 (tasted in 1990) is equally rich and dense, with oak flavours just beginning to dominate the cassis and spice fruit: another wine for the next century. The second wine is Ch la Croix.

CH DU GLANA   →**
St-Julien Beychevelle, 33250 Pauillac

Appellation and classification: St-Julien, Cru Grand Bourgeois Exceptionnel
Total v'yds owned: 45ha (111 acres)
Cabernet area: 31ha (77 acres)
Average production: 205,000 bottles

The strictly functional modern cellar is used for making wine that matures relatively quickly and is easily enjoyable. The 86 was, for the vintage, light and supple, with few tannins, the result of cask ageing for only about three months.

CH GLORIA   **→
St-Julien Beychevelle, 33250 Pauillac

Appellation and classification: St-Julien, Cru Bourgeois
Total v'yds owned: 45ha (111 acres)
Cabernet area: 29ha (72 acres)
Average production: 192,000 bottles

The vineyard of Ch Gloria was reconstructed by Henri Martin from parcels of land that had once been owned by *cru classé* châteaux. M. Martin, who has been a strong promoter of the Médoc, believes that the *cru bourgeois* classification does not do justice to his wines. Certainly they have been good, tarry, fruity, spicy wines that seem to mature quite quickly, but are very attractive. The 86 seemed to mark a change in style towards a bigger, more tannic wine, which showed greater firm fruit, and would repay bottle ageing. The 82 (tasted in 1989) on the other hand, lacked the depth of the vintage, even though it compensated with its attractive smoky, cassis fruit. The second wine is Ch Haut-Beychevelle-Gloria.

CH GRUAUD-LAROSE   ***→
St-Julien Beychevelle, 33250 Pauillac

Appellation and classification: St-Julien, Second Growth
Total v'yds owned: 82ha (203 acres)
Cabernet area: 51ha (126 acres)
Average production: 420,000 bottles

One of the two large neighbouring properties in St-Julien owned by the firm of Cordier (the other is Ch Talbot), Gruaud-Larose has a reputation for making fine wines even in bad years. That it is also generally good value is another reason why it is one of the best known estates in the commune. Georges Pauly, the oenologist for the Cordier estates, is now making some big, quite chunky and firm wines which exhibit excellent fruit even if they also show tannins and ageing ability. Of the wines tasted in 1990 there is a Cabernet Sauvignon firmness about the 86 full of tannins which are well integrated with the powerful fruit; the 85 by contrast, was very forward and warm; the 88 showed bags of spicy wood and fruit; and the 89 was huge, deep in colour, big and spicily woody, a powerful mouthful of wine that will go against the normal Gruaud-Larose propensity for relatively early maturation. The second wine is Sarget de Gruaud-Larose.

CH HORTEVIE   **
St-Julien Beychevelle, 33250 Pauillac

Appellation and classification: St-Julien, Cru Bourgeois
Total v'yds owned: 3.5ha (9 acres)
Cabernet area: 2.45ha (6 acres)
Average production: 18,000 bottles

For the Médoc, this is a tiny vineyard, more at home in St-Emilion across the water. But stylistically, Hortevie is every sip a St-Julien, smooth, velvety and ripe. The 81, not the most welcoming of vintages, produced a delightful wine that matured over a period of six years. The wine is made at Ch Terrey-Gros-Cailloux, which is under the same ownership.

CH LAGRANGE   →***
St-Julien Beychevelle, 33250 Pauillac

Appellation and classification: St-Julien, Third Growth
Total v'yds owned: 49ha (121 acres)
Cabernet area: 32ha (79 acres)
Average production: 230,000 bottles

Owned by the Japanese wine and spirits firm, Suntory, Ch Lagrange is in the process of being completely renovated. Michel Delon of Ch Léoville-las-Cases has been retained as a consultant, so we can expect fireworks. I have tasted two wines from the new regime and they certainly show considerable improvements: the 85 (tasted in 1988) was very tannic for the vintage, but with heavyweight fruit to balance it, while 86 (also tasted in 1988) took the tannins of the vintage and exaggerated them, so that it tastes like a wine that will not mature until the 21st century. A second wine, Les Fiefs de Lagrange, was introduced with the 83 vintage.

CH LALANDE-BORIE   **→
St-Julien Beychevelle, 33250 Pauillac

Appellation and classification: St-Julien, Cru Bourgeois Superieur
Total v'yds owned: 18ha (44 acres)
Cabernet area: 12ha (30 acres)
Average production: 96,000 bottles

Jean-Eugène Borie of Ducru-Beaucaillou owns this new vineyard planted in 1970 on land that had once belonged to Ch Lagrange. He is making wines that mature relatively quickly, have an attractive St-Julien perfume, and plenty of ripe fruit.

CH LANGOA-BARTON →***
St-Julien Beychevelle, 33250 Pauillac

Appellation and classification: St-Julien, Third Growth
Total v'yds owned: 20ha (49 acres)
Cabernet area: 14ha (34 acres)
Average production: 96,000 bottles

Langoa-Barton is one of two properties owned by the Barton family who are of Irish descent. It has belonged to the same family since 1821, longer than any other *cru classé* in Bordeaux. Longevity in ownership also breeds traditions, and Langoa and its sister estate Léoville-Barton have a reputation for producing some of the more traditional wines in St-Julien. If that means maintaining consistent quality, then I am all for tradition, because that is the hallmark of both estates. Which is better, Langoa or Léoville, is a moot point, although general opinion is that Léoville wins by a short head. I have always enjoyed tastings of Langoa: of the wines tasted in 1990 the 87 was extremely good for the year, with tobacco-y tannins and fruit; the 88 had delicious firm fruit, excellent tannins and a generally rich, welcoming style; the 89 was full of big, chewy fruit, altogether a big, serious wine. Of older vintages, there was an excellent 81 (tasted in 1984) rich, firm and spicy for the vintage, and probably still drinkable.

CH LÉOVILLE-BARTON ***→
St-Julien Beychevelle, 33250 Pauillac

Appellation and classification: St-Julien, Second Growth
Total v'yds owned: 39ha (96 acres)
Cabernet area: 27ha (67 acres)
Average production: 192,000 bottles

If Ch Léoville-Barton is better than Langoa-Barton, it shows that the 1855 classification sometimes still gets things right. The second-growth Léoville makes wines that are designed for a long life and development. Perhaps this is marginally less true under Anthony Barton's control than it was under his father Ronald, but tastings of recent vintages show plenty of big fruit and tannins there. Perhaps its proximity to Pauillac has something to do with the weighty style, certainly the high percentage of Cabernet Sauvignon has much to do with its ageing ability. Of the wines tasted in 1990, the 87 was big, rich and closed, a much riper wine than normal in that vintage; the 88 has excellent colour, but was dominated by tannin at the time – a wine to keep; the 89 was very rich and broad, tasting of new wood, and promising bags of ripe fruit in years to come. The 82 (tasted in 1986) was a triumph, concentrated, dense and hugely rich. The wines for Léoville are made at Langoa, but treated separately. Wines not used in the Grand Vin are sold as plain St-Julien.

CH LÉOVILLE-LAS-CASES →****
St-Julien Beychevelle, 33250 Pauillac

Appellation and classification: St-Julien, Second Growth
Total v'yds owned: 85ha (210 acres)
Cabernet area: 55ha (136 acres)
Average production: 360,000 bottles

This is one half of the former Léoville estate, which was owned by the Marquis de las Cases and was split into three in the 1820s: the other half was divided again into Léoville-Barton and Léoville-Poyferré. All three châteaux are classified second-growth, but in the past few years it is Léoville-las-Cases which has made the running, under the direction of the forceful Michel Delon. The proximity to Pauillac, as with Léoville-Barton, partly explains the depth and firmness of the wines, whether the vintage is good or less good. But another reason is the almost obsessive perfectionism practised by M. Delon and the very strict selection of grapes. The quality is obvious from tasting the wine: the 85 (tasted in 1988) typical of the vintage in that it is maturing fast, but with superb warm, ripe fruit; the 86, bigger, harsher, more tannic, designed to last seemingly for ever. As an example of an averge vintage, the Léoville-las-Cases 81 is one of the best and most long-lived of that vintage, still firm and tannic, with considerable weight and intensity. The second wine, Clos du Marquis, stands up well to its illustrious Grand Vin.

CH LÉOVILLE-POYFERRÉ **→***
St-Julien Beychevelle, 33250 Pauillac

Appellation and classification: St-Julien, Second Growth
Total v'yds owned: 63ha (156 acres)
Cabernet area: 41ha (101 acres)
Average production: 222,000 bottles

Until recently this was the weak link in the Léoville estates. But since the 80 vintage, new management, new wood and new equipment have generated a turnround in fortunes. While 82 and 83 showed considerable promise, the 86 was better yet, and the 89 (tasted in 1990) certainly the best wine this château has made for 20 years. Some commentators in Bordeaux believe that the Poyferré land is the best of the three Léoville estates: if that is the case, the next few vintages could see some stunning wines.

CH ST-PIERRE **→***
St-Julien Beychevelle, 33250 Pauillac

Appellation and classification: St-Julien, Fourth Growth
Total v'yds owned: 20ha (49 acres)
Cabernet area: 14ha (34 acres)
Average production: 60,000 bottles

Until it was purchased by Henri Martin (of Ch Gloria), this estate was known as St-Pierre-Sevaistre. Whether the shortening of the name will also change the style of the wine, it is too early to say definitively. But the quality of the wines, always good and reliable, chunky and dominated by the high proportion of Cabernet Sauvignon, seems to be getting better. The 86 (tasted in 1988) is full of dense, rich fruit, not too tannic and probably ready to drink in the mid-90s. The 89 (tasted in 1990) has elegance and cassis fruit, balanced with some wood tastes, and tannin enough to see it ageing well.

CH TALBOT   ***
St-Julien Beychevelle, 33250 Pauillac

Appellation and classification: St-Julien, Fourth Growth
Total v'yds owned: 101ha (250 acres)
Cabernet area: 72ha (178 acres)
Average production: 400,000 bottles

Talbot, the largest estate in St-Julien, is owned by the Cordier firm, who also own the neighbouring second-growth Gruaud-Larose. While Gruaud-Larose is a big, chunky, fruity wine, always attractive even when young, Talbot is more austere, showing less fruit and more tannin when young and evolving into a more classic style. This is almost certainly derived from the higher percentage of Cabernet Sauvignon in the Talbot vineyard. Wines that are tasting well for the early 90s are the 78, with direct cassis flavours and ripe, jammy fruit; and the 79, with the soft, velvety texture that is also a sign of St-Julien. Of younger wines, the 86 is very good, classic red Bordeaux of great style and class. In 1990 tastings the 88 was deep, rich and fat, with considerable new wood tastes, while 89 was extraordinarily fruity and rich, perhaps waiting for wood tastes to take over. The second wine is Connetable Talbot.

CH TERREY-GROS-CAILLOUX   **→
St-Julien Beychevelle, 33250 Pauillac

Appellation and classification: St-Julien, Cru Bourgeois
Total v'yds owned: 15ha (37 acres)
Cabernet area: 9.7ha (24 acres)
Average production: 96,000 bottles

The owners of Terrey-Gros-Cailloux also own Ch Hortevie, and both wines are made in the *chai* at Terrey-Gros-Cailloux. The vineyard is in parcels spread all over the commune. Commentators write of the quality of the wine and the good value it represents: I have never tasted it.

Margaux

The southernmost of the great village *appellations*, Margaux is also the most widely spread. It takes in not only the village of Margaux but the neighbouring hamlets of Soussans to the north and Cantenac, Arsac and Labarde to the south.

The soil here is the lightest gravel in the Médoc. This quality is used to explain the lighter, some say ethereal, style of Margaux, as contrasted to the heavier wines of St-Julien and Pauillac further north. The quality of the soil also explains the high proportion of Cabernet Sauvignon in many of the château vineyards; 65 percent is a common amount, while Ch Margaux has 75 percent and one estate, du Tertre, has 80 percent.

Here Cabernet Sauvignon shows another side to its character. It does not make the hard, muscular, tannic wines (albeit with enormous fruit) that characterize Pauillac: in Margaux they are more elegant, stylish – as they also say of race horses, wines with breeding. That is certainly true of the wines of the hamlet of Cantenac, home of Ch Palmer, Ch d'Angludet and Ch d'Issan, all three making some of the most attractive of Margaux wines. Here, the depth of gravel is at its greatest.

By contrast Margaux – the village – tends to make wines with greater tannin, slower to mature: of course that is true of Ch Margaux, but it is also true of other estates – Ch Rausan-Ségla and Ch la Gurgue spring to mind. The soil here, while always gravel, has some limestone in the subsoil.

One of the problems with Margaux, at least in the recent past, was that the 1855 classification gave very little clue as to quality. Some highly classified vineyards were in steep decline, others further down the list were doing much better than their grading suggested. The 1980s have seen many improvements in the quality of wine from those vineyards which have been poorly regarded since the 1960s. It looks as if owners are investing wisely and usefully.

PRODUCERS

CH D'ANGLUDET →***
Cantenac, 33460 Margaux

Appellation and classification: Margaux, Cru Bourgeois Superieur
Total v'yds owned: 30ha (74 acres)
Cabernet area: 15.6ha (39 acres)
Average production: 144,000 bottles

If Angludet had existed as an estate in 1855, it would certainly have been classified. But the estate had been divided up by then and lost the importance it had in the 18th century. It is really only since 1961, when the Sichel family bought the land and revived the vineyard, that it has regained its renown, if not achieved a classification. The wine is certainly better than most *cru bourgeois*, always well made, with great style and finesse.

The relatively high proportion of Merlot (30 percent), dictated by the clay and sand in the vineyard soil along with the gravel, produces a wine that can mature relatively quickly, but which then can survive on a peak of maturity for a number of years. Vintages like the 78 (tasted in 1989) show how well the wine can mature, with its soft fruit and tannins, while younger wines, like the 87 (tasted in 1990) have excellent new wood flavours and light colour, a good example of a light vintage; and the 88 (tasted in 1990) offers ripe fruits and tannins, a wine of some depth and complexity.

CH BOYD-CANTENAC **→
Cantenac, 33460 Margaux

Appellation and classification: Margaux, Third Growth
Total v'yds owned: 18ha (44 acres)
Cabernet area: 12ha (30 acres)
Average production: 90,000 bottles

The complicated intermingling of the wines of Ch Boyd-Cantenac and Ch Pouget finally ended after the 82 vintage when, for the first time, the two wines were vinified in separate *cuveries*, rather than in the same vats in the same building. So it is really only with the 83 vintage (tasted in 1985) that we can see the true character of Boyd-Cantenac on its own: full-bodied, quite chunky for Margaux, with good concentrated spicy fruit, a fine wine in a mixed vintage. The 85 unusually was better than the 86 when tasted in 1989, but perhaps this was just a stage in the wines.

CH BRANE-CANTENAC ** → ***
Cantenac, 33460 Margaux

Appellation and classification: Margaux, Second Growth
Total v'yds owned: 85ha (210 acres)
Cabernet area: 59ha (146 acres)
Average production: 348,000 bottles

After a long period of decline, the wines from one of Margaux' largest vineyards has now been dramatically improved. The best include the 83 (tasted in 1986) sweet, medium-bodied with smooth fruit and some tannin, a wine that will mature relatively quickly; and the 86 (tasted in 1989) deep, rich and intensely powerful. The second wine is Ch Notton.

CH CANTENAC-BROWN → **
Cantenac, 33460 Margaux

Appellation and classification: Margaux, Third Growth
Total v'yds owned: 32ha (79 acres)
Cabernet area: 24ha (59 acres)
Average production: 180,000 bottles

The extraordinary building at Cantenac-Brown, more like a minor English private school than a Bordeaux château, was in fact not built by the Mr Brown who owned the estate at the beginning of the 19th century, but by his French successors. It is now owned by the du Vivier family, former owners of the de Luze négociant house. The wine is not one that I have encountered often, but it seems to have a hard, tannic style when young which softens slowly and reluctantly. Of recent vintages, the 86 showed considerable improvement on the wines of the 1970s, with its rich tannins and elegant fruit; however the 89 (tasted in 1990) was a disappointment, with a very light style and not much tannin.

CH DESMIRAIL **
33460 Margaux

Appellation and classification: Margaux, Third Growth
Total v'yds owned: 18ha (44 acres)
Cabernet area: 14.4ha (36 acres)
Average production: 48,000 bottles

This vineyard disappeared sometime after the 1855 classification placed it as a third-growth. It has been revived by Lucien Lurton, owner of Brane-Cantenac and other Margaux properties, from four different vineyards within Margaux. The first vintage was 81. At present the wine is pleasant, perfumed and relatively fast maturing, but given time, the ageing of the vineyards and the continued expert advice of Professor Emile Peynaud, it should deepen and improve: it will certainly be helped by the high percentage (80 percent) of Cabernet Sauvignon in the vineyards.

CH DURFORT-VIVENS ** →
33460 Margaux

Appellation and classification: Margaux, Second Growth
Total v'yds owned: 20ha (49 acres)
Cabernet area: 16ha (39 acres)
Average production: 66,000 bottles

After a long, lean period, Durfort-Vivens seems to have returned to something approaching the quality that would justify its exalted status in the 1855 classification. Owner Lucien Lurton bought the property in 1961, and has begun restoring its fortunes. The wine is relatively tough when young, and needs a good many years before maturity. The 82 (tasted in 1986) was a fine wine for the château, with plenty of tannin sitting on top of ripe cassis fruit. The 88 (tasted in 1990) had a good balance between wood and fruit, with a perfumed ripe flavour. This looks like a château on the way up. The second wine is Domaine de Cure-Bourse.

CH GISCOURS   ***
Labarde, 33460 Margaux

Appellation and classification: Margaux, Third Growth
Total v'yds owned: 81ha (200 acres)
Cabernet area: 61ha (150 acres)
Average production: 350,000 bottles

The Tari family, which has owned Ch Giscours since 1952, makes one of the best, and certainly one of the most reliable, wines in Margaux. Their vineyard, part of a huge estate of 250ha (618 acres), is one of the largest in the *appellation*. They make a wine which is more powerful than some in Margaux, with greater density. I always enjoy Giscours, but traditionally it has needed time. The 78 (tasted in 1985) was still very deeply tannic and firm, despite the presence of huge quantities of ripe fruit. The 82 is more forward, as is the 86 (tasted in 1988) with smooth, surprisingly un-tannic fruit. The 88 (tasted in 1990) seemed to return to harder tannins and greater austerity, even though with good colour and richness, while the 89 (tasted in 1990) also has good tannins over spicy, elegant fruit.

CH LA GURGUE   →***
33460 Margaux

Appellation and classification: Margaux, Cru Bourgeois Superieur
Total v'yds owned: 12ha (30 acres)
Cabernet area: 8.4ha (21 acres)
Average production: 60,000 bottles

Since the change of ownership, and the arrival of Bernadette Villars of Ch Chasse-Spleen as manager, this small estate has looked set for great things. The vineyard is next door to Ch Margaux, on the slope leading down to the river. The wines are now certainly some of the best *cru bourgeois* wines in Margaux: the 82 was full of ripe fruit that had been allowed free rein; the 85 (tasted in 1989) is a smooth, concentrated, warm wine; the 86 (tasted in 1989) is a pleasing, medium-bodied wine with initially some tough tannins which are now softening. The 89 (tasted in 1990) was among the top Margaux of the vintage, brimming with fruit, in a very concentrated style that suggests extensive bottle ageing will be necessary.

CH D'ISSAN   →***
Cantenac, 33460 Margaux

Appellation and classification: Margaux, Third Growth
Total v'yds owned: 32ha (79 acres)
Cabernet area: 24ha (59 acres)

Unusually for Margaux, the Issan vineyard is planted only with Cabernet Sauvignon (75 percent) and Merlot (25 percent), without the usual Cabernet Franc. This must obviously have an effect on the wines, which are normally tannic when young, even though they can mature relatively quickly. The château is a beautiful eighteenth-century building which has been lovingly restored by the present owners, the Cruse family, and decorated with numerous works of art. The wines, too, have been given care and attention, so that now Issan is producing a reliably consistent wine that is Margaux in its perfume, even if tannic in its taste. Good recent vintages include the 85 (tasted in 1988) warm, soft and rich, with good spicy wood flavours; and the 89 (tasted in 1990) quite lean for the year, but showing good perfume. The 88 (tasted in 1990) was spoilt by an overripe taste. The second wine is Ch de Candale.

CH LABÉGORCE-ZÉDÉ   **→

Soussans, 33460 Margaux

Appellation and classification: Margaux, Cru Bourgeois Superieur
Total v'yds owned: 26ha (64 acres)
Cabernet area: 13ha (32 acres)
Average production: 114,000 bottles

The name Labégorce crops up a number of times in Margaux. It is a corruption of the Abbé Gorsse who once owned this estate, together with Ch Labégorce and Ch l'Abbé Gorsse de Gorsse. It is experiencing something of a renaissance, producing a chunky wine, with plenty of fruit, even if it lacks the elegance of some other Margaux cru bourgeois wines. The 86 (tasted in 1989) was certainly tannic, very firm and closed, but was hinting at a full-bodied rich wine in the future. The 89 (tasted in 1990) was showing some balance between cassis fruit and tannin, with a rather austere aftertaste.

CH LASCOMBES   **→***

33460 Margaux

Appellation and classification: Margaux, Second Growth
Total v'yds owned: 94ha (232 acres)
Cabernet area: 61ha (151 acres)
Average production: 430,000 bottles

Ch Lascombes is a large estate, but it is only recently that some form of amalgamation and swapping of vineyards has cut down on the 1,000 or so different plots of land in Margaux that made up its 94 ha. As well as rationalization, there has been considerable investment by Lascombes' current owners, the UK Bass Charrington company: they have built a spectacular new chai and installed the most modern vinification equipment. The wines have been less spectacular than the buildings, solid and generally reliable, but not really sparkling as a second-growth should. Recent vintages show little improvement: the 88 (tasted in 1990) was appley and tart with too much wood and too little fruit; the 89 (tasted in 1990) showed a strange balance between wood and fruit that may disappear as it ages. The best vintage of the 1980s was the 83 (tasted in 1986) fat and fruity for the vintage with good spicy wood. The second wine is Ch Ségonnes.

CH MALESCOT-ST-EXUPÉRY   **→

33460 Margaux

Appellation and classification: Margaux, Third Growth
Total v'yds owned: 34ha (84 acres)
Cabernet area: 17ha (42 acres)
Average production: 180,000 bottles

The reputation of Malescot-St-Exupéry has been for making long-lived wines in a traditional way. Chances to taste this wine are rare, but the 82 (tasted in 1985) showed the full but forward cassis fruit typical of the vintage, coupled with some wood and hints of spice.

CH MARGAUX ****
33460 Margaux

Appellation and classification: Margaux, First Growth
Total v'yds owned: 85ha (210 acres)
Cabernet area: 64ha (158 acres)
Average production: 210,000 bottles

Since the arrival in 1977 of the Mentzelopoulos family as owners, Ch Margaux has been able to take its place again at the top of the Médoc tree: some would argue that it is now making the best wine anywhere in Bordeaux. Money, vast sums of it, have been spent but, unlike some estates where money never seems to produce results, here the effects of spending have been spectacular, not only in the restored buildings, but in the wine. It is, perhaps inevitably, weightier than most wines of Margaux (the commune, that is), but it has, to a greater degree than other wines of the village, that lovely, delicate perfume and elegance that gives Margaux wines their character. Any vintage since 78 has been of the best. The most recent tasted was of the same class: the 89 (tasted in 1990) with its power and concentration, spicy and tarry, coupled with perfume, elegance and a terrific sense of style. The second wine is Pavillon Rouge du Château Margaux, itself a superior example of the commune.

CH PALMER ****
Cantenac, 33460 Margaux

Appellation and classification: Margaux, Third Growth
Total v'yds owned: 45ha (111 acres)
Cabernet area: 25ha (62 acres)
Average production: 150,000 bottles

For many years Ch Palmer has been the next best thing to Ch Margaux in the Margaux *appellation*. Its status as merely third-growth has been belied by the high prices it attracts (more than most second-growths) and by the praise it gains from consumers and other producers alike. Its ownership is complicated, with French, Dutch and British connections, but the wine production is under the control of the British owner, Peter Sichel (who also owns the up-and-coming *cru bourgeois* Ch d'Angludet). Everything at Palmer is traditional, from the old-fashioned presses to the long maceration of the grapeskins after fermentation to extract extra colour. The style is old fashioned, too, very opulent (the high level of Merlot – 40 percent – would see to that) and smooth, but with built-in structure and tannins that see the wine ageing gracefully over many years. The last three vintages tasted maintain the reputation: a spicy, smoky, rich 87 (tasted in 1990); a huge, firm, tannic structured 88 (tasted in 1990); and a mammoth 89 (tasted in 1990) with concentration and complexity, coupled with potential elegance and charm. The second wine is the Réserve du Général.

CH POUGET   **→
Cantenac, 33460 Margaux

Appellation and classification: Margaux, Fourth Growth
Total v'yds owned: 10ha (25 acres)
Cabernet area: 7ha (17 acres)
Average production: 42,000 bottles

Until the 83 vintage, this wine was indistinguishable from Ch Boyd-Cantenac, as both wines were made in the *chai* at Pouget. Now there is separate production, with a new *chai* for making Ch Pouget. Reports suggest the wines are in a rich style, certainly more consistent than they used to be.

CH PRIEURÉ-LICHINE   **→***
Cantenac, 33460 Margaux

Appellation and classification: Margaux, Fourth Growth
Total v'yds owned: 60ha (148 acres)
Cabernet area: 33ha (82 acres)
Average production: 300,000 bottles

For the late Alexis Lichine, author, ambassador for French wine in the United States, one-time owner of Ch Lascombes, Prieuré-Lichine was home. He restored the ancient religious buildings at the château, and improved the vineyard and the wine. For years, his was the only château that actually welcomed casual visitors. He has been succeeded by his son Sacha, and the wines have maintained their reliability and quality. It has a soft style, probably influenced by the high Merlot content, and the wines mature relatively fast. Three vintages (tasted in 1988) showed the style well: the 86, quite acid, quite deep as befits the vintage, with rich, attractive spicy wood balance, and excellent colour. The 82 was quintessential Margaux, perfumed, elegant, not too concentrated. The 78 was just mature, hinting at age, with rich mature fruit and some acids – a wine to drink up. The second wine is Ch de Clairefort.

CH RAUSAN-SÉGLA   **→
33460 Margaux

Appellation and classification: Margaux, Second Growth
Total v'yds owned: 42ha (104 acres)
Cabernet area: 28ha (69 acres)
Average production: 120,000 bottles

As with many Margaux estates which had seemed to be in decline, the 1980s have brought a revival in fortunes, and vintages from 81 show something of which the château is capable – and which gave it an exalted classification in 1855. Owned by the British Lonrho group, its wines are made by and distributed exclusively through the négociant firm of Louis Eschenauer. The 82 (tasted in 1989), which is now mature, has excellent cassis fruit and smoky wood flavours; the better 83 (tasted in 1986) had more tannin and ripe firm fruit. The 86 (tasted in 1988) is powerful, tannic, deep in colour, with a forward, fresh perfume. The 89 (tasted in 1990) combines elegance with strong tannins.

CH SIRAN →***
Labarde, 33460 Margaux

Appellation and classification: **Margaux, Cru Bourgeois Superieur**
Total v'yds owned: **35ha (86 acres)**
Cabernet area: **17.5ha (43 acres)**
Average production: **150,000 bottles**

The wines have some weight and style, maturing with elegance and charm: the 81 was a wine that had less austerity than others in that year. The 88 (tasted in 1990) showed considerable weight and tannins, with deft touches of new wood. The 89 (tasted in 1990) was extremely successful, marrying the ripe, soft fruit well with the oak, producing a wine that will mature in the late 1990s.

CH DU TERTRE →***
Arsac, 33460 Margaux

Appellation and classification: **Margaux, Fifth Growth**
Total v'yds owned: **48ha (119 acres)**
Cabernet area: **38.4ha (95 acres)**
Average production: **168,000 bottles**

This *cru classé* is owned by Philippe Capbern-Gasqueton, owner of Calon-Ségur in St-Estèphe. The wine is generally tannic when young, and takes a long time to mellow. The 82 (tasted in 1988) was typical in this respect: while there was certainly plenty of fruit, the wine was still firmly tannic, with deep colour and cedarwood flavour. I liked the 88 (tasted in 1990) rather less: it was spoilt by a rather agricultural smell; the 89 (tasted in 1990) was better, with good concentration, very firm with excellent cassis and cherry fruit.

Moulis and Listrac

Both Moulis and Listrac lie to the west of the main line of Médoc vineyards which run close to the river Gironde. They are on high ground, near the towns of Castelnau and St-Laurent. The soil here has less gravel and more clay, a number of the better growths have a higher percentage of Merlot than the wines from the main Médoc villages and are therefore not included in this directory.

However all the estates are profiting from the improved financial climate in Bordeaux. Their wines are now fetching sufficiently high prices for there to be considerable investment in new plantings in the vineyard and new plant in the *chai*. New wood was much more in evidence in the 1980s than ever before. The consequent quality improvement is a pleasure to report. While their price has gone up, these *cru bourgeois* of Listrac and Moulis still can offer good value.

As a rough and ready rule, the wines of Moulis are powerful but smooth, and manage to show off considerable fruit character. Some estates, notably Ch Chasse-Spleen and Ch Brillette are making wines worthy of classed-growth status. Listrac's wines are rather more astringent and tough when young, but the two Fourcas estates, Ch Fourcas-Dupré and Ch Fourcas-Hosten, are showing the potential of this commune.

PRODUCERS

CH BRILLETTE →***
Moulis-en-Médoc, 33480 Castelnau

Appellation and classification: Moulis, Cru Grand Bourgeois
Total vineyard owned: 30ha (74 acres)
Cabernet area: 16.5ha (40 acres)
Average production: 132,000 bottles

Great names have advised at this up-and-coming estate. The results show in the wines: the 86 (tasted in 1988) was a spicy, concentrated wine, showing rich fruit and good oak, even if designed for relatively rapid maturation.

CH CHASSE-SPLEEN ***
Moulis-en-Médoc, 33480 Castelnau

Appellation and classification: Moulis, Cru Grand Bourgeois Exceptionnel
Total v'yds owned: 62ha (153 acres)
Cabernet area: 31ha (77 acres)
Average production: 300,000 bottles

Ch Chasse-Spleen regularly makes the best wines in Moulis, and some of the best from any *cru bourgeois*. Its reputation is not new – it was seen as a candidate for promotion before World War 1, but its quality level has never been higher. The wines tend towards considerable tannin when young, but there is always excellent fruit quality, and this emerges to give gorgeously forward fruit, the product of 45 percent Merlot in the blend, topped up by the new wood tastes. The 86 (tasted in 1988) was a great wine, full of fruit and tannin, with huge, burstingly ripe tastes. The 88 (tasted in 1990) showed surprising softness and the fruit was still held back, but it had weight and richness that will show in time. The second wine is L'Ermitage de Chasse-Spleen.

CH CLARKE **→
Listrac, 33480 Castelnau

Appellation and classification: Listrac, Cru Bourgeois
Total v'yds owned: 121ha (299 acres)
Cabernet area: 60ha (148 acres)
Average production: 360,000 bottles

This is the biggest thing to hit Listrac for a very long time. Baron Edmond de Rothschild has revived an ancient vineyard and château, and completely renovated it, installing the most modern equipment. He has also planted huge swathes of vineyard and is aiming to produce considerable quantities of wine. While early vintages tasted light, the inevitable product of a young vineyard, vintages from the mid-1980s onwards are showing much more depth and complexity. The second wine is Ch Malmaison.

CH FOURCAS-DUPRÉ **→
Listrac-Médoc, 33480 Castelnau

Appellation and classification: Listrac, Cru Grand Bourgeois Exceptionnel
Total v'yds owned: 42ha (104 acres)
Cabernet area: 21ha (52 acres)
Average production: 265,000 bottles

A very "proper" *cru bourgeois*, owned by the Pages family, making a wine that is firm and somewhat austere when young. The gravelly soil is good for the Cabernet Sauvignon which dominates the blend. The wine matures into a light-weight but attractively spicy and fruity wine. The 86 (tasted in 1988) was better than usual, with a wealth of fruit and tannin.

CH FOURCAS-HOSTEN →***
Listrac-Médoc, 33480 Castelnau

Appellation and classification: Listrac, Cru Grand Bourgeois Exceptionnel
Total v'yds owned: 40ha (99 acres)
Cabernet area: 22ha (54 acres)
Average production: 216,000 bottles

The Pages family, of Fourcas-Dupré, manage this property, and make wine here that outshines the produce of their own vineyard. There is a quality of delicious fruit in most vintages, certainly since the late 1970s. The 85 (tasted in 1988) was full of cassis fruit, with deceptive power and excellent wood flavours.

CH MOULIN-À-VENT **
Moulis-en-Médoc, 33480 Castelnau

Appellation and classification: Moulis, Cru Grand Bourgeois
Total v'yds owned: 24ha (59 acres)
Cabernet area: 15.6ha (39 acres)
Average production: 120,000 bottles

A château that has improved considerably in the 1980s. Both 85 and 86 vintages are powerful, rich, somewhat tannic wines, the 85 warmer and lighter, the 86 more dense. There is a second label, Moulin-de-St-Vincent.

Graves

The Graves is the most exciting area in Bordeaux at the moment. From being the source of indifferent sweet white wines and rather lightweight reds, it has changed into a powerhouse of excitement. Dry white wines, fermented and matured in wood, are now boosting the reputation of white Bordeaux on the international scene; while reds are undergoing a transformation as new wood and new ideas on fermentation come into play.

The Graves is now two areas: in the north, there is a new *appellation*, Pessac-Léognan, which takes in the communes in and around Bordeaux and to the south. Here the most famous red Graves is made: Ch Haut-Brion, Domaine de Chevalier, and the rest. To the south of Léognan is now the Graves *appellation*. In fact, while many improvements are being made in the Pessac-Léognan *appellation*, the greatest excitement is to be found further south, in the backwoods of this strangely remote area. If this were a study of Bordeaux rather than of Cabernet Sauvignon, there would be a host of estates from this region. But, while Cabernet Sauvignon is an important element in this area, it normally forms only about 30–40 percent of the vineyard, rather than being in the majority.

The Graves, as its name suggests, is a land of gravelly soil which runs in ridges away from the River Garonne. The base of this gravel is sand or sandstone and clay. Most of the vineyards, apart from those in the Bordeaux suburbs, are planted in clearings in the forest of Les Landes which stretches from here to the ocean and down almost to the Spanish border.

The Cabernet Sauvignon has its strongest hold in the classed growths of the northern Graves – what is now Pessac-Léognan. Here, the older estates have long made wines to last, even though they all possess a lightness, finesse and elegance that is typical Graves. In the communes of Pessac, Léognan and Martillac, the concentration of gravel soils is greatest, and so is the amount of Cabernet. Down south, around Langon and on the edge of the Sauternes region, the soil is more clayey, which is why there is more Merlot to be found here.

PRODUCERS

CH CARBONNIEUX   ** →
33850 Léognan

Appellation and classification: Pessac-Léognan, Cru Classé
Total v'yds owned for red: 35ha (86 acres)
Cabernet area: 17.5ha (43 acres)
Average production of red: 180,000 bottles

The beautiful medieval château, formerly a monastery, has been restored from total dilapidation – as have the vineyard and the *chai* – by the Perrin family who bought the property in 1956. Production here is divided equally between white and red, with the red gradually gaining increasing importance. The red has also been getting better, as vines planted in the late 1950s mature, and as the proportion of Cabernet Sauvignon has increased. The wines of the late 1980s showed greater depth and weight than ever: the 85 (tasted in 1988) somewhat lightweight attractive forward fruit; the 86 (tasted in 1989) complex, rich and sweet, with a powerful spicy, smoky oak bouquet, and the 88 (tasted in 1990) very firm and tannic, still very closed up.

DOMAINE DE CHEVALIER   *** →
33850 Léognan

Appellation and classification: Pessac-Léognan, Cru Classé
Total v'yds owned for red: 15ha (37 acres)
Cabernet area: 9.75ha (24 acres)
Average production of red: 60,000 bottles

While the lucky few who get a chance to taste the white Domaine de Chevalier regard it as the greatest white Graves, the red wine just misses that level of ultimate greatness. Not to say that it is not very good indeed. Vintages from anytime since the mid-1970s are still showing power and richness while many other red Graves have fallen by the wayside. The use of new barrels contributing delicious vanilla and spice flavours to the fruit, the deep colour from long maceration, and above all the high proportion (65 percent) of Cabernet Sauvignon, all mean that these are some of the most long-lived red wines made in the Grâves. The 86 (tasted in 1988) was oozing rich fruit and new wood; the 88, while lighter, still had excellent tobacco-y fruit; the 89 (tasted in 1990) was already showing good balance between the new wood and rich, cassis fruit.

CH DE FIEUZAL   ***
33850 Léognan

Appellation and classification: Pessac-Léognan, Cru Classé
Total v'yds owned for red: 21ha (52 acres)
Cabernet area: 14ha (34 acres)
Average production of red: 96,000 bottles

The red wines made here have traditionally been on the light side. But things have changed with vintages of the 1980s: the 83 (tasted in 1985) had elegance and style with good tannin; the 86 (tasted in 1988) was big and powerful, designed for a long life; the 88 (tasted in 1990) was elegant with a splash of acidity on top of ripe fruit; the 89 (tasted in 1990) was the best yet, deep colour, ripe tannic fruit with complex spice and blackcurrant flavours.

CH HAUT-BAILLY   →***
33850 Léognan

Appellation and classification: Pessac-Léognan, Cru Classé
Total v'yds owned for red: 25ha (62 acres)
Cabernet area: 15ha (37 acres)
Average production of red: 132,000 bottles

The wines from this estate, south of the town of Léognan, are characterized by their softness and stylish elegance even when young. The 85 (tasted in 1988) had classic Graves qualities: the tobacco smells, the perfumed, silky fruit and the shot of acid to stop it being too soft and sweet. The 86 (tasted in 1988) while bigger and more tannic, is still full of understated elegance. Despite this obvious early attraction, the wines can age well over a 10-year period, or longer.

CH HAUT-BRION   ****
33600 Pessac

Appellation and classification: Pessac-Léognan, First Growth
Total v'yds owned for red: 41ha (101 acres)
Cabernet area: 22.5ha (56 acres)
Average production: 144,000 bottles

This was the only Graves red wine to be classified in 1855, and it owes this to the unique position the estate of Haut-Brion has held since the 17th century, when it was considered the best wine in Bordeaux. Now surrounded by the suburbs of Bordeaux, the vineyard still produces one of the very best reds to be made anywhere in the Bordeaux region; and, since a slight dip in its quality in the late 1960s, it has been making wine that merits first-growth status. It is much lighter than any of the Médoc first-growths, showing the Graves finesse and elegance to a fine degree. The wines are sometimes deceptively attractive at an early stage: the 85 (tasted in 1988) could almost have been drunk then and there. But they do have an ability to age, and I would not expect the 86 (tasted in 1988) to be fully mature until after 2000. The 89 (tasted in 1990) had impeccable balance alongside very rich fruit and ripe tobacco and wood tastes. There is a second wine, Bahans-Haut-Brion.

CH LARRIVET-HAUT-BRION   ** →
33850 Léognan

Appellation and classification: Pessac-Léognan, unclassified
Total v'yds owned for red: 15ha (37 acres)
Cabernet area: 9.2ha (23 acres)
Average production of red: 91,000 bottles

A high proportion of Cabernet Sauvignon and gravelly soil mean that this is often a firm, tannic wine when young, and it never shows the fleshy character of those Graves wines with a higher proportion of Merlot. That said, it matures well, into a very direct-tasting wine, with good balance and a positive fruit character. The 88 (tasted in 1990) was typical in this respect: quite light in colour, it had hints of new wood, and a fine balance of acidity and slightly austere fruit.

CH LA LOUVIÈRE   → ***
33850 Léognan

Appellation and classification: Pessac-Léognan, unclassified
Total v'yds owned for red: 37ha (91 acres)
Cabernet area: 26ha (64 acres)
Average production of red: 192,000 bottles

There has been something of a stylistic change at La Louvière. While the Cabernet Sauvignon (at 70 percent) continues to dominate the blend, the importance of Merlot (at 20 percent) has been increased, and the result is a wine that is becoming increasingly fruity, juicy and warm. The 88 is an example of this new style: tasted in 1990, it showed excellent Cabernet colour, but then had deep, smooth fruit balanced with new wood tastes, influenced by the Merlot. Older vintages of La Louvière, by contrast, often seemed very hard and tannic when young.

CH LA MISSION-HAUT-BRION   → ****
33400 Talence

Appellation and classification: Pessac-Léognan, Cru Classé
Total v'yds owned for red: 17ha (42 acres)
Cabernet area: 10.2ha (25 acres)
Average production of red: 84,000 bottles

Now under the same ownership as Ch Haut-Brion across the road, the style of La Mission-Haut-Brion, long-standing rival of its neighbour, has changed ever so slightly in favour of a firmer, more weighty, more structured style. Until the 83 vintage, when the new owners took over, La Mission's style was very rich, very full bodied, very warm, even if always balanced with intense fruit and tannin. Now it is likely to be even more long-lasting than before. The deep gravel in the vineyard aids the concentration of wines such as the 89 (tasted in 1990) a superb wine, it has all the intense and spicy sweet blackcurrant fruit, combined with tough tannins and a very dense colour.

CH OLIVIER   → **
33850 Léognan

Appellation and classification: Pessac-Léognan, Cru Classé
Total vineyard owned for red: 18ha (44 acres)
Cabernet area: 11.7ha (29 acres)
Average production of red: 102,000 bottles

One of the lightest red Graves in this directory, Ch Olivier has, however, improved with the vintages of the 1980s, so that the 88 (tasted in 1990) for example, had excellent deep colour and a good, new wood taste, even if there was still a streak of rather too assertive acidity. The 89 (tasted in 1990) was more rewarding, with good firm and solid fruit, rather closed up but showing good potential.

CH PAPE-CLÉMENT ** → ***
33600 Pessac

Appellation and classification: Pessac-Léognan, Cru Classé
Total v'yds owned for red: 28ha (69 acres)
Cabernet area: 16.8ha (41 acres)
Average production of red: 144,000 bottles

As with so many other châteaux in the Graves, the 1980s have seen an enormous improvement in the fortunes and the quality of Ch Pape-Clément. One of the oldest estates in the Graves, the vineyard's records go back to 1300. The present owners have renovated the *chai* and improved the vineyard. Wines like the very fine 86 (tasted in 1988) have the elegance and perfume of a great Graves red, with the characteristic tobacco smells, but now coupled with power and concentration. The 88 (tasted in 1990) had the same elegance, plus the fruit and tannin in excellent balance.

CH SMITH-HAUT-LAFITTE **
Martillac, 33650 La Brède

Appellation and classification: Pessac-Léognan, Cru Classé
Total v'yds owned for red: 45.5ha (112 acres)
Cabernet area: 33ha (82 acres)
Average production of red: 264,000 bottles

A generally lightweight wine, but with enough of the characteristic Graves tobacco and spice smells and good fruit to make it attractive for comparatively short-term drinking. The 88 (tasted in 1990) was light, perfumed and with a pleasing oak character.

CH LA TOUR-HAUT-BRION ** →
33400 Talence

Appellation and classification: Pessac-Léognan, Cru Classé
Total v'yds owned for red: 4ha (10 acres)
Cabernet area: 2.8ha (7 acres)
Average production: 18,000 bottles

Since the change in ownership of Ch La Mission-Haut-Brion, this small estate, which was formerly treated as a second wine for La Mission, is now being vinified separately. The 86 (tasted in 1988) had rich fruit and smoothness, with delicious blackcurrant flavours. It would appear that the high percentage of Cabernet Sauvignon in the vineyard (70 percent) will mean that the wines are long-lived.

CH LA TOUR-MARTILLAC → **
Martillac, 33650 La Brède

Appellation and classification: Pessac-Léognan, Cru Classé
Total v'yds owned for red: 20 ha (49 acres)
Cabernet area: 12 ha (30 acres)
Average production of red: 102,000 bottles

The Kressman family estate produces wines that are very traditional in style, heavy and tannic when young. High temperature fermentation means that they have good deep colour, but sometimes the fruit extract seems to be missing. In good vintages, though, some elegance with the firm fruit makes for good ageing ability. The 85 (tasted in 1988) was one of the best wines from this château in the 80s, with its deep flavour, cherry fruit and concentrated colour. The second wine is Ch La Grave-Martillac.

Other French Cabernets

Outside Bordeaux, very few wines have a preponderance of Cabernet Sauvignon. However, in the regions listed below, its presence makes an increasingly important contribution.

SOUTHWEST FRANCE

The hinterland east and south of Bordeaux is a kaleidoscope of *appellations* rooted in strong historic traditions. Close to Bordeaux, the grape varieties of these *appellations* follow the Bordeaux pattern, using Cabernet Sauvignon, Cabernet Franc and Merlot along with Malbec and other more local varieties.

BERGERAC AND PÉCHARMANT
Largest of these *appellations* is due east of St-Emilion on the road that follows the River Dordogne. The small market town of Bergerac is the centre of a number of *appellations*, making anything from rich reds to sweet whites. The two principal red *appellations* are Begerac and Pécharmant. The latter, and smaller of the two, also has the higher quality. There is also a less widely seen *appellation* of Côtes de Bergerac. The basic grape varieties for all three appellations are the same: Cabernet Sauvignon, Cabernet Franc, Malbec and Merlot, with Merlot normally predominating, or at least equal, in the blend. The style of wine varies from light and fresh, to be drunk young (in the case of Bergerac) to quite serious, rich deep wines which are matured in new *barriques* and repay some bottle ageing.

Domaine des Bertranoux *→**
A small property in Pécharmant, owned by Guy Pécou, making a smooth, silky wine with redcurrant flavours.

Ch Champerel **
This small Pécharmant vineyard makes a 50 percent Cabernet Sauvignon, 50 percent Merlot wine very intense in its flavours, and designed for some bottle ageing.

Ch Court les Muts **
Côtes de Bergerac red, made in a fruity, smooth style, very drinkable when young, but with a slight backbone of tannin.

Domaine du Haut Pécharmant →**
The top *cuvée* here, Cuvée Veuve Roches, commemorates one of

those famous wine widows who built up the reputation of the estate. The Pécharmants here are a blend of 40 percent Cabernet Sauvignon, 20 percent Cabernet Franc, 30 percent Merlot and 10 percent Malbec.

Ch La Jaubertie   **→

Bergerac estate owned by an Englishman, Henry Ryman, making excellent, deeply fruity wines with considerable elegance, although when young they can be somewhat green. Oak barrels are used for four years. The blend is 65 percent Merlot, 25 percent Cabernet Sauvignon and 5 percent Cabernet Franc.

Ch de Panisseau   →**

Bergerac made by the Becker family, whose home is this pretty thirteenth century château. The wine is generally well-balanced, with a good fresh style.

Jean Revol   *→→**

An unusual Bergerac, in that it is 80 percent Cabernet Sauvignon and 20 percent Cabernet Franc. The wine is not complex, but it is pleasantly fruity, and worth drinking young.

Ch de Tiregand   →***

One of the oldest-established producers of Pécharmant, the St-Exupéry family blend 45 percent Merlot, 30 percent Cabernet Sauvignon, 15 percent Cabernet Franc and 10 percent Malbec. The wine is aged in wood, using barrels from Ch Mouton-Rothschild.

BUZET

Another of the areas which owes its allegiance to Bordeaux grape varieties, Buzet is situated on the left bank of the Garonne, southeast of Bordeaux. It is one of the many areas of southwest France that was in drastic decline and was rescued by the cooperative movement. In this case the Vignerons Réunis des Côtes de Buzet is a model cooperative, dominating the production of the *appellation*. It matures all its wines in 225-litre (49.5 gallons) *barriques*, almost unheard of for cooperatives elsewhere in France.

The top wine here is the Cuvée Napoléon (→***) which receives six months in barrel. The cooperative also makes some wines for the estates, of which one of the best is Ch de Gueyze (**→), a vineyard set up in 1973.

CÔTES DE DURAS

Next-door to the Entre-deux-Mers region of Bordeaux, the Côtes de Duras area could just as easily be a Bordeaux vineyard apart from the quirk of political geography which put it in the Lot-et-Garonne *département* rather than the Gironde. Red wines come from Cabernet Sauvignon, Cabernet Franc, Merlot and Malbec, and are made in the style of simple, quaffing red Bordeaux.

While the cooperative dominates the scene, the most highly reputed producer is now Ch la Grave-Béchade (**→), owned by David Amar, who uses second-hand barrels from Ch Lafite for maturing his reds. The blend for the reds is 40 percent Cabernet Sauvignon, 40 percent Merlot, 20 percent Cabernet Franc. Domaine de Ferrant (**) produces a 60 percent Cabernet Sauvignon wine, aged in tank rather than wood, quite rich, with good direct fruit tastes.

CÔTES DU MARMANDAIS

The Marmandais, centred on the town of Marmande, is on both sides of the River Garonne, bordering the Graves and Entre-deux-Mers areas of Bordeaux. Again, production is very much in the hands of the cooperatives, of which the Coopérative du Cocumont is the more important of the two. They make a range of wines, based on the local blend of Cabernet Sauvignon, Cabernet Franc, Merlot, plus the local Cot, Fer Servadou and Abouriou and the Gamay and Syrah from eastern France. The best wine I have tasted is a single estate wine vinified by the Cocumont cooperative, called Ch la Bastide (→**).

LANGUEDOC AND ROUSSILLON

Cabernet Sauvignon is not normally an approved variety for the *appellations* of France's Midi vineyards. The only place in which it can be used as part of even the lesser quality level of a VDQS wine is in the small areas of Cabardès and Côtes de la Malapère in the Aude *département*. However as a grape it is putting in an appearance in a number of wines whose producers regard the *appellation* laws in much the same way as Italian producers regard their DOC laws – as somewhat anachronistic and to be ignored if necessary. So these wines appear under a regional Vin de Pays, such as Vin de Pays de l'Hérault: but their high prices soon indicate that they are just as superior as the Italian super *vini da tavola*.

Ch de Gourgazaud   **→

Producer of Minervois in the Hérault *département*, has plantings of a number of "foreign" grape varieties – Chardonnay and Cabernet Sauvignon among them. The Cabernet Sauvignon, a Vin de Pays de l'Hérault, spends six months in two-year old wood; it is not designed for long ageing, but is a fruity wine, with a good shot of wood.

Domaine St-Marin de la Garrigue   **

This 35ha (86 acres) estate is in the Hérault *département*, in the VDQS area of Picpoul de Pinet. The owner, François Henry, ignores the local wine tradition and makes a white from Chardonnay and a red Cuvée Réserve, from a blend of Cabernet Sauvignon and Merlot, with some Grenache and Cinsaut thrown in to add to the fun.

Mas Chichet   →**

The Roussillon vineyard of Paul Chichet, 32ha (79 acres) in total, consists of a wide variety of different vines, among them 14ha (34 acres) of Cabernet Sauvignon and Cabernet Franc, which are blended together in a 70 percent – 30 percent ratio to make a Vin de Pays des Pyrénées-Orientales, which M. Chichet calls Cuvée Réserve. The style is in the direction of Bordeaux, but the extra heat south of Perpignan makes the wine much heavier, less elegant.

Mas de Daumas Gassac   →****

The most famous Vin de Pays of them all, on the edge of the *garrigues*, 30 kilometres (19 miles) northwest of Montpellier and away from the coastal plain of the Hérault. A simple Vin de Pays de l'Hérault in name, the Cabernet Sauvignon from Mas de Daumas Gassac is in fact a world-class wine. The 12ha (30 acres) vineyard, owned by Aimé Guibert, was first planted in 1974 on a rare outcrop of red glacial powder. The blend for red wines is 80 percent Cabernet Sauvignon, with a cocktail of other grapes. Grapes are vinified separately and then aged in Bordeaux *barriques*. The wines are huge, long-lived (I have yet to taste a mature example) and definitely southern French rather than Bordeaux. The 80 (tasted in 1987) was still very intense, vibrant, quite firm, but with an excellent spicy flavour; the 82 (also tasted in 1987) was huge, seriously rich, but still dominated by wood and tannin.

PROVENCE

While much of the wine of Provence is eminently forgettable but enjoyably gluggable, there are pockets of much more serious things. Around Aix-en-Provence and in the strange moonscape of Les Baux-en-Provence, there are some producers who are developing quite individual styles, often using unusual blends. There are also the iconoclasts who are quite happy to make Vins de Pays rather than *appellation* wines.

LES BAUX-EN-PROVENCE

This is almost the hottest place in France, with little or no topsoil, and owners normally need dynamite to blast out a vineyard. However the dry climate does make it possible for most vineyard owners to practise organic-farming methods. The grape varieties in use here range from the more conventional Syrah, Grenache and Mourvèdre to the locally suspect Cabernet Sauvignon. Most vineyards use a percentage of Cabernet in their blend.

The style of wine is definitely warm and southern. There are plenty of tannins when young, from both Syrah and Cabernet, but there is a good spicy undertow, and rich, vital fruit which blossoms out with herbs and spices.

Producers using Cabernet Sauvignon include Mas de Gourgonnier (with 30 percent Cabernet plus 30 percent Syrah and 40 percent Grenache), Domaine des Terres Blanches (which is a blend of Cabernet with Grenache, Syrah, Mourvèdre and Cinsaut) and Mas de la Dame (23 percent Cabernet).

Of all the producers using Cabernet, Domaine de Trévallon (****) uses most. The sole wine made on this 16ha (39 acres) estate is a blend of 60 percent Cabernet with 40 percent Syrah, very big and chewy when young, needing around 10 years for maturity. Aged in small oak for 18 months, a wine like the 85 (tasted in 1990) was revelling in its intensity and dense flavours.

COTEAUX D'AIX EN PROVENCE

While most of the producers of Côteaux d'Aix-en-Provence use local grape varieties to make reds which are superior in quality to the normal Côtes de Provence reds, there are two estates which use a proportion of Cabernet Sauvignon in the mix, with results that set them apart from the rest.

Ch Vignelaure   →***
In Rians, makes a wine with 60 percent Cabernet Sauvignon, 30 percent Syrah and 10 percent Grenache. The style is rich and full of cassis fruit and thyme and other herb flavours. The 83 (tasted in 1988) was a lovely wine, nowhere near mature, but showing its quality with deep, dense, almost opaque colour and very rich fruit.

Commanderie de la Bargemone **

The top red is made in a lighter style than Ch Vignelaure, with 50 percent Cabernet Sauvignon, while the standard *cuvée* is a blend with Cinsaut, Grenache and Syrah as well as Cabernet. Both wines are eminently fruity, ageing relatively quickly but with firm, herby fruit.

CÔTES DE PROVENCE

In this huge *appellation* that stretches all the way behind the beaches of the Riviera, there are a very few pockets of interest.

Commanderie de Peyrassol **→

The vineyard in Le Luc, produces two reds with some Cabernet. The standard *cuvée*, Eperon d'Or has one-third Cabernet, a fruity wine with some hints of spicy oak; the superior Cuvée Marie-Estelle has 60 percent Cabernet, is tannic and firm, with good cassis flavours.

Domaines Ott **

Domaines Ott is the biggest name in Côtes de Provence as négociants and estate owners. The Ch de Selle estate produces two wines – a regular *cuvée*, and the Cuvée Speciale, only made in good years, and full of ripe tannins that give it good ageing ability.

CÔTES DU LUBERON

In the vineyard area north of Aix-en-Provence, the enterprise of the Chancel family has created a huge vineyard planted with the local varieties as well as grapes such as Cabernet Sauvignon. The quality of the wines here, the reds especially, is good, and improving as the vineyard ages. Officially the Cabernet can only be used in Vin de Pays: Syrah is the main constituent of the Côtes du Luberon red.

CORSICA

Traditional varieties hold sway in the AC wines of France's Mediterranean island. But the charmingly-named Vin de Pays de l'Ile de Beauté, the Vin de Pays which covers the island, allows Cabernet Sauvignon. The cooperatives make much of the wine, and those from the Union des Vignerons Associés du Levant have good quality and a drinkable, if unexciting, style.

LOIRE

Cabernet Franc is the red-wine grape of the western Loire as the Pinot Noir is of the east. Cabernet Sauvignon gets a small-time part in association with Cabernet Franc in Anjou and Touraine, but rarely appears in a majority position. It is permitted in all the regional *appellations* – Anjou Rouge, Touraine Rouge – as well as in the village *appellations* such as Saumur-Champigny, Chinon and Bourgueil, although it rarely appears there.

California

The 1980s proved to be the most exciting decade for California Cabernet since the ending of prohibition in 1933. A succession of first-rate vintages – 84, 85, 86 – and the arrival on the scene of a number of new superstars have injected a heady enthusiasm into the California wine industry. While Chardonnay and Fumé Blanc may still be the most popular styles of wine, Cabernet is certainly the best that the State can produce.

Of course, there have been great Cabernets in California for a long time. What has changed is that while once they were the only great Cabernets, now they are some among many. And those new arrivals, from Ridge Monte Bello in 1962 onwards, have introduced ideas and attitudes that are new to California.

First – and for Europeans the most important – is the notion of vineyard site. While it has long been recognized that the Napa Valley is home to the greatest Cabernets, pinning down or recognizing particular vineyard sites has taken longer. Even longer to materialize was the idea of single-vineyard wines. Ridge Monte Bello is now the norm rather than, as it then was, the exception.

Second is the idea of small quantities of a particular wine. The arrival of boutique wineries, another way of saying pretty small, coupled with individual bottlings of either single-vineyard or reserve wines, has meant that quantities of some wines are in hundreds rather than thousands of cases. No longer is there just one Cabernet from John Doe Vineyards, available in decent quantities and at a good price: now John Doe makes five Cabernets in tiny quantities and charges large sums for them. Be prepared to pay for some of the best, and to order them as soon as they are released.

Third is the concept of blending. Most of the pioneering Cabernets were 100 percent Cabernet, and defiantly varietal in character. It was, and still is, a very legitimate style in an area which, unlike Bordeaux, can rely on really ripe Cabernet fruit every year and rarely sees greatly diminished crops. But it also produces a wine which, with naturally high tannins and often impenetrable fruit, is a contender for the longevity stakes rather than for pleasurable mid-term drinking. Use of the Bordeaux blending grapes of Merlot and Cabernet Franc (even occasionally Petit Verdot) can often introduce greater complexity to a wine as well as advancing its maturity. Some producers have gone as far as creating genuine Bordeaux blends with up to 40 percent or even 50 percent of grapes other than Cabernet Sauvignon.

Changes in approach have led to a change of style for many California Cabernets, indeed, more than one change of style. From making superb, rich, powerful wines in the sixties and seventies, some producers did a complete turnround in the early eighties and made what are often lean, mean numbers, too austere for their own good, but considered to be ''food wines''. Thankfully the idea survived only a few vintages. By the 84 vintage things were back on course: but there were differences in style.

For one thing, the attitude towards wood had changed. Many earlier Cabernets were matured in American wood, not generally new and often in large casks, for anything up to four years. Some wines, Martha's Vineyard, for example, are still kept for a long time in wood. But the trend now has been to age Cabernet in French wood, in the Bordeaux-sized small casks, and for no more than 18 months to two years. This allows the fruit in a wine to speak much more readily, for fresher tastes and greater complexity.

There has also been much more foreign influence. Foreign investment in Calfornia vineyards has increased dramatically in the past decade, whether it is from Japanese conglomerates or from French wine producers. The arrival of French Champagne houses, such as Moët, Roederer, Mumm, Piper Heidsieck, is well known to any follower of California sparkling wine. But the greatest influence on table wines has come from the now famous joint venture between Robert Mondavi of the Napa Valley and Château Mouton-Rothschild of Bordeaux to produce Opus One, a California Cabernet made with a cross-fertilization of French and Californian knowhow. That has been closely followed by Dominus, utilizing the wine skills of Christian Moueix of Château Petrus, but making a Cabernet-based wine, not one derived from the Merlot of Petrus.

Do changes like the introduction of Bordeaux blending grapes and the arrival of French wine skills mean that California Cabernets and Bordeaux are growing together? In some ways they are: the increased complexity of the wines is one way, the search for elegance as much as power is another. A repeat of a famous blind tasting back in 1976 when a California Cabernet beat all Bordeaux first-growth clarets, might find it more difficult now to tell the difference between the two countries' wines.

But it is unlikely that a distinctive California style will be lost. The climate, the general conditions and attitudes to winemaking will prevent that. The influence of the Old World on the New (and, of course, vice versa) is much more likely to mean that California Cabernet will truly be able to compete as a world-class wine style.

THE CABERNET ARRIVES

It is usually agreed that the first Cabernet grew in California in the vineyards of Jean-Louis Vignes, a native of Bordeaux who planted out land in what is now greater Los Angeles in the 1830s. At that time, its pre-eminence in Bordeaux was only just being established, so California Cabernet was quick off the mark. That it worked even in the hot conditions of southern California can be deduced from the fact that Vignes offered wines for sale in 1857 which he claimed were 20 years old, surely a product of Cabernet's ageing ability.

Cabernet gradually moved north up the California coast. It was not until 1860 that Count Agoston Haraszthy, the Hungarian creator of the Buena Vista winery in Sonoma, introduced Cabernet both to Sonoma and Napa, the two counties which were to become the grape's natural American home.

However, the closing years of the nineteenth century and the opening of the twentieth were not good times for the California wine industry. Phylloxera decimated the vineyards, while growing prohibitionism decimated the market. During the Prohibition years of 1919-33, the only vineyards that survived were those that could produce grapes for sacramental wine and home winemaking, the only two types of wine permitted under the law. Cabernet plantings were a mere 40ha (99 acres) when André Tchelitscheff, a French-trained Russian oenologist, arrived in California in 1937 at the request of Beaulieu Vineyards and initiated the sequence of Private Reserve Cabernets, which continue to this day.

Other old-established wineries followed suit: Beringer, Charles Krug, Louis M Martini, Inglenook all made what would now be called Reserve Cabernets, designed to age, which they produced in addition to more commercial Cabernets.

However, it was the table wine explosion of the sixties which opened the most recent chapter in the history of California Cabernet. Ridge was the first serious Cabernet producer of the new era, but it was closely followed by Heitz, Mondavi, Chappellet, Freemark Abbey and many others.

The late seventies and the early eighties saw another wave of Cabernet producers – businessmen or professional people who wanted to work on the land, or to indulge their passion for Cabernet by actually making it, or at least owning land on which Cabernet grew. Most have remained small, only a few have expanded.

There are now hundreds, perhaps thousands, of Cabernet producers in California. As with any high-investment cottage industry, they come and go at an alarming rate. But even if the owners change, the vines remain, able to produce better and better Cabernets as the vines mature, creating a long-term tradition of California Cabernet.

THE CABERNET VINEYARDS

California has been late in getting to grips with the idea that certain vines perform better in some areas than others. The creation of an appellation system (called AVAs, or Authorised Vineyard Areas) has set up some areas as particularly good for grape growing, but has not yet specified which grapes any AVA is actually good for. Deciding where Cabernet works best has been partly hit and miss, partly luck and partly knowledge of the conditions that the Cabernet likes.

Popular impressions outside California of the Golden State basking in perpetual hot sunshine are quite wrong. Some areas of the Central Coast, between Los Angeles and San Francisco, are positively cool. The main North Coast wine counties of Napa, Sonoma and Mendocino have a series of microclimates dictated by the mountains and by the influence of the cool waters of the Pacific Ocean and San Francisco Bay.

Some areas are definitely too cool for Cabernet. Carneros, which forms the southern end of Napa and Sonoma counties, is one such area: there Chardonnay and Pinot Noir flourish, Cabernet fails to ripen. Northern Mendocino is another. For many, Monterey and Santa Barbara on the Central Coast are also too cool, although that argument is still being waged. But definite Cabernet country is northern and central Napa and northern and central Sonoma: and a glance at the addresses and vineyard locations of the vast majority of producers in the directory which follows will show that to be completely understood.

Within those areas, there are certain more specific sites which produce top quality Cabernet. Although Alexander Valley in Sonoma and parts of Sonoma Valley could lay claim to success with Cabernet, most of the best sites are in Napa: the central townships of Oakville, Rutherford and St Helena have the greatest concentration of Cabernet vineyards; and on the east side of the valley the Stag's Leap AVA is seen as great Cabernet country.

There are arguments in Napa about whether vineyards on the valley floor or vineyards on the mountainsides produce the better Cabernet. Stylistically, mountain vineyards make tougher, more tannic, possibly more long-lasting Cabernet; they are better drained, but are also harder to farm. The styles seem to be different – whether one is better than the other is best proved by opening a few bottles to taste.

There are problems with the health of the California vineyards. Phylloxera, the incurable disease which results from the attacks of small beetles on the roots of European vines, is spreading again in the Napa Valley. Prevented, if not cured, by the grafting of American vine roots onto the European plants, it has been kept at bay for a century. But it now appears that one of the most widely used rootstocks is no longer resistant to phylloxera. New plantings are on better, resistant rootstocks, but many of the vineyards on the Napa Valley floor, with poorer drainage than the hillside vineyards, are becoming infested, and are having to be replanted at great expense.

Other diseases are around, mainly those affecting Cabernet in the normal course of events. But they are compounded in the conditions of the Napa by the fact that this is a mono-cultural area – it is all vineyards: there are no alternative crops to reduce the spread of pests and diseases, and heavy spraying is having its effect on natural life as well as the resistance of vines to disease.

Heavy cropping is another problem for Cabernet vines planted on the valley floor; the streams that provide ready moisture for the roots encourage leaf growth as well as large crops of grapes.

All this means that selection is as important in the Napa Valley, or indeed anywhere in California, as it is in any vineyard area. Good husbandry is a vital factor in the success of the wine.

MAKING CABERNET

Winemaking techniques for red wines in California now differ little from those elsewhere in the world. But that is very much to do with the fact that California pioneered techniques which are now accepted as the norm in France as they are in California. Many Cabernets are fermented in stainless steel before going into wood for maturing: the idea of barrel fermentation for reds is less advanced than it is for white Chardonnay. Stainless steel also allows California producers to go for high fermentation temperatures – up to 33° C (91° F) for red wines, much higher than all the textbooks say, but which is done in Bordeaux as well as in California to increase the extract and colour from the grapes.

Techniques for getting colour out of the grapes ranges from the super high-tech use of rotofermentors (which rotate the fermenting must to keep the skins mixed up with the juice) to old-fashioned submerged-cap fermentation grids, used at Ridge, which press the skins back down into the must whenever they rise to the surface.

After the first alcoholic fermentation, most wineries allow their Cabernet to go through the malolactic fermentation in order to reduce the natural acidity of the grape. While most wineries employ specially cultured yeasts to start both fermentations, there are those who prefer to depend on the naturalness, if greater unreliability, of the yeasts on the skins of the grapes.

Once fermentations are finished, virtually all California Cabernet goes into wood for maturing. A few producers still use large casks, more for the benefits of the slight oxidizing effect of storing a wine in wood than for the change in taste. But most use small Bordeaux-sized 225-litre (49.5 gallon) barrels, sometimes of American wood, but increasingly of French wood, with Nevers the preferred source. Demand for wooden barrels from France is now so great that at least one French cooper has set up a California branch.

After 18 months to two years in cask, wines are bottled. Most wineries will keep their Reserve or similar wines back after bottling for anything from a few months to two years so that they will have some maturity before release. Wineries know that once consumers have bought a wine most of them want to drink it. But an increasing number of connoisseurs now appreciate what the Californian would call the "collectability" of great Californian Cabernet, and will put it in their cellars alongside their bottles of great Bordeaux. That, if nothing else, shows that California Cabernet has now arrived.

PRODUCERS

ALEXANDER VALLEY VINEYARDS   → ★★★
8644 Highway 128, Healdsburg, Sonoma

Total v'yds owned: 101ha (250 acres)
Cabernet area: 26ha (64 acres)
Cabernet production: 168,000 bottles

The Wetzel family's vineyards have been producing wine since 1975, and have consistently led with their Cabernets. From the 1982 vintage, using a blend with 12 percent Merlot, they have received considerable critical acclaim for producing wines that are drinkable on release, but which look likely to last for around ten years. Of the vintages in the mid-1980s, 84 was widely praised for its rich, complex flavour; 85 took longer to develop, but (tasted in 1990) showed excellent colour and an intense ripe flavour.

BEAULIEU   ★★ → ★★★★
1960 St Helena Highway, Rutherford, Napa

Total v'yds owned: 607ha (1,500 acres)
Cabernet area: 162ha (400 acres)
Cabernet production: 2.4 million bottles

Georges de Latour is the name to conjure with at Beaulieu. He founded the winery in 1900, and his family controlled it until 1969, when it was purchased by the Heublein Company, now part of the UK-based Grand Metropolitan group. He introduced the wine in 1936, and for many years it was made by the legendary André Tchelistcheff, a Russian-born, French-trained oenologist who has helped revolutionize attitudes to wine in California. De Latour's name lives on in the Georges de Latour Private Reserve wines which are some of California's best: the 85 (tasted in 1990) from a great vintage, positively oozes cherries and blackcurrants, with surprising elegance in such a rich, powerful wine. Older vintages, such as the 80, are equally massive, while 78 shows excellent poise with its cigar-box flavours and concentrated fruit. Other Cabernets produced at Beaulieu include Rutherford Cabernet, made in the same style as Private Reserve but maturing more quickly, and the easy-drinking Beautour Cabernet.

BERINGER   ★★ → ★★★
PO Box 111, St Helena, Napa

Total v'yds owned: 890ha (2,200 acres)

Beringer's reputation is now riding high after a period in the 1960s when it seemed in decline. Much of this increased fame is due to the improved quality of the Cabernets now produced. These range from the top-quality Private Reserve, through various single-vineyard wines, to the more widely available Beringer Cabernet Sauvignon. The Private Reserve is based on two vineyards – the Chabot Vineyard in St Helena and State Lane Vineyard between Oakville and Yountville. Occasionally there have been separate bottlings from these two vineyards, but a wine such as the 84 Private Reserve (tasted in 1989) is a blend of the two, with its huge, rich fruit, excellent acidity and wood balance, and intriguing sweet and sour flavour. A separate bottling of some fruit from the Chabot Vineyard is also made, and there is a Cabernet from its Knights Valley vineyard in Sonoma. The regular Cabernet is, inevitably, not in the same class. Look also for their second label, Napa Ridge.

BUENA VISTA ** →
1800 Old Winery Road, Sonoma

Total v'yds owned: 444ha (1097 acres)
Cabernet area: 68ha (168 acres)
Cabernet production: 252,000 bottles

Buena Vista is another of the long-established wineries that went through a sticky patch, but during the 1980s was suddenly pulled together and is now making some sound, occasionally exciting, wines. The catalyst here was new ownership in the hands of the Racke family from Germany, and a new winemaker, Jill Davis. The vineyards are in Carneros, and provide much cooler-climate Cabernet than other Napa or Sonoma wineries. The effect is apparent in the Private Reserve wines, which can sometimes taste lean, although in years such as 84, with its juicily rich flavour, or 85 (tasted in 1989) smooth and elegant, the wines are satisfactorily rich. The standard Buena Vista Cabernet exhibits the Carneros leanness to a greater degree, the 82 (tasted in 1985) showing a rather tannic taste, and not ripe enough fruit.

BURGESS CELLARS ***
1108 Deer Park Road, St Helena, Napa

Total v'yds owned: 9ha (22 acres)
Cabernet area: 8ha (20 acres)
Cabernet production: 84,000 bottles

Since its founding in 1972, Burgess Cellars has made a consistently interesting series of Cabernets. There has been some stylistic change – from the heavy, rich style of the 1970s, to a lighter, more elegant style in the 1980s (beginning with 81). Their Cabernet goes under the Vintage Selection label, and while early vintages were 100 percent Cabernet, more recently Cabernet Franc and Merlot have been part of the blend. Best wines still available are the 85, with its spice and cassis flavours, minty and rich, but with a modifying streak of tannin; the 86, more tannic, but with plenty of blackcurrant fruit.

CAKEBREAD CELLARS ** →
8300 Highway 29, Rutherford, Napa

Total v'yds owned: 27ha (67 acres)
Cabernet area: 18ha (44 acres)
Cabernet production: 132,000 bottles

In common with other Napa wineries, Cakebread has moved away from its hugely luscious Cabernets of the 1970s to much leaner offerings in the 1980s. Some commentators find this disappointing, but Cakebread Cabernets still pack quite a punch of fruit. Certainly the 85, though quite lean, has elegant cigar-box flavours; the 86 is richer and perhaps more satisfying, even though the tannins are going to mean that it will not be really drinkable until the mid-1990s.

CARMENET VINEYARD → ****
1700 Moon Mountain Road, Sonoma

Total v'yds owned: 20ha (49 acres)
Cabernet production: 114,000 bottles

Carmenet is part of the group that owns the Chardonnay and Pinot Noir specialists, Chalone and Acacia. However here, half way up Mount Pisgah in a dramatic Mayacamas Mountain setting with views over the Sonoma Valley, it is all about Cabernet, here called Sonoma Red Table Wine. Wines are aged in the constant temperature of cellars carved out of the mountainside, and the vineyards make a strong case for the quality of hillside, rather than valley floor, land. The first vintage in 82 set the pace for quality in a blended wine with 87 percent Cabernet Sauvignon, plus Merlot and Cabernet Franc, and when tasted in 1989, was showing chewy, tannic fruit, intensely sweet at the same time and beginning to mature. Other vintages which are showing well are the 84, tobacco-y fruit, good flavoursome extract and a peppery aftertaste; the 85, rich from the vintage, terrific varietal flavour, and the potential for long ageing; 86, serious and elegant; 88 (tasted in 1989 in cask) spicy and herby, with fine tannin structure, one which will last.

CAYMUS   *** → ****
8700 Conn Creek Road, Rutherford, Napa

Total v'yds owned: 28ha (69 acres)
Cabernet area: 16ha (39.5 acres)
Cabernet production: 324,000 bottles

Caymus has had a high reputation for its Cabernets since the first vintage in 1970. Owner Charles Wagner and his son Chuck now produce three Cabernets at three different quality levels. The finest – and the rarest – is the Special Selection, the first vintage of which was in 1975, a selection of the finest casks for a vintage, and which get four years in barrel. The 84 (tasted in 1989) showed the quality of these wines, lean and elegant, with balanced tannin and acidity, underpinned by almost perfect fruit. The Estate, with 20 months in wood, is more immediately approachable, but, with its tannin and acidity still firmly there, a wine such as 85 will go well into the late 1990s. A third Cabernet, the Napa Valley Cuvee, still shows tannin when young, the 85 (tasted in 1989) with its spicy fruit and cassis flavours, promising much for the mid-1990s.

CHAPPELLET VINEYARD   ** →
1581 Sage Canyon Road, St Helena, Napa

Total v'yds owned: 44ha (109 acres)
Cabernet area: 14.5ha (36 acres)
Cabernet production: 72,000 bottles

Since its early days, when the 68, 69 and 70 Cabernets made the headlines, Chappellet has been something of a slumbering giant, only occasionally producing vintages to match those early ones. Yet that this mountainside vineyard in the forests east of St Helena is still capable of producing fine wines is shown by an 86 Reserve (tasted in 1990) very much in the tannic mould of Chappellet wines, but with cedar wood and mint flavours, on top of elegant, very intense fruit. It will need until the mid-1990s before being drinkable. These Signature Reserve wines are the top range that Don Chappellet produces in better years: he also produces, in larger quantities, and every year, an Estate wine.

CHATEAU MONTELENA   ** → ***
1429 Tubbs Lane, Calistoga, Napa

Total v'yds owned: 40ha (99 acres)
Cabernet area: 28ha (69 acres)
Cabernet production: 120,000 bottles

Right at the northern end of the Napa Valley, in the hottest region and up against the foot of Mount Helena, Chateau Montelena's vineyard has been producing Cabernets since 1978. Prior to that, grapes were purchased from both Napa and Sonoma counties and bottled separately. The Montelena Estate wines, from the 1978 vintage, have a record of longevity, of high tannins and weighty, sometimes almost too heavy fruit. Best vintages are the lighter ones: the 83, for example, has good direct cassis fruit tastes, coupled with a firm backbone of elegant tannins; the 86, too, is well balanced, with supple fruit and acid balance, coupled with some spicy oak.

THE CHRISTIAN BROTHERS   **→
St Helena, Napa

Total v'yds owned: 969ha (2,390 acres)

With two huge vineyard holdings in Napa Valley for table wines, and in the San Joaquin Valley for dessert and fortified wines, the Christian Brothers was one of the largest landowners in California. The vineyards were sold by the Catholic teaching order in 1989 to Heublein, the UK-owned company, which has started an investment programme that should do much to put the winery back on the tracks after some years in the doldrums. The winemaker Tom Eddy had already produced an 85 estate-bottled Cabernet which reveals promising cherry and cassis flavours, and a good wood balance. He has also made a more curious wine, called Montage, an unvintaged blend of Cabernet from Bordeaux and from the Napa.

CLOS DU BOIS   **→
51 Fitch Street, Healdsburg, Sonoma

Total v'yds owned: 218ha (539 acres)
Cabernet area: 96ha (237 acres)
Cabernet production: 456,000 bottles

Perhaps better known for its Chardonnays, Clos du Bois, now part of the UK-owned Hiram Walker group, also produces a range of Cabernet-based wines that deserve attention. The Marlstone comes from a 40ha (99 acre) vineyard of the same name in nearby Alexander Valley, and is planted with the classic Bordeaux range: the two Cabernets, Merlot, Malbec and Petit Verdot. Like many of the Clos du Bois wines which are ready for drinking on release, the 84 Marlstone (tasted in 1989) showed plenty of rich, soft fruit, very jammy and raisiny. The other single vineyard wine is Briarcrest, 100 percent Cabernet, much tauter, with some bitterness in heavy vintages such as 85, but with some success in earlier vintages, especially 81. There is also a blended Alexander Valley Cabernet which is designed for lighter, early drinking.

CLOS DU VAL   ***→
5330 Silverado Trail, Stags Leap, Napa

Total v'yds owned: 103ha (255 acres)
Cabernet area: 46ha (114 acres)
Cabernet production: 300,000 bottles

The word elegance would not be amiss to describe the style of Cabernet-based wine produced at Clos du Val. Bordeaux-born Bernard Portet (brother of Dominique who runs Taltarni in Australia) has managed this Stag's Leap District winery since it was started in the early 1970s by New York businessman John Goelet. Straightaway a style was established which, with a hiccough or two in the early 1980s, has been remarkably consistent. Complexity and balance mark out wines such as the 85 Cabernet (tasted in 1989) soft, with a shot of acidity, and a good minty, eucalyptus fruit, welded into the right structure to mature well into the late 1990s. Reserve wines are also made from selected fruit in Clos du Val's Stag's Leap vineyards: the 82 (tasted in 1989) showing perhaps too much maturity and developing a vegetal character which will come to dominate the undoubtedly rich fruit. A lighter style of Cabernet, Joli Val, is now made using bought-in Napa fruit.

B R COHN WINERY   ** → ***
15000 Sonoma Highway, Glen Ellen, Sonoma

Cabernet area: 16ha (39.5 acres)
Cabernet production: 29,000 bottles

Bruce Cohn's first Cabernet vintage was 1984, and he quickly put himself in the front runners with a row of three splendid wines, blended with 4 percent Cabernet Franc, from his Oliver Hill Vineyard in Glen Ellen. The 85 (tasted in 1989) showed what is already an established style – smooth, rich, velvety, with concentrated fruit, with a good underlying acidity suggesting it will age well. The wines are bottled unfiltered, suggesting minimum handling in the winery.

CONN CREEK   ** →
8711 Silverado Trail, St Helena, Napa

Total v'yds owned: 48ha (120 acres)
Cabernet area: 1.2ha (3 acres)
Cabernet production: 85,000 bottles

Nearly all the grapes required for Conn Creek Cabernets come from long-term contract vineyards, many of them famous in their own right, such as the Hess Collection on Mount Veeder, Chalk Hill in Sonoma, Spottswoode in St Helena, and Collins Vineyard near St Helena. They make two reserve wines – called, confusingly, Barrel Select and, in smaller quantities, Private Reserve Barrel Select. The best wine they have made in the 1980s was yet another style, the 84 single-vineyard Collins Vineyard Private Reserve (tasted in 1988) with ripe extract, plenty of tannin to help ageing and cherry and vanilla flavours to give some immediate attraction. A rather dry 83 rejoiced in the considerable title of Conn Creek Winery Collins Vineyard Proprietor's Special Selection. Conn Creek also makes a straight Napa Valley Cabernet.

CUVAISON   → ***
4550 Silverado Trail, Calistoga, Napa

Total v'yds owned: 162ha (400 acres)
Cabernet area: None
Cabernet production: 60,000 bottles

Cuvaison has been making top-class Cabernet since the 84 vintage, after a long period when what was on offer was hard and generally clumsy. Both 85, with its balanced fruit, acidity and tannin and the judicious use of spicy new wood flavours, and the 86, even better because it is riper and smoother, are up with the best. Cuvaison owns no Cabernet vineyards, although it owns vineyards for Chardonnay in Carneros, and buys from growers on a regular basis.

DIAMOND CREEK →****
1500 Diamond Mountain Road, Calistoga, Napa

Total v'yds owned: 8ha (20 acres)
Total Cabernet area: 8ha (20 acres)
Cabernet production: 36,000 bottles

Al Brounstein only produces a Cabernet-based wine (with 8 percent Merlot and 4 percent Cabernet Franc) from his mountainside vineyard. He has divided it into four: Gravelly Meadow, Red Rock Terrace, Volcanic Hill and Lake Vineyard, with the last named (less than 0.4 ha/1 acre) generally blended with Gravelly Meadow except in special years. The largest production comes from Volcanic Hill. All the wines are highly regarded, but their tannin and serious slowly-evolving nature (derived from the mountain site) are never likely to make them immediately popular – probably a good thing, given the small quantities produced. In 85, the Gravelly Meadow produced the most tannic wine, while Red Rock Terrace was intense and concentrated richness and Volcanic Hill offered more obvious fruit to go with the tannin. All three will last well into the next century.

DOMINUS ***
Yountville, Napa

Total v'yds owned: 65ha (160 acres)
Cabernet area: 16.6ha (41 acres)
Cabernet production: 75,000 bottles

A collaboration between Christian Moueix, the young inspirational manager of Château Petrus in Bordeaux, and two Californians of the family of Inglenook winemaker John Daniel, Dominus is based on the Daniel family vineyard of Napanook, due west of Yountville. There M. Moueix blends Cabernet Sauvignon with about 20 percent Merlot and 10 percent Cabernet Franc to make what many see as the next star of the Napa, and certainly the priciest. The first vintage was 83, a wine that is still formidably tannic, released after the lighter, more elegant 84. The best wine so far is 85 (tasted in 1989) which shows the complexity a Bordelais can add to Napa fruit, and which is destined to go on and on; 86 is almost as good.

DUCKHORN **→***
3027 Silverado Trail, St Helena, Napa

Total v'yds owned: 11ha (27 acres)
Cabernet area: None
Cabernet production: 48,000 bottles

Perhaps better known as a Merlot producer, Dan Duckhorn also produces a Cabernet (which has a small amount of Merlot and Cabernet Franc in the blend) from grapes which he and his wife Margaret buy in. The style is quite heavy, rich and tannic, the 85 (tasted in 1990) one of the best of the 1980s, very concentrated in colour and taste, with rich fruit to back up the tannin, lots of ripe tastes – a wine that will last up to and beyond the turn of the century.

DUNN VINEYARDS   ***→
805 White Cottage Road, Angwin, Napa

Total vineyard owned: 2ha (5 acres)
Cabernet area: 2ha (5 acres)
Cabernet production: 48,000 bottles

The tiny production of Randall Dunn's 100 percent Cabernet wine comes from a small mountainside vineyard up Howell Mountain on the east side of Napa. He buys in more grapes as well as managing a vineyard to supplement the small quantities from his own vineyard. The first vintage of the Howell Mountain wine was in 1979 and, from then on, Dunn has produced a succession of much praised vintages, the 84 perhaps the best of the early part of the decade, all demanding years and more years in bottle before maturity. For those who cannot wait, there is the equally good, but somewhat lighter Dunn Napa Valley, from grapes purchased from valley-floor vineyards.

FAR NIENTE   **→
Off Oakville Grade, Oakville, Napa

Total v'yds owned: 40ha (99 acres)
Cabernet area: 18ha (44 acres)
Cabernet production: 120,000 bottles

Far Niente is as well known for its elaborate 19th century looking label and its renovated stone cellar in Oakville as for its wines. Owner Gil Nickel owns the Stelling Vineyard whose neighbours include Martha's Vineyard, so his Cabernet is in good company. The first few vintages were not quite up to the standard of the neighbour's wines, but since the ripe, earthy 85 (tasted in 1989) things have moved upwards.

FETZER VINEYARDS   →**
1150 Bel Arbres Road, Redwood Valley, Mendocino

Total v'yds owned: 404ha (998 acres)

Fetzer is by far the largest producer in Mendocino, and it dominates the scene with vineyards in Redwood Valley and Hopland. The secret of the rapid growth of Fetzer has been in making a range of wines to suit all tastes, and the new Bel Arbors range, blending California and Washington State fruit for very reasonable prices, bears witness to that policy. At a more serious level, they make two good-value Cabernets, using Mendocino fruit: a Barrel Select wine, the 85 (tasted in 1989) with ripe, forward fruit and definitely ready to drink; and the Reserve Cabernet, tasting more of new wood, but with attractive fruit structure.

FISHER VINEYARDS   →***
6200 St Helena Road, Santa Rosa, Sonoma

Total v'yds owned: 30ha (75 acres)
Cabernet area: 12ha (30 acres)
Cabernet production: 18,000 bottles

From a tiny vineyard high up on the western slopes of the Mayacamas Mountains, Fred Fisher makes a Cabernet blend (with 5 percent Merlot and some Cabernet Franc) which he calls Coach Insignia (his family owns a coachworks). The first vintage was in 84, but already he has established a style – light and delicate rather than blockbusting, some would say restrained, certainly not flaunting the subtle fruit and tannin. A thinking man's Cabernet.

FLORA SPRINGS   ***

1978 West Zinfandel Lane, St Helena, Napa

Total v'yds owned: 162ha (400 acres)
Cabernet area: 63ha (156 acres)
Cabernet production: 56,000 bottles

While much of the grapes from the Napa vineyards owned by the Komes family go to other producers, they keep a select amount back to make small quantities of premium wines at their Flora Springs winery on the west side of the Napa Valley. They make two Cabernet-based wines: Trilogy is an equal blend of Cabernet Sauvignon, Cabernet Franc and Merlot, the first vintage being in 84: the 86 (tasted in 1989) is a subtle, soft wine, with fruit and tobacco flavours, ripe and rich with some tannins, dominated at this stage by Merlot, needing some time to balance out. Their Cabernet Sauvignon has 7 percent Merlot and 1 percent Cabernet Franc, the 85 (tasted in 1989) deep, full and still closed, with an attractive minty, herby flavour, a wine to age until the mid-1990s.

FORMAN VINEYARD   →***

1501 Big Rock Vineyard, St Helena, Napa

Total v'yds owned: 19ha (47 acres)
Cabernet area: 9ha (22 acres)
Cabernet production: 19,200 bottles

Rick Forman, ex-Sterling Vineyards and Newton Vineyards, has a small parcel of land in hills to the east of St Helena. His Cabernet, blended with 15 percent Merlot and 10 percent Cabernet Franc, was first made with the 83 vintage. Already he has hit the jackpot, with every wine a winner: possibly the 85 leads by a short head from the 86, but both exhibit splendid style, elegance and balance, and forward touches of new wood, which should soften out in the ten years at least they need for maturity.

FRANCISCAN VINEYARDS   **→

1178 Galleron Road, Rutherford, Napa

Total v'yds owned: 391ha (966 acres)
Cabernet area: 41ha (101 acres)
Cabernet production: 150,000 bottles

Now under the joint ownership of the German Peter Eckes Company and Franciscan's president Agustin Huneuus, the vineyards are producing some of the best value Cabernet in Napa. With vineyards adjoining the new Opus One vineyard in Rutherford, the quality of their fruit is not in question. The Cabernet is spicy and meaty, with well balanced oak, a change from the over-spiced wines made in the 1970s, using American rather than the present French wood. The 85s show distinctive rich fruit tastes, while the Meritage, a blend of Cabernet Sauvignon with 40 percent Merlot and some Cabernet Franc, shows considerable refinement and elegance. Franciscan also has a 200ha (494 acres) estate in Monterey County and 80ha (199 acres) in Alexander Valley which are producing inexpensive wines under the Estancia label.

FREEMARK ABBEY   ** → ***
3022 St Helena Highway North, St Helena, Napa

Total v'yds owned: 53ha (130 acres)
Cabernet area: 33ha (82 acres)
Cabernet production: 170,000 bottles

Freemark Abbey has built a consistent reputation for its top
Cabernet, Cabernet Bosche, since the first release in 1969. The
vineyard itself, in Rutherford, does not actually belong to the winery,
but to John Bosche, who has a regular contract to supply Cabernet
for this wine. The style is full-bodied, with intense yet balanced fruit
that ages well – certainly well over a decade from vintage to maturity.
Since 1984, a succession of excellent vintages have put the wine
back in the top place it enjoyed in the 1970s: the 85 (tasted in 1989)
showed great concentration and ripe, earthy fruit flavours, and
needs a lot of time to develop.

The 84 vintage also saw the release of another single-vineyard
wine, Sycamore Vineyard: tasted in 1989, this is a bigger style than
Bosche, meaty and very tannic. The regular Napa Valley Cabernet
follows the house style of considerable initial tannins when young,
but develops more quickly and becomes pleasantly perfumed.

FREY VINEYARDS   ** →
14000 Tomki Road, Redwood Valley, Mendocino

Total v'yds owned: 12ha (30 acres)

The Frey family, with their hand-built winery and vineyard in the
middle of a redwood forest clearing, at the far northern end of the
Redwood Valley, are in as remote a spot for winemaking as any in
California. They are the most organic wine producers, largely by
default they say – "we just neglected to irrigate and spray the vines"
– when they started in 1967, but now as a matter of definite policy.
Their wines come from their own vineyards and from those of some
neighbours, whose land is also certified as organic. Cabernets, as
with all their wines, have a terrific intensity of flavour, almost black
tastes when young, needing a good decade to reach maturity. The
83, from the Easterbrook Vineyard (tasted in 1989) was still firmly
tannic and acid, perhaps somewhat austere, but the 86 Easterbrook, despite some firmness, has huge fruit buried underneath the
tannin, while the 85 just oozes delicious, ripe fruit.

FROG'S LEAP   ** → ***
3358 St Helena Highway, St Helena, Napa

Total v'yds owned: 4ha (10 acres)
Cabernet area: 3ha (7.5 acres)
Cabernet production: 30,000 bottles

A 10-year old winery, founded with the 81 vintage, Frog's Leap takes
its whimsical name from the fact that the property was formerly a
frog breeding-ground supplying California French restaurants.
When it comes to wines, though, owners Larry Turley and John
Williams are somewhat more serious: their Cabernet, partly made
from their own fruit, and partly from bought-in fruit is improving all
the time. The 86 (tasted in 1990) is their best so far, still young in
colour, hinting at wood underneath excellent fruit and soft tannins,
a welcoming perfumed bouquet and considerable style.

GRACE FAMILY VINEYARDS →***
1210 Rockland Road, St Helena, Napa

Total v'yds owned: 0.8ha (2 acres)
Cabernet area: 0.8ha (2 acres)
Cabernet production: 3,600 bottles

Tiny production of a highly praised wine inevitably means that the Grace Family's Cabernet is one of the most expensive on the market. The first vintage in 78 was made by Caymus Vineyards, and released as a separate bottling from that winery, but with the 85 vintage, Richard Grace has built his own small winery, and now bottles his own wine, sold through mail order. The 85 (tasted in 1989) consisting of a total of 1,500 bottles, is typical in its richly juicy fruit, its smoky oak tastes and its cassis and ripe plum flavours. Surprisingly drinkable now, it should still mature well into the late nineties.

GRGICH HILLS CELLAR →***
1829 St Helena Highway, Rutherford, Napa

Total v'yds owned: 145ha (358 acres)
Cabernet area: 17ha (42 acres)
Cabernet production: 120,000 bottles

The partnership between winemaker Mike Grgich and grape grower Austin Hills started in 1977. Since then, they have developed an impressive line of Cabernets from the Hills vineyard in Yountville and from contract growers. The first Cabernet vintage in 80 set the tone of the others that followed: well structured, with excellent forward fruit, and rich smooth taste as it matures. The 85 (tasted in 1989) balanced fresh fruit tastes with considerable depth and elegance that suggests it will mature well over the next five years.

GROTH VINEYARDS AND WINERY **→***
Oakville, Napa

Total v'yds owned: 66ha (163 acres)
Cabernet area: 35ha (86 acres)
Cabernet production: 96,000 bottles

A small family-owned concern, less than ten years old (the first vintage was 82), which has set a fast track record for its Cabernet from vineyards in Oakville and Yountville. They make two styles: an Estate wine, with production of around 7,500 cases, and a Reserve wine of about 500 cases made from selected barrels. The blend for the wines includes 15 percent Merlot. The 85 vintage in the Estate range (tasted in 1989) shows attractive, elegant fruit, with a streak of acidity and balancing tannin which suggests good ageing potential. The 86 Estate is even better – more intensity, more richness and smoky oak flavours. The 85 Reserve has the same qualities as the 85 Estate, only, as befits a Reserve wine, more so.

GUNDLACH-BUNDSCHU VINEYARD **
2000 Denmark Street, Sonoma

Total v'yds owned: 151ha (373 acres)
Cabernet area: 10ha (25 acres)
Cabernet production: 72,000 bottles

Jim Bundschu only uses fruit from his own estates in southern Sonoma Valley to make his wines. The Cabernets mainly come from the Rhinefarm estate, in flat land southeast of Sonoma town, and although other Cabernets are made, the Rhinefarm label is the top style. Until the 84 vintage, there was also a Batto Ranch Cabernet, but this has been discontinued. The best Rhinefarm I have tasted was the 85, and, although some critics have found vegetal tastes in the wine, I enjoyed the rich, spicy, cassis and vanilla flavours of the wine. Not necessarily for long ageing, it shows a very direct style that possibly derives from the fact that it is 100 percent Cabernet.

HEITZ WINE CELLARS   *** → ****
500 Taplin Road, St Helena, Napa

Total v'yds owned: 46ha (114 acres)
Cabernet area: 28ha (69 acres)
Cabernet production: 156,000 bottles

Joe Heitz and his family produce what is probably California's best known single-vineyard Cabernet, Martha's Vineyard, from land on the west side of the valley in Oakville on the slopes of the Mayacamas Mountains. The land in fact is owned not by the Heitz family but by the Mays family, who have supplied the grapes to Heitz on the basis of a gentlemen's agreement since 1966. The agreement is probably made more binding by the fact that the Mays are shareholders in the winery. The Martha's Vineyard wine has a long track record, and it is possible to see how it develops and matures: anyone who tastes that first 66 will find it still developing, still showing minty flavours that characterize these wines, still with some tannin. Small wonder then that later vintages seem always young: in ageing terms alone, the wine is the nearest to first-growth Bordeaux reached by any producer in California. Heitz makes another single-vineyard wine, Bella Oaks, from a Rutherford vineyard, which is a faster maturing wine, with less concentration and tannin when young, but by any standards, except those of Martha's Vineyard, one of the top California Cabernets. If these two wines, produced in small quantities and with an immense lifespan, are unattainable for many consumers, they should look instead at the Heitz Napa Valley Cabernet, the 84 (tasted in 1989) showing warm fruit, approachable tannins and ripe tobacco flavours.

HESS COLLECTION WINERY   *** →
4411 Redwood Road, Napa

Total v'yds owned: 113ha (279 acres)
Cabernet area: 52ha (128 acres)
Cabernet production: 144,000 bottles

From his vineyards on the slopes of Mount Veeder and the old Christian Brothers La Salle winery, Donald Hess (who regards his wines as part of his art collection – hence the name) has started a series of Cabernets, with a first release in 83. The vineyard blend of 23 percent Merlot and 12 percent Cabernet Franc is reflected in the finished regular Estate wine, but the superior Reserve is 100 percent Cabernet. The 85 regular Estate wine (tasted in 1989) is a stunning wine, very oaky, very concentrated, showing intense fruit flavours, so full and rich that the tannins hardly stand a chance. The Reserve 84 (tasted in 1989) consists of 3,000 bottles, and echoes and enhances the richness that seems an inherent part of these Hess wines: so rich, in fact, that it was enjoyable young, even though it will obviously age well into the late 1990s.

WILLIAM HILL WINERY ***
1775 Lincoln Avenue, Napa

Total v'yds owned: 172ha (425 acres)
Cabernet area: 28ha (69 acres)
Cabernet production: 260,000 bottles

Bill Hill, tall, quiet and with the looks of a Country and Western singer, has vineyards northeast of Napa City, on Mount Veeder and in Carneros. His Cabernets come mainly from the Mount Veeder vineyard, although a new plot is being planted on the southern edge of Napa City. He makes two styles, a lighter wine called Silver Label, and a Reserve wine, designated with a Gold Label. With the 85 and 86 vintages of the Reserve, William Hill struck a high note. The 85 (tasted in 1989) has more fruit, somewhat less oak than the 86 which shows better tannins and therefore better ageing potential. The 85 Silver Label dwells more on the fruity, fresh aspects of Cabernet, and would certainly be very drinkable now.

INGLENOOK NAPA VALLEY ** →
1991 St Helena Highway, Rutherford, Napa

Total v'yds owned: 486ha (1,200 acres)
Cabernet area: 28ha (69 acres)
Cabernet production: 600,000 bottles

Now part of the UK-owned Heublein Company, Inglenook's decline in fortunes, recorded during the late 1960s and 1970s, has now been firmly reversed with a succession of excellent vintages of the Reserve Cask Cabernet, and the launch in 1983 of a new Cabernet wine, Reunion, which blends together fruit from three of the company's top vineyards. The 85 Cabernet Reserve Cask (tasted in 1989) had an open, warm style, not chewy, but elegant and ripe, smooth and concentrated. The 84 Reunion has delicious tobacco fruit and ripe flavours, exhibiting some tannin and acidity, while the 85 (tasted in 1989) was bigger, very closed, and will develop slowly probably until the turn of the century.

JEKEL VINEYARDS **
40155 Walnut Avenue West, Greenfield, Monterey

Total v'yds owned: 141ha (348 acres)

Bill Jekel, one of the most important growers in Arroyo Seco region of Monterey, is a great advocate of playing down the importance of the area in which grapes are grown, and playing up what happens to them in the winery. Yet, curiously enough, his Cabernets are absolutely typical of this cool climate area, with their strong vegetal flavours, which intensify rather than soften with age. For many this is a drawback, for others a character to be enjoyed. Certainly an 84 Jekel Cabernet (tasted in 1990) was a very pleasing wine, certainly vegetal, now mature and in a light style, but still attractive to drink. Cabernet Franc and Merlot are now blended into the wine.

JOHNSON TURNBULL VINEYARDS ** → ***
8210 St Helena Highway, Oakville, Napa

Total v'yds owned: 15ha (37 acres)
Cabernet area: 8ha (20 acres)
Cabernet production: 38,000 bottles

Cabernet from their Oakville vineyard is the mainstay of this winery, although they now also make Chardonnay from a Knights Valley vineyard. They used to make just one Cabernet which was characterized by minty, herby tastes, faintly reminiscent of Heitz Martha's Vineyard not far away. With the 86 vintage, two wines were produced: a Vineyard Selection 67 which continued this minty character, and a softer, fruitier Vintage Selection 82 (both figures derived from the years in which the vines were planted) which will mature more quickly, but may also remain at its peak for longer.

JORDAN VINEYARD AND WINERY   **→

1474 Alexander Valley Road, Healdsburg, Sonoma

Total v'yds owned: 111ha (274 acres)
Cabernet area: 76ha (188 acres)
Cabernet production: 660,000 bottles

If you put on one side the amazing chateau-like winery and the considerable snobbism that goes with it, you will find a well-made wine that (almost) deserves the marketing success it has achieved. The wines are made for early drinking, and do not seem to age well, but that is a philosophy that can be respected. The 84 (tasted in 1990) was definitely maturing, with a brown coloured edge, but retaining pleasing ripe fruit. The 81 (tasted in 1983) showed excellent fruit quality, but again was about ready to drink. The blend includes 12 percent Merlot.

KENWOOD VINEYARDS   →***

9592 Sonoma Highway, Kenwood, Sonoma

Total v'yds owned: 95ha (235 acres)
Cabernet area: 7ha (17.5 acres)
Cabernet production: 230,000 bottles

Most of the fruit for Kenwood's Cabernets is bought in from other Sonoma growers. Their regular bottling is, as with the 86 (tasted in 1989) a fairly tannic wine in youth but with good minty, herby overtones, which needs 8-10 years to develop. Smaller quantities of two reserve wines are also made. The Jack London is a single-vineyard wine that shows considerable tannic, rich fruit, the 86 (tasted in 1989) very deep in colour, with spicy, herby flavours. Top of the line is the Artists Series, a special selection which features a newly-designed illustration on the label each year (but never again, after the first year, a naked lady, which was banned by the Bureau of Alcohol, Tobacco and Firearms, the US regulatory body). The wine has been much better since the 81 vintage saw the introduction of French oak for ageing, and wines like the richly complex 84 and the sensuously fruity 86, make this one of the great Sonoma Cabernets.

LAUREL GLEN   →***

PO Box 548, Glen Ellen, Sonoma Valley

Total v'yds owned: 16ha (40 acres)
Cabernet area: 14ha (34.5 acres)
Cabernet production: 48,000 bottles

Owner Patrick Campbell makes just two wines here, both based on Cabernet Sauvignon and which include some Cabernet Franc in the blend. Merlot and Tempranillo are also grown, but not so far used in the finished wines. The style was set with the first vintage of 81, ripe and elegant, ready to drink on release, but with some tannin structure to ensure ageing potential. The 85 (tasted in 1989) has been the best wine so far: well balanced, rich, concentrated, designed for ten years ageing. A second label Counterpoint (Campbell is a musician) is for wines not selected for the main label.

MARKHAM VINEYARDS ** →
2812 North St Helena Highway, St Helena, Napa

Total v'yds owned: 101ha (250 acres)
Cabernet area: 65ha (161 acres)
Cabernet production: 46,000 bottles

Now owned by the Japanese Sanraku Company (Japan's largest winemaker), Markham was started by Bruce Markham with the 78 vintage. Vineyards in Yountville supply the fruit for the Markham Cabernet, which, since the 82 vintage, has shown regular signs of quality. The 84 (tasted in 1989) was a smooth, elegant style of wine, not overly obvious tannins, but with good fresh fruit and acidity, designed for drinking within a decade rather than for long-term ageing. The 85 and 86 are reputed to be better and more tannic.

LOUIS M MARTINI → **
254 South St Helena Highway, St Helena, Napa

Total v'yds owned: 323ha (798 acres)
Cabernet area: 110ha (272 acres)
Cabernet production: 550,000 bottles

One of the great names in Napa Valley winemaking, it is perhaps surprising to realize that the best Martini Cabernets come not from the Napa at all, but from a mountain vineyard in Sonoma, called Monte Rosso, which the winery purchased in 1937. For a long time this vineyard was the backbone of the succession of great Cabernets produced at the winery, but with the 79 vintage was the first to be bottled separately as a single-vineyard wine. During the late 1960s and 1970s, Martini Cabernets had an increasingly large share of Merlot, but this has since dropped back to 3 percent in the Special Selection wines, and none at all in Monte Rosso. The best Monte Rosso from the 1980s that I have tasted was the 84, now beginning to mature but showing lovely ripe, elegant fruit. The regular Cabernet is described as North Coast Cabernet and blends Sonoma and Napa fruit: the 85 (tasted in 1989) was disappointingly vegetal.

MAYACAMAS → ****
1155 Lokoya Road, Napa

Total v'yds owned: 19ha (47 acres)
Cabernet area: 6ha (15 acres)
Cabernet production: 24,000 bottles

Mayacamas' mountainside vineyards on Mount Veeder regularly produce an austerely tannic wine, big on flavour, long on ageing. The winery is housed in a century-old stone building, but the present operation is somewhat newer than that (it was re-founded by the Taylor family in 1941 and bought by the present owners in 1968). The ability of the wines to age is more akin to Cabernets of Bordeaux than of California, and I have yet to taste a fully mature Mayacamas wine. Recent vintages would suggest that the ageing timespan is shortening from vintages such as the 70 and 68 which are reckoned not to be ready yet. The 85 (tasted in 1990) with its big, chunky fruit, almost earthy tannins, and heady aromas, looks likely to show some maturity by 1998.

ROBERT MONDAVI WINERY ***→****
7801 St Helena Highway, Oakville, Napa

Total v'yds owned: 560ha (1385 acres)
Cabernet area: 151ha (373 acres)
Cabernet production: 1.1 million bottles

Considering that the Robert Mondavi winery must be one of the largest producers of Cabernet in California, let alone Napa, I never cease to be amazed at the regular high quality of what is made. All the way down the range, what is done is done properly with the attention to detail and time for innovation that belong more properly to a small boutique winery. We should all be grateful for this, and admire the way that Bob Mondavi, since he broke away from the family Charles Krug winery in 1966, has created such a success story, continued now by his son Tim Mondavi as winemaker. There are two styles made, a regular bottling from Napa Valley fruit, and a Reserve bottling, much of the fruit for which comes from the To-Kalon Vineyard in Oakville next door to Martha's Vineyard. Recent tastings of the Reserve suggest some vintages stand out: the 79 (tasted in 1987) with an amazing cigar-box/tobacco bouquet, smooth, concentrated fruit; the 86 (tasted in 1989) chewy with ripe minty flavours and again tobacco smells, coupled with splendid acidity; the 85 (tasted in 1989) richer than the 86, more minty, a huge, classic wine, piled high with fruit.

MONTICELLO CELLARS **→***
4242 Big Ranch Road, Napa

Total v'yds owned: 91ha (225 acres)
Cabernet area: 14ha (34.5 acres)
Cabernet production: 120,000 bottles

The Jefferson connection at Monticello goes beyond the name, with a scale model of Jefferson's Virginia mansion and acknowledgment of his love of wine. Monticello wanted to recognize this with a quotation in praise of wine from Jefferson on its label, but was prevented by the Bureau of Alcohol, Tobacco and Firearms. Cabernets come in two styles: a regular bottling, called Jefferson Cuvee, the 86 (tasted in 1989) a splendidly full wine, with plenty of tannins and fruit that would put some other winery's reserve bottlings to shame; and the Corley Reserve, the 85 (tasted in 1989) attractively perfumed, with strawberry and blackcurrant fruit flavours, not for long ageing but for very enjoyable drinking.

MOUNT VEEDER WINERY **→
1999 Mount Veeder Road, Napa

Total v'yds owned: 10.5ha (26 acres)
Cabernet area: 7.3ha (18 acres)
Cabernet production: 32,000 bottles

This small winery, on the slopes of Mount Veeder, close to Mayacamas, has been making full-bodied, tannic, wines from mountainside fruit since 1973. Started by Michael and Arlene Bernstein, it is now under the same ownership as Franciscan Winery, but the style does not seem to have changed. The best vintages are the most recent, especially the 85 and 86; but some earlier vintages, especially 82 and 81, disappoint. Perhaps the finest vintage was 79 (tasted in 1989) now beautifully balanced, with austere fruit and delicate flavours.

NEWTON VINEYARD ** → ***
2555 Madrona Avenue, St Helena, Napa

Total v'yds owned: 25ha (62 acres)
Cabernet area: 25ha (62 acres)
Cabernet production: 66,000 bottles

For anybody with a poor head for heights, travelling the Newton Vineyard either on foot or in a pickup truck is not the best place to be. Vertiginous slopes make this one of the most beautiful Napa vineyards, but one which has to be worked entirely by hand. Halfway up the Spring Mountain is a delicately beautiful winery, the work of Peter Newton. The Cabernet produced here contains proportions of Merlot (12 percent), Cabernet Franc (12 percent) and Petit Verdot (1 percent). First vintage was with the 79, but the best wines have been made since 84, which (tasted in 1989) showed a light, elegant style, with spicy vanilla overtones. The 86 (tasted in 1990) is bigger, more tannic, more serious, with excellent tannins and firm cassis flavours.

OPUS ONE → ****
Oakville, Napa

Cabernet area: 44ha (109 acres)
Cabernet production: 135,000 bottles,

The famous link-up between Robert Mondavi and the late Baron Philippe de Rothschild of Château Mouton-Rothschild in Bordeaux has continued and grown to encompass a projected winery and separate vineyards on the valley floor in Oakville. The intention has always been to combine Californian grapes with Franco-American wine skills, and this aim has succeeded with great elan. The very first vintage in 1979 was a stunning wine, and the superlatives have continued. Both the 85 and 86, the most recent releases in 1989/90 have shown continued advances – the 85 (tasted in 1990) showing how enormously rich fruit can still be contained into something refined and elegant – very French, in fact. The 86 (tasted in 1990) seems likely to mature more quickly, but its beautiful cedary, tarry fruit and black cherry and cassis flavours show its quality.

JOSEPH PHELPS ** → ****
200 Taplin Road, St Helena, Napa

Total v'yds owned: 131ha (325 acres)
Cabernet area: 44ha (109 acres)
Cabernet production: 240,000 bottles

Joseph Phelps' beautiful hideaway in a side valley off the main Napa Valley has been producing fine Cabernets since 1973, and the winery now makes four different styles. The regular bottling draws on fruit from Napa Valley growers, the 85 (tasted in 1990) with a perfumed, meaty bouquet, some tannins and hints of mint, has a proportion of Merlot in the blend. Then there are three reserve wines: the single-vineyard Eisele, from the independently owned 16ha (39 acres) vineyard near Calistoga, a wine containing 4 percent Merlot, the 85 (tasted in 1989) very firm and concentrated, with spice and blackcurrants under some tense, heavy tannins – a wine to keep for years. The other single-vineyard wine is from the 3ha (7.5 acres) Backus Vineyard in Oakville, warm, concentrated wine which matures more quickly than Eisele. Insignia, the proprietary red, is a blend with 25 percent Cabernet Franc and 15 percent Merlot, very much aiming at a French style, first made in 1974, and in 85 and 86 vintages proving to be two of the best reds made in the Napa.

PINE RIDGE WINERY   ***
5901 Silverado Trail, Napa

Total v'yds owned: 50ha (124 acres)
Cabernet area: 43ha (106 acres)
Cabernet production: 144,000 bottles

Four different bottlings of Cabernet are made at this winery on Silverado Trail in the Stag's Leap area. Owner Gary Andrus trained for a time in Bordeaux and it shows in his elegant, and often restrained, built-to-last wines. The best cuvee he makes is Andrus Reserve from fruit grown on the west side of Napa Valley at Rutherford: the 80 was the first vintage, and was a splendid debut, but 84 was not far behind. Pine Ridge Stags Leap Vineyard comes, as its name suggests, from vineyards near the winery: the 85 (tasted in 1990) shows complexity and delicacy, with lively fruit and great style. The third special bottling is new: Diamond Mountain Vineyard first made with the 86 vintage. The fourth bottling is the largest, the Rutherford Cuvee, the 85 (tasted in 1989) full of cigar-box and tobacco flavours, very pleasing, and relatively quick to mature. Apart from the Diamond Mountain wine, the wines all have a mixture of Merlot, Cabernet Franc, and in the case of Andrus, Malbec.

PRESTON VINEYARDS   ** →
9282 West Dry Creek Road, Healdsburg, Sonoma

Total v'yds owned: 50ha (124 acres)
Cabernet area: 5.6ha (14 acres)
Cabernet production: 48,000 bottles

Preston launched its first Cabernet with the 82 vintage, and has subsequently produced a series of wines that are designed for relatively early drinking, and which exhibit attractive flavours, always on the lighter side. The best vintage so far has been 85, as much a product of the vintage as the winery.

RIDGE VINEYARDS   ****
17100 Monte Bello Road, Cupertino, Santa Clara

Cabernet area: 20ha (49 acres)
Cabernet production: 144,000 bottles

Surely some of the best California Cabernets come from this unlikely spot in a winery high above the city of San Jose, and right on the San Andreas Fault. Following takeover winemaker Paul Draper now works for a Japanese pharmaceutical firm, but what he is making is just as good as ever. The best wine is Monte Bello, from a 20ha vineyard near the winery, at an altitude of 770 metres (2525 feet). Since the first vintage in 1962, this has been consistently among the top two or three in California. Recent vintages show continuing quality and consistency in the rich, elegant style of the grapes and the hands-off method of winemaking, letting, for example, the grapes' natural yeasts control the fermentation. The 78 (tasted in 1988) showed great warmth of fruit, generous flavours and still no sign of peak maturity. Ten percent Merlot and 5 percent Petit Verdot are included in the blend. Other Cabernets are good, even though they are lesser wines compared with Monte Bello. York Creek Vineyard Cabernet comes from Spring Mountain in Napa, the 84 (tasted in 1990) with 9 percent Merlot, was maturing relatively quickly, and was certainly ready to drink. Three other Cabernets are produced: Howell Mountain Vineyard, from the Napa, Santa Cruz Mountain, and Jimsomare also from Santa Cruz near the winery.

RUTHERFORD HILL WINERY   ** →
200 *Rutherford Hill Road, Rutherford, Napa*

Total v'yds owned: 323ha (798 acres)
Cabernet area: 47ha (116 acres)
Cabernet production: 230,000 bottles

Rutherford Hill, owned by the same group of partners as Freemark Abbey, makes Cabernets which have generally been less highly regarded than those of its sister winery. The style has been easy to drink, with wines ready once released. The regular cuvee was first released with the 74 vintage, and the most recent offerings, such as the 84, show good concentration and ripe, juicy fruit. With the 85 vintage, they introduced a cuvee called XVS (Exceptional Vineyard Selection), and this is definitely a cut above the regular cuvee, the 85 full of fruit with balancing tannin and rich chocolate flavours – a wine that will comfortably mature over ten years or more.

SANTA CRUZ MOUNTAIN VINEYARD   → ***
2300 *Jarvis Road, Santa Cruz*

Total v'yds owned: 4.8ha (12 acres)
Cabernet area: none
Cabernet production: 16,000 bottles

Owner Ken Burnap buys in all the Cabernet grapes he needs to make his single-vineyard Bates Ranch wine. The style is big and beefy, with hugely ripe fruit and very fruity, tarry flavours. The 85 Bates Ranch is the best vintage since the first vintage in 77: a robust, healthy wine style, very deep in colour and with considerable concentration, a wine that will last for a good ten years or more.

SHAFER VINEYARDS   ***
6154 *Silverado Trail, Napa*

Total v'yds owned: 54ha (133 acres)
Cabernet area: 17ha (42 acres)
Cabernet production: 84,000 bottles

Shafer's two Cabernets come from vineyards in Stag's Leap, and bought-in grapes to supplement what they grow themselves. They also have vineyards in Carneros for their Chardonnay. The first Cabernet vintage, the 78 (tasted in 1988) was still full of tannins. The style since then has changed and opened out, with the excellent 85 regular wine having all the lovely cassis and tar flavours one would expect from a Stag's Leap wine. Since the 83 vintage, they have also produced a Hillside Select bottling, which comes from grapes grown on hillside sites near the winery. The 85 of this (tasted in 1990) showed considerable intensity of flavour and greater tannins.

SILVER OAK CELLARS

*** →

915 Oakville Cross Road, Oakville, Napa

Total v'yds owned: 80ha (198 acres)
Cabernet area: 80ha (198 acres)
Cabernet production: 264,000 bottles

There is only one fruit processed at this winery, and that is Cabernet. Owner/winemaker Justin Meyer obviously likes the grape, and he gets excellent results with it. He makes two Napa wines: one a regular bottling and one from the single-vineyard Bonny's Vineyard, named after his wife. Meyer also owns vineyards in Sonoma's Alexander Valley, which supplies fruit for his third Cabernet, and it is this wine (which carries the designation North Coast because fruit crosses the county line from Sonoma to Napa to be processed) which is made in large quantities. Only 12,000 bottles are made of each of the other wines: Bonny's Vineyard is probably the finer, but it would be difficult to differentiate in quality in some vintages. Both wines, as well as the Alexander Valley wine, performed exceptionally well with the 84 and 85 vintages.

SILVERADO VINEYARDS

→ ***

3103 Silverado Trail, Napa

Total v'yds owned: 135ha (334 acres)
Cabernet area: 26ha (64 acres)
Cabernet production: 120,000 bottles

This winery owned by the Disney family released its first vintage with the 81, and yet it has already reached the top league of Napa wineries for its Cabernet. Money was not a problem for winemaker John Stuart, but quality vineyards and his skills were also a vital part of the equation. The result has been some excellent wines, such as the 86, very fruity, but with some austere tannins that make it a serious wine for long-term maturing. The 87 (tasted in 1990) is a shade disappointing, with a taste that is almost burnt, but even this has considerable cassis and ripe fruit flavours.

SIMI WINERY

→ ***

16275 Healdsburg Avenue, Healdsburg, Sonoma

Total v'yds owned: 111ha (274 acres)
Cabernet area: 51ha (126 acres)
Cabernet production: 420,000 bottles

The historic Simi Winery first opened its doors in 1881. Originally called the Montepulciano winery, and owned by the Italian Simi brothers, it is now part of the huge Moët-Hennessey/Louis Vuitton empire, and shares many technical facilities with Domaine Chandon, the Moët sparkling wine operation in Napa. However, when it comes to Cabernet, Simi is on its own. With vineyards in the Alexander Valley supplying much of the fruit – especially for the Reserve wine, which is top of the range – Simi has developed a style which is possibly French in definition, complex and elegant. The Reserve 82, for instance (tasted in 1990) with its 25 percent Merlot, showed lean, young tannins and concentrated crisp fruit, with hints of smoothness coming through as it matures. The 80 Reserve (tasted in 1989) was possibly more concentrated, more tannic, while the splendid 84 (tasted in 1989) is a great wine by any standards, beautifully balanced, richly proportioned and bursting with fruit. The regular bottling shows a lighter, smoother character, ready for drinking on release, and most enjoyable.

SPOTTSWOODE VINEYARD AND WINERY   ***
1410 Hudson Avenue, St Helena, Napa

Cabernet area: 12ha (30 acres)
Cabernet production: 28,800 bottles

With a first vintage in 82, Spottswoode is still new to the Cabernet scene. But owner Mary Novak, whose vineyard is squeezed into the new housing development on the edge of St Helena, was one of those who made a striking run of vintages from the start. The 82, made with winemaker Tony Soter, shows a concentrated style, with attractive perfume, and (tasted in 1989) still plenty of tannin and acidity to hold it all together. The 85, has similar qualities, but also an extra richness derived from the excellent vintage.

STAGS LEAP WINE CELLARS   →****
5766 Silverado Trail, Napa

Total v'yds owned: 31ha (77 acres)
Cabernet area: 30ha (74 acres)
Cabernet production: 216,000 bottles

Stag's Leap Wine Cellars, under its owner Warren Winiarski, have been up with the top in Cabernets since their inaugural vintage in 72. Their vineyards in the Stag's Leap District display the elegance and surprising power that seem to be hallmarks of this newly-designated area within Napa Valley. Stag's Leap makes two special bottlings, Cask 23 and Stag's Leap Vineyards, as well as a larger quantity of a regular bottling which comes from contract growers elsewhere in Napa. The regular bottling itself is a fine wine: the 85 (tasted in 1990) showed big, ripe fruit, the edge of maturity, excellent tannins, and very attractive perfumes. Of the two special bottlings, Cask 23 is the greater, especially in recent vintages like 84, 85 and 86, with their rich cedar and tar flavours, considerable concentration and smoothness masking long-term tannins. Stag's Leap Vineyard (SLV) is perhaps not quite so fine, but good nevertheless, with somewhat more acidity to counter the still considerable concentration of fruit. As ranges, both these bottlings are among the finest in California.

STERLING VINEYARDS   **→***
1111 Dunaweal Lane, Calistoga, Napa

Total v'yds owned: 444ha (1097 acres)
Cabernet area: 105ha (259 acres)
Cabernet production: 200,000 bottles

For some years Sterling, with its dramatic hill-top winery, cable cars and general razzmatazz seemed more designed for tourists than for wines. But in the past five or so years winemaker Bill Dyer has put the winery back on the track started in 1969 when it was first opened. He has decided to go for single-vineyard wines, derived from the excellent range of holdings around Napa. So Cabernets now include the Diamond Mountain vineyard wine as well as the top-of-the-range Reserve and a regular bottling. While I find the regular bottling still disappointing (the 86, tasted in 1990, was unpleasantly vegetal), the Diamond Mountain wines are something again. The Reserves are the best, though: the 84, 85 and 86 make a trio of wines which show that Sterling can certainly compete with some of the top Cabernets in Napa.

SWANSON WINERY ** →
Oakville, Napa

Total v'yds owned: 65ha (161 acres)

The first Cabernet release from this new Napa winery was of the 87 vintage, a 100 percent Cabernet wine, big on tobacco flavours and strong oak tastes, and showing off a splendidly intense colour. The 88 (tasted in 1989 from cask) is likely to turn out to be a big, chewy wine, with very deep colour and considerable tannins, one for the long term. The vineyards are right next to the Opus One vineyard.

PHILIP TOGNI VINEYARD ** → ***
3780 Spring Mountain Road, St Helena, Napa

Total v'yds owned: 4ha (10 acres)
Cabernet area: 2.8ha (7 acres)
Cabernet production: 4,500 bottles

Philip Togni, one-time winemaker at such Cabernet wineries as Chappellet, set up his own vineyard high up on Spring Mountain with the 83 vintage. With his predilection for mountainside fruit, he is able to coax small quantities of rich wines out of low-yielding vines. The 86 Estate wine is the most successful of those released: very rich, very voluptuous, with considerable power. A single-vineyard wine, Tanbark, was produced in the 85 vintage.

TREFETHEN VINEYARDS ** →
1160 Oak Knoll Avenue, Napa

Total v'yds owned: 263ha (650 acres)
Cabernet area: 46ha (114 acres)
Cabernet production: 130,000 bottles

The Trefethen family bottles half the production of its large estate on the valley floor north of Napa City and on the western slopes of the valley, selling the rest to other producers. They have been perhaps more associated with Chardonnay, and vintages of the winery's Cabernet in the early 1980s showed rather harsh tannins and some vegetal undercurrents. But with the 85 vintage and the release of the first Reserve wine, Trefethen has shown that there is fine Cabernet to be produced: this has plenty of balancing fruit and a good firm streak of tannin. The proprietary brand, Eschcol Red, is a blend of Cabernet with Pinot Noir and generally represents good value.

Washington State

Washington State is marginal Cabernet country. Its northerly vineyards need every bit of sunshine they can to ripen the late-ripening Cabernet; and, by October, when the fruit is ready, there is an increasing risk of early frosts which could kill off the whole crop. Yet it can be done, and with increasing success, to judge by the wines I have tasted from vintages after the mid-1980s.

The main Washington vineyards are in the eastern part of the State, on the dry side of the Cascade Mountains, and away from the foggy, damp coast. The Columbia River basin forms the main geographical designation, and there are two smaller areas in Yakima Valley and Walla Walla. All the vineyards need irrigation, but there is sufficient water from the river systems. All three geographical designations can appear on the wine label; if the wine is a blend from two or more areas it is simply described as a Washington wine.

Producers' problems have something in common with New Zealand, with their search to avoid the excessively herbaceous character that comes with underripe Cabernet. That some producers are now regularly making ripe, long-lasting wines shows that specific sites have sufficient sunshine to ripen the grapes fully.

Most producers follow the growing practice of blending some Merlot into the wines to soften the tannins and to flesh out what is sometimes quite hard fruit. They also use French oak – Nevers or Limousin seem to be interchangeable – for fermentation as well as maturing the wines. Maturing can take up to two years although unless the fruit is particularly ripe, this does seem to be excessive.

PRODUCERS

CH STE MICHELLE/COLUMBIA CREST **→
1 Stimson Lane, Woodinville, Seattle

Total v'yds owned: 1174ha (2900 acres)

The largest Washington State producer has wineries all along the Columbia River vineyard area, but its main offices and headquarters are on the outskirts of Seattle housed in a building that looks a little like a French château. They use both names – Columbia Crest and Ch Ste Michelle – as labels. The Ch Ste Michelle Cabernet 87, a wine made from fruit from anywhere within the State, is a tannic wine to begin with, the 87 (tasted in 1990) very chewy and tough, but the 85 (tasted in 1989) showed good rich and lively fruit and was ready to drink. There is a Benton County Cold Creek Vineyards Cabernet, which seems to develop more slowly. Under the Columbia Crest label, the 85 Cabernet (tasted in 1990) showed excellent vibrant colour, good spicy fruit, a ripe taste with some balancing tannins.

COLUMBIA WINERY ***
1445 120th Avenue NE, Bellevue, Seattle

Total v'yds owned: None

Formerly called Associated Vintners, this was the first winery to make vintaged varietal wines from European grape varieties in Washington. It has subsequently made a considerable name for itself for its Cabernets. These include both valley-wide Columbia Valley wines and a number of single-vineyard wines, under the name of winemaker David Lake, from Yakima Valley. The general style is smooth, rich with intense fruit. The 86 Columbia Valley Cabernet (tasted in 1990) was perhaps least successful – hard and acid, lacking complexity, even though the fruit quality was there. However the single-vineyard wines are more interesting: the Otis Vineyard 85

David Lake signature (tasted in 1990) showed a maturing taste, with a hint of cassis fruit and tobacco flavours. Other single-vineyard wines are from Red Willow Vineyard and Sagemoor Vineyard (with 23 percent Merlot). The special one-off Millenium 79, a blend with 15 percent Merlot, and designed for maturity in 2000, has intense flavour, aromatic, ripe, dense taste and classic tannins.

COVEY RUN →**
Box 2287, Zillah, Yakima Valley

Total v'yds owned: 70ha (173 acres)

From its privileged position on the slopes of the Rattlesnake Hills, the Covey Run winery has splendid views across its south-facing vineyards to the Horse Heaven Hills on the opposite side of the valley. The vineyards produce a Yakima Valley Cabernet, blended with 7 percent Merlot, and aged for 12 months in Limousin oak: the 86 (tasted in 1990) shows bursting, very jammy fruit, likely to soften in a year or two as wood flavours balance it out.

KIONA VINEYARDS WINERY **→
Box 2169 E, Benton City, Yakima Valley

Total v'yds owned: 12ha (30 acres)

Using Yakima Valley fruit from its own vineyard, the small family-owned Kiona makes a Cabernet which is in a relatively fast-maturing style, the 86 (tasted in 1989) has elegance and concentration, coupled with some tannin and ripe fruit.

LATAH CREEK WINE CELLARS **
E 13030 Indiana Avenue, Spokane

Total v'yds owned: none

From his winery in the Columbia River valley area, north of the Yakima Valley, winemaker Mike Conway produces a big, chewy style of Cabernet, blended with Merlot: the 87 (tasted in 1990) had plenty of cassis and blackcurrant flavours, supported by strong tastes of new wood. It is a wine that needs ageing.

LEONETTI CELLAR **→
1321 School Avenue, Walla Walla

Total v'yds owned: 1ha (2.5 acres)

The tiny production of Gary Figgins' blended Cabernet and Merlot shows up the quality of the Walla Walla vineyards on the border with Oregon. His Seven Hills Vineyard 85 (tasted in 1989) was a rich, warm wine, with very strong varietal spicy fruit tastes, with plenty of tannin to suggest good ageing potential.

STATON HILLS WINERY →**
71 Gangl Road, Wapata, Yakima Valley

Total v'yds owned: 14.6ha (36 acres)

In their Yakima Valley vineyards, Dave and Margy Staton have devised a system of A-frame trellises for training Cabernet, which turns whole walls of leaves and fruit to the sun, to give them a greater chance to ripen. The 87 Cabernet (tasted in 1990) was smooth and rich, but had a somewhat herbaceous quality suggesting underripe fruit. Some Merlot was used in the blend.

STEWART VINEYARDS →**
1382 West Riverside Avenue, Sunnyside, Yakima Valley

Total v'yds owned: 28ha (69 acres)

Vineyards are near the town of Sunnyside in Yakima Valley and on the Wahluke Slope of Columbia River valley. The 87 Cabernet (tasted in 1990) had excellent soft fruit, almost sweet in its ripeness, with hints of tannin, but essentially designed for relatively rapid maturation.

PAUL THOMAS WINERY **→
1717 136th Pl. NE, Bellevue

Total v'yds owned: none

Wine star Paul Thomas started out making fruit wines but has moved on to make some of the most individual grape wines in Washington State. His Chardonnay is highly praised, as is his Cabernet, using fruit grown in eastern Washington and trucked to his winery near Seattle. The 85 Cabernet (tasted in 1989) balances some ripe fruit with obvious acidity which needs time to soften down, but should then produce a well-integrated, concentrated, if always lively wine.

WOODWARD CANYON →***
Box 387, Lowden, Walla Walla

Total v'yds owned: 4.5ha (11 acres)

Rick Small's winery, housed in a pioneering tin shed, uses fruit from his own vineyard in Walla Walla and from Mercer Ranch in the Columbia River valley. His 86 Cabernet (tasted in 1989) exuded new French oak smells and tastes, but balanced these with concentrated cassis and cherry fruit flavours and firm ripe tannins. The result is a wine that will age well, and which shows considerable potential.

Australia

Cabernet is sometimes described as Australia's premium red table-wine variety. This is, of course, to ignore the fact that the country's finest red wine is made from the Shiraz (Syrah) grape and Shiraz which has created the most distinctive Australian red-wine style. The best expression of Cabernet Sauvignon is not in the 100 percent Cabernet wines but in the blends with Shiraz, a combination which when well done is Australia's finest offering to the wine world.

In fact, many so-called Cabernets in Australia are not 100 percent Cabernet. Don't believe what the label says: Australians can call their wine Cabernet even if it contains as much as 20 percent of something else. It may be Shiraz or one of the Bordeaux varieties, Merlot, Cabernet Franc and Malbec. Only when the magic amount of 20 percent of something else is passed, do the other grapes have to appear on the label, which explains omnibus wine names such as Cabernet/Shiraz or Cabernet/Merlot/Malbec.

Australians are great blenders. They will blend different grape varieties, and they will blend grapes from, it seems, virtually anywhere on the continent with grapes from virtually anywhere else. While some purists object that a wine should come from a particular spot and express that place, frankly it does not worry most consumers, as long as the final result is good; and that is the blessing of Australian wine – that so much is so good and such good value. The back label of a bottle will probably tell you where the grapes come from: while a designation such as South-East Australian, for example, will at least tell you that the grapes come from more than one state, and a more precise definition, such as Barossa Valley or Coonawarra, will identify the wine as being made 95 percent from that area's grapes.

Even if you won't find the very greatest Cabernets, you will almost certainly not find better value anywhere else in the world. The Australians seem to get the magic balance of price and quality pretty well right pretty often. One reason is that some of the best wines, certainly some of the best Cabernets, come from the biggest firms, so there are large quantities of above average quality wines ready to set standards which smaller wineries have to strive hard to beat.

The spread of Cabernet has been a result of the phenomenal growth in table-wine production in a country which had traditionally relied on fortified wines as its main production. As with many happenings in the Australian wine scene, it has been entirely random: if producers want to plant Cabernet they go ahead and do it, regardless of whether the soil or climate are right. Parts of the main producing areas are too hot for a vine whose greatest expressions are to be found in the marginal, almost cool climate of Bordeaux. Cabernet does not want the searing heat that Shiraz enjoys: it needs a long summer of warm days which can allow it to ripen slowly, to deepen in flavour and colour. That is possible in Australia in selected areas. Trial and error are now showing where those are. They are the areas where the producer can avoid the major problem of fruit lacking in acidity through being overripe.

The ripeness of grapes and the nature of Australian winemaking generally mean that Australian Cabernets are not for long-term ageing. There are some exceptions, generally from the cooler producing areas, where acidity and tannins are in balance, but as a rough rule an Australian Cabernet matures over five to ten years, rather than the ten years or more for a Bordeaux Cabernet. Even when young they become attractive, because of the rich fruit and forward flavour, often a product of the blending with Shiraz.

THE CABERNET ARRIVES

Although vines arrived with the First Fleet in 1788, there are few precise details of what was planted under Captain Arthur Phillip's instructions. Indeed, at the time, Cabernet was still a relative newcomer in Bordeaux. It is probably much more accurate to date the first plantings of Cabernet to the work of John Macarthur in 1816 and James Busby in 1831. The latter is regarded as the father of both the Australian and New Zealand wine industries. He collected vines from Europe and planted them at his property at Kirkton in the Hunter Valley; although he left Australia soon after to go to New Zealand, cuttings from his vines survived at Kirkton right up to 1924.

Although the first century of Australian wine production was mainly of table wines, there was a dramatic change after World War I, with the development of Empire Preference which encouraged the industry to concentrate on fortified wines. That meant a move towards red varieties such as Grenache and Shiraz, which were good for port-styles, and away from Cabernet. Plantings of Cabernet dwindled. When, for example, in 1952 Penfolds, the largest Australian wine producer, wanted to find some Cabernet Sauvignon in South Australia, the only place they could find it was at their vineyard of Kalimna in the Barossa Valley.

CABERNET VINEYARDS

The 1960s and 1970s saw the return of Cabernet as the boom in table wine grew. Plantings were made in entirely the wrong places, in the hot Riverlands, for example, where Cabernet has a tendency to produce grapes with immense berry fruit flavours and little shape, taste or structure; but they were also made in what proved to be just the right places for the vine; and there are enough of the right places for Cabernet to have established itself as the second most widely planted red variety in Australia after Shiraz.

The two most highly regarded areas are both cool in Australian terms, with temperatures similar to Bordeaux, even if they have much lower rainfall. In South Australia the strip of terra rosa soil at Coonawarra, right at the southern end of the state; and, in Western Australia, the more recently-established Margaret River vineyards are home to some of the country's finest Cabernet producers.

Other areas also produce good Cabernet. There is plenty of the vine in the Barossa, especially on the slopes rather than the valley floor; there are plantings in Clare, and the McLaren Vale is proving to be a second home for the vine, as is the Padthaway area north of Coonawarra. In Victoria much of the Geelong area makes good wines, as do isolated areas such as the Pyrenees, or even, to the northeast, Milawa. The Yarra Valley produces Cabernet, but this is super-cool country, and Pinot Noir reigns supreme here.

In New South Wales, there are plantings of Cabernet in the Hunter Valley, but it is significant that one of the best Cabernets to be made by a Hunter-based producer, Rosemount, is actually produced from Coonawarra grapes. The Hunter's climate, humid and hot at the picking season, is quite wrong for Cabernet: the Shiraz should remain supreme here.

MAKING CABERNET

As in other wineproducing countries, red-wine making in Australia involved less technology than white-wine production. But the Australians have developed certain techniques which they use to obtain the best from the red grapes.

At the fermentation stage, the choice is between fermenting the grapes with their stalks and pips or removing these before fermentation starts. The first method increases tannin in the wine (from the stalks), the second reduces it. There is little need for extra tannin in Australian Cabernet, and the common practice is to destem the grapes before crushing and fermentation.

During fermentation a red-wine producer needs to extract colour from the skins. This will be done by macerating the skins in the juice to extract colour. Various pieces of equipment aid an Australian producer. Foremost among these is the Potter, a vertical cylindrical stainless steel tank which acts a little like a coffee percolator, draining the juice off the skins at the moment the producer decides there is enough colour in the wine. Potters are a common feature of many Australian wineries. More traditional producers still use open fermenting tanks and either stir the skins about in the fermenting must or plunge them back to the bottom of the must to gain the right colour extraction. Some producers leave the fermented finished wine on the skins for a few extra days in order to increase tannins, but this is not normally necessary with Cabernet in Australia.

Acid though can be a problem, and while the grapes have to be picked at a certain degree of ripeness, some producers are picking as early as possible in the ripeness curve. If they can get the acidity of the grapes right, producers will put their wine through the second, malolactic fermentation, to reduce acidity levels and increase the consequent complexity of the wine.

Most Cabernets are matured in oak. French oak is preferred, certainly for more expensive wines: Nevers and Limousin are both used. Barrels are brought from France ready made up, at great expense. Wood ageing can be anything up to two years, although one year to 18 months is more normal for better Cabernets. American oak is also popular, because of the vanilla and spice tastes this wood gives off, though it is more commonly used with Shiraz which can take the very strong taste of the wood.

PRODUCERS

ASHBOURNE **
Lenswood, Ashbourne, South Australia

Total v'yds owned: 8ha (20 acres)

Geoff Weaver, who works at nearby Thomas Hardy, has this small vineyard among the apple trees of Lenswood in the Adelaide Hills on his own account. Currently, the wines are made at Petaluma, the state-of-the-art winery of Brian Croser. Cabernet and Merlot are planted and are blended in a wine which is only available in Australia.

ASHBROOK ESTATE **→
Harman's South Road, Willyabrup, Western Australia

Total v'yds owned: 12ha (30 acres)
Cabernet area: 2ha (5 acres)

Vines form only a tiny part of this 200ha (494 acres)estate in the middle of a red gum forest in the Margaret River area. The winery has been operating since 1975, and the Devitt family make a Cabernet, based mainly on Cabernet Sauvignon with anything up to 20 percent of Cabernet Franc and Merlot. It spends two years in French oak, the 84 vintage producing a blackcurrant cassis tasting wine, quite restrained, with elegance rather than richness. More recent vintages show greater ripeness and roundness.

BOTOBOLAR **
Botobolar Lane, Mudgee, New South Wales

Total v'yds owned: 26ha (64 acres)

The only totally organic vineyard in Australia is owned by Gil and Vincie Wahlquist. They make a number of reds, including St Gilbert, which is an unusual blend of Cabernet, Shiraz, Mourvèdre (locally known as Mataro) and Pinot Noir – the 84, a rich, meaty robust wine, peppery and big rather than elegant. They also make a straight Cabernet which can develop well in the bottle – around eight years from harvest.

BALGOWNIE   **→
Hermitage Road, Maiden Gully, Bendigo, Victoria

Total v'yds owned: 14*ha* (34.5 *acres*)
Cabernet area: 6*ha* (15 *acres*)
Cabernet production: 20,000 *bottles*

Stuart Anderson set up this vineyard near Bendigo in 1969, and is still in charge. His training took him to Château Cissac in Bordeaux, and it was there that he probably learned how to use the taste of wood so that it never shows but is there as an underpin to the fruit. The wines tend to show medium-weight fruit, some tannin but never too much and a long, cherry/cassis fruit taste. A blended Cabernet/ Shiraz wine is also made.

BANNOCKBURN   **→
Midland Highway, Bannockburn, Geelong, Victoria

Total v'yds owned: 18*ha* (44 *acres*)
Cabernet area: 4.5*ha* (11 *acres*)
Cabernet production: 20,000 *bottles*

On the south bank of the Moorabol River, inland from Geelong, this is one of the southernmost vineyards in Victoria. Because of the comparatively cool climate of the vineyard, owner Stuart Hooper and winemaker Garry Farr concentrate mainly on "Burgundian" wines, but they also make a Cabernet, which normally includes 10 percent Merlot and 10 percent Malbec in the blend. The 84 (tasted in 1990) shows an elegant style with already mature colour, somewhat vegetal, and beginning to dry out. Younger vintages still show light fruit, although wines from the early 1980s were heavier.

JIM BARRY WINES   →**
Main North Road, Clare

Total v'yds owned: 105*ha* (259 *acres*)

Jim Barry runs one of the larger Clare wineries, producing local specialities like the Watervale Rhine Riesling, but also making a number of red wines which, on the whole, are better than his whites. There are two Cabernet-based wines: the 100 percent Cabernet, the 86 suitably rich, but deliberately soft and easy to drink, and a less expensive Cabernet (60 percent) and Merlot (40 percent) blend, again soft and smooth in the house style.

BERRI-RENMANO   **→
Berri, South Australia

Total v'yds owned: 8*ha* (20 *acres*)

Producing over 15 percent of Australia's total wine from grapes supplied by its members, Berri-Renmano is a cooperative operating in the flat, irrigated vineyards of the Riverlands. In such a setting it would be expected that quantity would be more important than quality. But, in fact, both under the Berri Estates and the Renmano Chairman's Selection labels, the firm produces some excellent, easy-drinking Cabernets that represent good value for money. Berri Estates 86 blended with some Shiraz (tasted in 1990) is full of sweet, pleasantly mature fruit with a spicy, cinnamon note at the end. Renmano Chairman's Selection also shows well in a more elegant way, but again with sweet, forward fruit.

BOWEN ESTATE   ** → ***
Naracoorte Road, Penola, Coonawarra, South Australia

Total v'yds owned: 24ha (59 acres)

With vineyards entirely on the famed Coonawarra terra rosa soil, Doug and Joy Bowen own one of the few private estates in Australia's best Cabernet district. They make a typical wine of the region, blended with 10 percent Merlot, sometimes with an herbaceous character, but full of minty, eucalyptus tastes. The 86 (tasted in 1990) was firm, still with plenty of acidity and tannin, with some of the those vegetal flavours and a hint of eucalyptus. I preferred it to the 87 (tasted in 1989) which showed less fruit character despite stalky concentration and a raisiny taste. The 84 is their best vintage so far, but it is certainly mature now.

BRAND'S LAIRA   ** →
Naracoorte Road, Coonawarra, South Australia

Total v'yds owned: 28ha (69 acres)

At the northern end of the Coonawarra terra rosa strip is Brand's Laira, named after Eric Brand who owns it, and the Laira, the ship owned by a Captain Stentiford who was the first owner of the property back in the 1890s. The Brands have made two Cabernets since the 1960s: a straight Cabernet and a Cabernet/Merlot blend. They have been described as "classic" wines, and they exhibit all the right tobacco-y, spicy, tealeaf flavours, coupled with considerable elegance. The fruit can tend to austerity in cooler vintages.

BROKENWOOD   **
McDonalds Road, Pokolbin, Hunter Valley, New South Wales

Total v'yds owned: 16.5ha (41 acres)
Cabernet area: 7ha (17.5 acres)

Set up by three Sydney lawyers in 1970 (including James Halliday, now owner of Coldstream Hills in Victoria and a leading wine writer), Brokenwood is now managed by winemaker Iain Riggs and new partners are in charge. It continues to sustain the high reputation for its Semillon and Shiraz established quickly with the first release of wines in 1975. The Cabernets, a product of the Hunter, are not quite so exciting; but from the Graveyard vineyard, the 87 Cabernet (tasted in 1989) shows some pleasing soft fruit, with good cassis flavours and only slight signs of wood.

BROWN BROTHERS   → ***
Glenrowan-Myrtleford Road, Milawa, Victoria

Total v'yds owned: 157ha (388 acres)

With its considerable vineyard holdings and additional supplies from other growers, especially in the neighbouring King Valley, Brown Brothers is able to produce a wide range of Cabernets, which go from the basic Victorian range (with fruit blended from a number of vineyards) right through to their top single-vineyard wines. Their hot country vineyards on the flat plain of Milawa are nicely balanced by the Whitlands vineyard at 770 metres (2526 feet) in the Australian Alps, an hour's drive from the winery. Their Victorian Family Selection wine is typical of the style of their volume wines: the 86 (tasted in 1989) with intense colour, rich fruit, some tannin, but a very straightforward style. The best Brown Brothers Cabernet is from the Koombahla vineyard in the King Valley whose position in a fold of the mountains protects it from too much sun, producing in 88 a fine, minty, rich, smooth wine which looks set to mature well.

CAPE CLAIRAULT   ***
Henry Road, Willyabrup, Margaret River, Western Australia

Total v'yds owned: 7ha (17.5 acres)
Cabernet area: 2ha (5 acres)

Self-taught winemaker and owner Ian Lewis is making a small quantity of classic Margaret River wines, using organic methods in his vineyard. The first commercial vintage was 81, and the 82 Cabernet was an award winner at the national show in Canberra. His 85 Cabernet (tasted in 1988) was a splendid wine, with terrific cassis fruit, smoky cigar-box bouquet and a well structured rich aftertaste.

CAPE MENTELLE   ****
Wallcliffe Road, Margaret River, Western Australia

Total v'yds owned: 40ha (99 acres)
Cabernet area: 14.4ha (35.5 acres)
Cabernet production: 60,000 bottles

David Hohnen was trained in Australia and in California and founded Cape Mentelle winery in the Margaret River and Cloudy Bay in Marlborough, New Zealand. He is still very much in charge, despite the purchase of both wineries by Veuve Clicquot Champagne in 1990. Just as he has done with Sauvignon Blanc in New Zealand, so Hohnen is producing one of Australia's best Cabernets in Western Australia. It shows that the cool climate of Margaret River is just as much a force to be reckoned with in Cabernet as the cool climate of Coonawarra in South Australia. Hohnen uses a very Bordeaux approach to Cabernets, blending them with some Merlot and a little Cabernet Franc, and producing wines that can mature over a long period even if they have the Australian character of direct fruit. The 83 (tasted in 1988) was just beginning to come round, but would benefit from another four to five years in bottle before drinking. The 84 (tasted in 1988) showed great style and delicacy from a cooler vintage. The 88 is going to be a top class wine – in about ten years' time.

CAPEL VALE WINES   →***
Lot 5, Stirling Estate, Capel North West Road, Capel, Western Australia

Total v'yds owned: 32ha (79 acres)
Cabernet area: 6ha (15 acres)
Cabernet production: 66,000 bottles

One of the many medical practitioners to become involved in wine, Dr Peter Pratten set up Capel Vale in 1973 in the southern coastal plain between Bunbury and Busselton north of the Margaret River area. He has vineyards around the winery, in Mount Barker much further south and in Margaret River, all of which supply Cabernet. The top Cabernet wine is a Bordeaux-style blend, which includes Shiraz with the Bordeaux grapes. Aged in small *barriques*, it is called Baudin after a French explorer of the area. There is also a straight Cabernet, the 85 (tasted in 1990) having excellent balance, attractive minty acidity and firm tannins.

CHITTERING ESTATE   **→

Chittering Valley Road, Lower Chittering, Western Australia

Total v'yds owned: 25ha (62 acres)

It is still early days for this winery set in the cool Darling Ranges, just north of Perth. The first release in 1987 showed that Chittering should become the showplace winery its spectacular buildings would suggest. Steven Schapera, joint owner of Chittering, has studied at the University of California Davis, and he has combined New and Old World technology to make his reds from Cabernet and Merlot.

CLYDE PARK   →***

Midland Highway, Bannockburn, Geelong, Victoria

Total v'yds owned: 3ha (7.5 acres)

The main job of Gary Farr, the owner of Clyde Park, is as winemaker at Bannockburn, and this is his spare-time vineyard. But he makes a very fine Cabernet in these cool-climate vineyards, the 86 (tasted in 1990) full of big, vegetal fruit, dusty and perfumed, with some wood and a youthful colour. The wines are bottled at Bannockburn.

COLDSTREAM HILLS   **→

Lot 6, Maddens Lane, Coldstream, Yarra Valley, Victoria

Total v'yds owned: 15ha (37 acres)
Cabernet area: 2ha (5 acres)
Cabernet production: 31,000 bottles

James Halliday, one of Australia's top wine writers, had already had first-hand experience of wine production at Brokenwood when he set up Coldstream Hills in 1985. While his main success has been with Chardonnay and Pinot Noir in the cool climate of the Yarra Valley, he does make three Cabernets. There is a blended Cabernet/ Merlot, a blended Cabernet Sauvignon/Cabernet Franc/Merlot, which, in a year like 88 can produce a deeply austere, tannic wine needing plenty of time in bottle, and a Coonawarra Cabernet, which is being sold under a second label, James Halliday.

CULLENS   **

Caves Road, Cowaramup, Margaret River, Western Australia

Total v'yds owned: 29ha (72 acres)

One of the doctor-and-wife-teams turned wine producer in Margaret River, Dr Kevin Cullen and his wife Diana have operated a very hands-on policy since their first plantings in 1971. Diana was winemaker for many years before being joined by their daughter Vanya who trained at Roseworthy College and at the Robert Mondavi winery in California. Their biggest-selling wine is a Cabernet/Merlot blend (65 percent Cabernet) strongly influenced by oak in its early years and needing bottle age to soften out.

DELATITE   **→

Stoney's Road, Mansfield, Victoria

Total v'yds owned: 24ha (59 acres)
Cabernet area: 2ha (5 acres)
Cabernet production: 10,800 bottles

The isolated Delatite vineyard in the foothills of the Great Dividing Range is a family-run business. The winery was designed by the top consultancy in the country, and it has helped them to produce a string of well-made, exciting wines. While the major part of production is of whites, they do make a Cabernet/Merlot blend, called Devil's River, which achieves good minty flavours, and a Cabernet/Shiraz blend (with 55 percent Cabernet), the 86 (tasted in 1987) still somewhat closed up, but showing good firm ripe fruit.

EVANS & TATE   ** → ***
Swan Street, Henley Brook, Western Australia

Total v'yds owned: 24ha (59 acres)

Of the two vineyards owned by Evans & Tate, the Gnangara Estate at the winery, north of Margaret River, supplies Shiraz, while the much larger Redbrook vineyard in the Margaret River area supplies all the other varieties including Cabernet – the largest planting. The Margaret River Cabernet normally has about 16 percent of Shiraz in the blend to give in 84 (tasted in 1990) a chewy, dusty, spicy wine with obvious potential for ageing. To repay the compliment, Cabernet is blended into the top-selling red, the Gnangara Shiraz.

FOREST HILL   ** →
Muir Highway, Mount Barker, Western Australia

Total v'yds owned: 20ha (49 acres)
Cabernet area: 10ha (25 acres)
Cabernet production; 24,000 bottles

Forest Hill was one of the pioneers in Mount Barker, the most southerly of Western Australia's vineyard areas. Half the vineyard belonging to Tony and Betty Pearse is planted with Cabernet which is made at the nearby Plantagenet winery. They produce a number of Cabernet-based wines, including a port-style ruby; the fresh, cherry fruit Light Dry Red, made from Cabernet by the carbonic maceration method for early drinking and freshness; and the Forest Hill Cabernet enhanced by strong fruit tastes, the 85 (tasted in 1990) showing some tannin and wood, together with flavoursome strawberry fruit.

HAINAULT VINEYARD   ** →
Walnut Road, Bickley, Western Australia

Total v'yds owned: 4ha (10 acres)
Cabernet area: 1ha (2.5 acres)
Cabernet production: 5,000 bottles

Hainault is in the cool Darling Ranges east of Perth. Peter Fennel, the owner, has French models in mind both with his whites and his reds, of which a Cabernet/Merlot blend is the winery's best-selling wine. This is a mix of 50 percent Cabernet, 45 percent Merlot and 5 percent Cabernet Franc, with each component vinified separately and blended just before bottling.

THOMAS HARDY & SONS   ** → ***
Reynell Road, Reynella, South Australia

Total v'yds owned: 824ha (2036 acres)

One of the giants of the Australian wine industry, the family-owned Thomas Hardy also owns Houghton in Western Australia and the

Stanley Wine Company in Clare Valley. At its main plant south of Adelaide, Thomas Hardy and Chateau Reynella wines are produced. There are various ranges, of which the Bird Series is the basic single varietal range; the middle range is the Stamp Collection; both these ranges have striking labels. The top varietal range is known as the Hardy Collection, with a McLaren Vale Cabernet Sauvignon, the 87 (tasted in 1990) having good fresh fruit balanced with some tannin. Of a similar quality is the Nottage Hill Cabernet, the 88 (tasted in 1990) soft and warm, more immediately attractive than the Hardy Collection Cabernet, and designed for earlier drinking. All the wines are well-made competent examples which just miss that final excitement.

HEEMSKERK   ∗∗→
Piper's Brook, Launceston, Tasmania

Total v'yds owned: 80ha (198 acres)

The Heemskerk/Louis Roederer sparkling-wine (the first vintage of which was released in 1990) takes up much of the production at this winery. However a Cabernet Sauvignon is made which exhibits the typical grassy, stalky, quite acid character of Tasmania's cool climate Cabernets, and it is one of the best on the island.

HENSCHKE   ∗∗∗→
Moculta Road, Keyneton, South Australia

Total v'yds owned: 81ha (200 acres)

Traditional open fermenters are still in use at this Adelaide Hills winery, one of the oldest in the area (founded 1868) and still owned by the family. The quality of that tradition is shown in virtually everything Henschke makes, especially among the red wines. While perhaps the Shiraz wines are the very best, the Cyril Henschke Cabernet, the 85 (tasted in 1988) still tannic, showed enormous colour and deep, intense fruit and style, even though it is not an obvious blockbuster. Cabernet is also used in a Merlot/Cabernet blend.

HOUGHTON   ∗∗→
Dale Road, Middle Swan, Swan Valley, Western Australia

Total v'yds owned: 144ha (356 acres)
Cabernet area: 14.4ha (35.5 acres)

Although owned by members of the Hardy family (of Thomas Hardy Houghton's wines are produced separately in the Swan Valley, Western Australia. At 3.2 million bottles, it is by far the largest Western Australia producer, and its White Burgundy is a national best seller. There are two Cabernets in the range: an inexpensive one made from Frankland River fruit, and somewhat pricier wines from Moondah Estate further north than the Swan Valley winery – a warm, open style of spicy, rich fruit. There is a blended Cabernet/Shiraz/Malbec in the Wildflower Ridge Range.

HUNGERFORD HILL   →∗∗
Broke Road, Pokolbin, Hunter Valley, New South Wales

Total v'yds owned: 100ha (247 acres)

Hungerford Hill owns a large estate in the Hunter Valley at Pokolbin, and a larger one in Coonawarra, where it grows most of the grapes for its Cabernets. The winery, which produces over a million bottles a year, also boasts a popular wine village, one of the major attractions on the wine route in the Hunter. The Coonawarra Cabernet is a typical green-pepper wine, rich with good cassis flavour – best seen in the Show Reserve wine. Less expensive wines carry the Hungerford Hill Collection label, and in this range there is a Cabernet/Merlot/Malbec blend.

HUNTINGTON ESTATE →***
Cassilis Road, Mudgee, New South Wales

Total v'yds owned: 40.4ha (100 acres)
Cabernet area: 13.5ha (33 acres)
Cabernet production; 32,000 bottles

One of the larger Mudgee producers, Huntington Estate is also the home of a concert hall inspired by owners Bob and Wendy Roberts' love of music. From their vineyard they make a range of wines, of which Cabernet is the largest quantity. The reds are fermented in large American oak casks, and this treatment is reflected in the way the wines need some time ageing in bottle. An 84 Cabernet/Merlot blend (tasted in 1987) still needed time, with its cassis and stalky fruit and ripe tannins. With age, the same wine has taken on an elegant, cigar-box taste, very fine and stylish. The straight Cabernet exhibits green-pepper flavours. There is also a Shiraz/Cabernet blend.

IDYLL VINEYARD **
Ballan Road, Moorabool, Geelong, Victoria

Total v'yds owned: 20ha (49 acres)

The Seftons planted this Geelong vineyard in 1966 and now produce a straight Cabernet and a Cabernet/Shiraz blend among other wines. The 85 Cabernet (tasted in 1990) was peppery, spicy, with certain hints of a cool climate vegetal quality, and residual chewy tannins. The bottles are adorned with Nini Sefton's beautiful labels.

KATNOOK ESTATE →***
Penola Road, Coonawarra, South Australia

Total v'yds owned: 350ha (865 acres)

The second-largest landowner in Coonawarra, Katnook produces about 144,000 bottles of wine a year, and also sells grapes to other producers. The two Cabernets are a Katnook Estate wine, and a Riddoch Estate Cabernet/Shiraz blend.

TIM KNAPPSTEIN **
2 Pioneer Avenue, Clare, South Australia

Total v'yds owned: 46ha (114 acres)
Cabernet area: 12.5ha (31 acres)
Cabernet production; 60,000 bottles

Tim Knappstein's family has long connections with Clare Valley, both through his own firm (called Enterprise when it was first established in 1976) and through the Stanley Wine Company. The majority holding in Tim Knappstein Wines is now held by Wolf Blass, but the Knappsteins remain in charge and own the vineyards in Clare and the Adelaide Hills. They make two Cabernets: a straight varietal wine (with small quantities of Merlot and Cabernet Franc) which, as in the 86 (tasted in 1990) can tend to the hot and chewy rather than the elegant; and a Cabernet/Merlot blend (with 85 percent Cabernet, 15 percent Merlot) of which the 87 (tasted in 1990) is smooth with fruit-cake tastes and a ripe, rounded flavour.

LAKE'S FOLLY → **
Broke Road, Pokolbin, Hunter Valley, New South Wales

Total v'yds owned: 14ha (34.5 acres)
Cabernet area: 10ha (25 acres)
Cabernet production; 50,000 bottles

Dr Max Lake was a pioneer in the Hunter when he set up his small vineyard and winery in 1963. Originally he made only Cabernet, to which was added Chardonnay in 1969. The two wines remain the sole production of the winery. The Cabernets continue to have a high reputation, but recent tastings suggest that perhaps they have been overtaken by competition: certainly the 87 (tasted in 1990) had strange, earthy tastes, compounded by off-balance vanilla from the oak, and a generally hot and sweaty feel.

LEEUWIN ESTATE *** → ****
Gnarawary Road, Margaret River, Western Australia

Total v'yds owned: 90ha (222 acres)
Cabernet area: 29ha (71.5 acres)
Cabernet production; 108,000 bottles

The elaborate setting, the restaurant, the concerts, the labels designed by artists such as Sydney Nolan and the high tech of the winery should not be allowed to hide the fact that Leeuwin also makes some very good wines. Since its first vintage in 1979, the winery has taken the headlines with its Cabernets which exhibit all the character that makes Margaret River such an important Cabernet area. A small proportion of Malbec is blended into the Cabernet, giving as in 84 a cassis and tobacco, carefully structured wine with obvious bottle-ageing ability. Just to prove the point, a recent release was a bottle-aged 79 Cabernet, which (tasted in 1990) showed beautiful deep coloured fruit, and big, rich, chewy, tobacco and raisin flavours, and the potential to survive even longer.

LINDEMANS *** → ****
300 Victoria Road, Rydalmere, New South Wales

Total v'yds owned: 1,010ha (2496 acres)

Now a part of the giant Penfolds group, Lindemans also takes under its wing the wineries of Leo Buring and Rouge Homme. It owns vineyards in Coonawarra and Padthaway, the Hunter Valley and in Mildura, Victoria. While its origins are in the Hunter Valley, probably the most important Cabernet vineyards are in the South Australian holdings. From Coonawarra come the single-vineyard Cabernets, which are among the best in Australia: St George Cabernet, the 85 (tasted in 1989) showing classic eucalyptus and mint tastes, with great firmness of the delicious fruit; the Limestone Ridge Cabernet/ Shiraz, the 86 (tasted in 1990) with huge rich colour and fruit, a blockbuster but with considerable elegance. At the very top is Pyrus, a Bordeaux blend from Coonawarra, which has Cabernet Franc, Merlot and Malbec as well as Cabernet Sauvignon.

GEOFF MERRILL

** → ***

Pimpala Road, Reynella, South Australia

Total v'yds owned: 22ha (54 acres)
Cabernet production; 24,000 bottles

Geoff Merrill, formerly chief winemaker at Thomas Hardy, set up this winery on the side before devoting himself more fully to it. He buys fruit to supplement his needs from surrounding McLaren Vale and from Coonawarra and the Barossa. The Geoff Merrill Cabernet is blended with Cabernet Franc: the 85 (tasted in 1987) was big, but with good raspberry fruit and not too much wood. The 82 (also tasted in 1987) showed that, the wines can also age well. Mount Hurtle Cabernet is a 100 percent single varietal wine, the 83 (tasted in 1987) showing typical bitterness and stalkiness, but with plenty of fruit there to sustain the wine in the future.

MILDARA

** →

Wentworth Road, Merbein, Victoria

Total v'yds owned: 255ha (630 acres)

Mildara is the group name for another Australian conglomerate, which takes in Yellowglen sparkling wines, Balgownie, Krondorf and Morton Estate in New Zealand. Under the Mildara label, they make two ranges of Cabernet: the Flower Label series Cabernet/Merlot, the 84, soft and easy drinking, more fruit than wood; and the more serious Coonawarra Cabernet, the 84 peppermint and tannin with good blackcurrant fruit flavours. Under the Krondorf name, there is a Cabernet blended from McLaren Vale and Coonawarra fruit, the 83 (tasted in 1988) showing good maturity and soft flavours, with just a hint of austerity. In the US market, they also sell a McLaren Vale wine under the Roo's Leap label; the 86 (tasted in 1990) herby and spicy with soft, easy-to-drink fruit.

MONTROSE

** →

Henry Lawson Drive, Mudgee, New South Wales

Total v'yds owned: 115ha (284 acres)
Cabernet area: 17ha (42 acres)
Cabernet production: 60,000 bottles

Montrose has passed through a chequered period in the past three years, with a takeover by the Hunter Valley Wyndham Estates group. The winemaker of many years, Carlo Corino departed, and stylistic changes may be made to achieve a smoother, easy drinking style fostered by Wyndham Estates. Past wines include the 86 Cabernet, with its perfumed fruit and intense ruby colour, coupled with ripe, earthy tannins; the Cabernet/Merlot 87 (with 70 percent Cabernet), still quite green in 1990, stalky with green-pepper taste; or the Cabernet Special Reserve 85 (tasted in 1987) weighty and jammy, heavy and rich, almost overripe, if with some cassis fruit.

MOSS WOOD ESTATE

***

Metricup Road, Willyabrup, Margaret River, Western Australia

Total v'yds owned: 8.4ha (21 acres)
Cabernet area: 3.4ha (8 acres)
Cabernet production; 19,200 bottles

One of the pioneers of Margaret River viticulture, Moss Wood was planted in 1969. Its small vineyard supplies all the winery's needs, which means that production quantities are kept deliberately small. The Cabernets are some of the best in the Margaret River. They are made in small, three-ton fermenters with regular plunging of the cap of skins to ensure good colour. The results are certainly classic, 100 percent Cabernet wines, the 85 (tasted in 1988) showing just the right amount of ripe fruit, excellent stalky acidity and hints of wood, promising a fine wine in the early 1990s. There is a Moss Wood Cabernet Reserve which is given extra oak ageing.

ORLANDO   ***→

Barossa Valley Highway, Rowland Flat, via Tanunda, South Australia

Total v'yds owned: 240ha (593 acres)

Orlando, already one of the three top producers in Australia, has grown bigger still with its absorption of Wyndham Estates in New South Wales, while at the same time it has itself been the subject of a major investment by the French Pernod-Ricard company. As producer of Australia's best-selling red wine, Jacob's Creek Shiraz/ Cabernet, a splendidly ripe, easy drink. Above this, admittedly good quality level, it makes a number of excellent value Cabernets which deny the claim that small is beautiful. The RF (for Rowland Flat) Cabernet is a fine, soft, blackcurrant fruit wine. At a higher level again there is the Saint range of varietal wines, with the St Hugo Cabernet, based on Coonawarra fruit, well balanced, the 86 (tasted in 1990) showing attractive mint character, if spoilt slightly by some mushy vegetal tastes. At the top is the new Jacaranda Ridge, another Coonawarra Cabernet, the 82 (tasted in 1988) full of tobacco, spice and pepper, with some green-pepper flavours, and excellent long-lived fruit.

PENFOLDS   ***→

Nuriootpa, Barossa Valley, South Australia

Total v'yds owned: 2,000ha (4942 acres)

The giant of the Australian wine industry, which owns Lindemans, Wynns, Kaiser Stuhl, Tollana, Seaview and Tulloch, also makes Australia's finest red wine, Grange, a Shiraz wine, made with obsessive selection and using techniques normally applied to top growths in Bordeaux. Shiraz is certainly the red-wine grape with which Penfolds is most at home, but it does some pretty good things with Cabernet as well and at all levels of the range. Many of them are blends with Shiraz, such as the popular Koonunga Hill and Dalwood Shiraz/Cabernets, or the St Henri (a Cabernet/Shiraz blend, known sometimes in Australia as "Claret"). Bin numbers are used to distinguish the wines, so Bin 389 is a Cabernet/Shiraz blend which is aged in casks used for Grange in the previous vintage, while Bin 707 is a straight Cabernet, with cigar-box flavours and rich fruit from Coonawarra, the Kalimna Vineyard and Clare Valley, the 85 (tasted in 1987) perfumed, spicy, tannic, intense flavour.

PETALUMA   ***

Lot 6, Spring Gully Road, Piccadilly, South Australia

Total v'yds owned: 93ha (230 acres)
Cabernet area: 37ha (91 acres)

Brian Croser, the inspiration behind much of the high-tech know-how in the Australian wine industry, and now behind the greater attention to good vineyard operation and selection, has his own winery in the Adelaide Hills where he puts into practice what he preaches and teaches; and he does it pretty well, because his wines certainly set standards against which others are judged. He has two labels, the main Petaluma label, which draws from vineyards in Clare, Adelaide Hills, and grapes bought in from Coonawarra; and the second label, Bridgwater Mill, named after the old mill at Piccadilly, now a restaurant. Petaluma Cabernets are possibly Brian Croser's best wines: originally with some Shiraz in the blend, they now tend towards a blend with 30 percent Merlot, the 87 (tasted in 1989) showing rich, complex fruit, deep purple colour, and huge tannins, obviously designed for long-term drinking. The Bridgwater Mill Cabernet is softer, rich and fruity, with fewer tannins, and earlier approachability.

PETERSONS ** →
Mount View Road, Mount View, Hunter Valley, New South Wales

Total v'yds owned: 16ha (39.5 acres)

Cabernet is among a range of wines produced at this family-run winery near Cessnock. Their style is soft, with good rich fruit, but not overly generous, in a pleasing perfumed manner.

PIPERS BROOK ** →
Pipers Brook, Launceston, Tasmania

Total v'yds owned: 12ha (30 acres)
Cabernet area: 2ha (5 acres)
Cabernet production: 4,800 bottles

Small quantities of a firmly austere Cabernet are made in this small vineyard. Close-spaced rows of vines and hand-picked grapes enhance the European feel of the wines from cool-climate Tasmania.

REDGATE ** →
Boodjidup Road, Margaret River, Western Australia

Total v'yds owned: 16ha (39.5 acres)

One of the smaller Margaret River vineyards, but one which keeps up the reputation of this area for Cabernet. The Ullinger family make wines in a traditional way; the style is classic, with a good minty flavour, hints of cassis, and good oak balance all combining in an elegant wine, which has good ageing potential.

REDMAN ** → ***
Naracoorte Road, Coonawarra, South Australia

Total v'yds owned: 32ha (79 acres)

The Redman family started planting this Coonawarra vineyard a year after they sold Rouge Homme winery to Lindemans in 1966. They concentrate here on red wines with Shiraz taking the lion's share of production, but there is also a Cabernet which now has an addition of some Merlot in the blend. The Cabernet style is somewhat fuller than many Coonawarra wines, and with its soft fruit matures relatively quickly.

ROSEMOUNT ESTATE →***
Rosemount Road, Denman, Upper Hunter, New South Wales

Total v'yds owned: 400ha (998 acres)

Although Rosemount has made its reputation with the Upper Hunter Chardonnays, it also produces a number of red wines, including Shiraz from Hunter fruit, and Cabernet from vineyards in Coonawarra, South Australia. Fruit is trucked all the way to the Hunter for processing – not uncommon in Australia. There are two Cabernets: a straight varietal, such as the 85 Cabernet (tasted in 1988) classic pencil-shavings bouquet and plenty of spicy cinammon fruit; and a Show Reserve wine to match their Chardonnay, with its cassis and cigar-box flavours combining splendidly. The popular Diamond Label red is a Cabernet/Shiraz blend.

ROUGE HOMME ***→
Naracoorte Road, Coonawarra, South Australia

Total v'yds owned: 130ha (321 acres)

Rouge Homme was started by the Redman family (Rouge Homme = Redman = Australian joke) back at the turn of the century, but was sold to Lindemans in the 1960s, while the family set up another vineyard called Redman. Lindemans' reputation for Coonawarra reds is maintained at Rouge Homme, which is operated independently, and the Cabernets are some of the best coming out of Coonawarra. The 85 (tasted in 1990) is typical, still very chewy with fine, firm, minty fruit which will last well into the 1990s, very much in a classic style. Occasionally mature, ready-to-drink wines are released in small quantities as Classic Wine Releases.

SALTRAM **→***
Angaston Road, Angaston, Barossa Valley, South Australia

Total v'yds owned: 28ha (69 acres)
Cabernet area: 7ha (17.5 acres)

Most of the fruit for this winery, is bought in from growers from all over South Australia. The winery makes a number of styles of wine starting with the well-made, inexpensive Hazlewood range. The varietal range includes a Cabernet, and there are two Cabernet/Shiraz blends – one based on Barossa fruit, the 84 (tasted in 1990) showing ripe chocolate and coffee flavours, and one, called Metala, based on Langhorne Creek fruit from south of Adelaide. The top range, the Pinnacle Selection, includes a Coonawarra Cabernet.

SEPPELT **→
Chateau Tanunda, Tanunda, Barossa Valley, South Australia

Total v'yds owned: 1,500ha (3,706 acres)

Visitors to the historic Seppeltsfield winery in the Barossa Valley, Australia's most splendid winery, could be forgiven for thinking that Seppelt was primarily a producer of fortified wines. What might have been true in the past has changed now, and just down the road in Tanunda their modern winery is home to a vast range of table wines reflecting Australia's more recent drinking patterns. Among this range a number of Cabernets stand out. There are Shiraz/Cabernet blends, such as Queen Adelaide Claret, an inexpensive, light, rather acid wine. Further up the scale is Moyston Claret, also a Shiraz/

Cabernet blend, the 85 attractively perfumed, and with good meaty flavours. The best 100 percent Cabernets are in the Black Label Range, the 85 well balanced, with some acidity, and big ripe tannins and fruit; and there is Drumbourg Cabernet, big, chewy, very firm when young, almost port-like in its rich concentration.

CHATEAU TAHBILK $***\rightarrow$
Tahbilk, Goulburn, Victoria

Total v'yds owned: 120ha (297 acres)

Historic Chateau Tahbilk, founded in 1860, is one of the great survivors, using premises that on the face of it appear to have changed little since the original winery was built, certainly in the way red wines are made. Open wooden fermenters are still used, and colour is gained by pressing down the cap of skins. The reds are big and tannic when young, and winemaker Alister Purbrick, believes – and I am sure he is right – that the wines can last for 40 or 50 years. The 85 Cabernet (tasted in 1987) showed little but huge tannins, but underneath were signs of excellent fruit, and potentially considerable elegance; when tasted in 1990, it was still very firmly closed up, but it was beginning to show a dusty, old-fashioned richness. The 84 (tasted in 1987) from a lighter vintage, had pleasing aromatic cassis flavours, and a more pronounced elegance. These are wines of great individuality and go against the normal Australian traditions of making wines for relatively early drinking.

TALTARNI $**\rightarrow***$
Moonambel Road, Moonambel, Victoria

Total v'yds owned: 138ha (341 acres)
Cabernet area: 44ha (109 acres)
Cabernet production: 72,000 bottles

This is one arm of a joint Australia/California project, both under the ownership of John Goelet, whose US base is Clos du Val in the Napa Valley. Two French brothers are in charge of winemaking, with Dominique Portet based at Taltarni, the largest of the wineries in the Pyrenees district of Central Victoria. A recent expansion in Tasmania will produce the base wine for a sparkling wine, but the Cabernet all comes from Victoria. As might be expected, the wines are made with a distinctly French emphasis, and the Cabernet is a blend with Merlot and Malbec. They can be well shaped wines, balancing fruit, acidity and tannins, the 85 (tasted in 1987) typically firm, almost austere. The 83 (tasted in 1987) showed intense fruit, very perfumed and elegant, very dry; when tasted in 1990, on the other hand, it seemed to be too dry, almost too old, and I preferred the 84, lighter with pleasing acidity, and fresh, elegant fruit.

TISDALL $\rightarrow**$
Cornelia Creek Road, Echuca, Victoria

Total v'yds owned: 129ha (319 acres)

Two vineyards in northern Victoria supply grapes for the Tisdall family winery. The Rosbercon vineyard near Echuca is the smaller, while Mount Helen vineyard in the Strathbogie Ranges provides grapes for the premium range of single-vineyard wines. The top wine is the Mount Helen Cabernet/Merlot, a pleasing soft, cassis-flavoured wine, which seems to be ready for early drinking.

TOLLANA   **
Sturt Highway, Nuriootpa, Barossa Valley, South Australia

Tollana started life as a brandy producer, Tolley, Scott & Tolley, but now concentrates on table wines, utilizing vineyard holdings in the Eden Valley, which produce the firm's best wines. The Eden Valley Cabernet Bin TL 222 is a pleasing soft wine, the 84 (tasted in 1988) ripe and elegant with excellent tannin and acid balance. There is also a Shiraz/Cabernet blend, from the Eden Valley.

TYRRELL'S   →***
Broke Road, Pokolbin, Hunter Valley, New South Wales

Total v'yds owned: 152ha (376 acres)
Cabernet area: 8.5ha (21 acres)
Cabernet production: 60,000 bottles

Tyrrells is one of the longest-established wineries in the Hunter Valley (they have an old hut outside the present winery just to prove it), and they have managed to preserve a traditional feel in their operations, with open fermenting tanks for reds, and a use of older wooden barrels for maturing as well as new wood. Their red wines are very much in a Hunter Valley mould, and their best are based on Shiraz. But Cabernet is here as well, in the best-selling Long Flat Red where it is blended with Shiraz and Malbec. And there are a handful of Cabernet wines, a Cabernet/Merlot blend (with 60 percent Cabernet), the 84 (tasted in 1988) quite green and stalky in youth, very much in an elegant French style; or the Vat 70 Private Bin Cabernet, the 85 (tasted in 1988) showing deep colour, intense concentrated fruit, and a rich, spicy, tarry style.

VASSE FELIX   →***
Harman's South Road, Cowaramup, Margaret River, Western Australia

Total v'yds owned: 8ha (20 acres)
Cabernet area: 5ha (12 acres)
Cabernet production: 42,000 bottles

Established in 1967, Vasse Felix was the first winery in the Margaret River area, and pioneered the growth of Cabernet in what is now seen as one of the top Cabernet regions in the country. The small vineyard is planted mainly with Cabernet, and Vasse Felix buys in more Cabernet from vineyards further south. The Light Dry Red, a fresh style of wine, made from Cabernet with Pinot Noir and Malbec is designed for early drinking. The straight Cabernets are somewhat more serious: the 86 (tasted in 1988) showing rich fruit extract, a full, concentrated style; the 87 (tasted in 1990) lighter, still young, but with good ripe fruit and attractive wood tastes.

VIRGIN HILLS   ***
Salisbury Road, Lauriston West, Victoria

Total v'yds owned: 16ha (39.5 acres)
Cabernet area: 14ha (34.5 acres)

Only one wine is made at this Macedon winery founded in 1968 – a Cabernet, with a small amount of Shiraz, Merlot and Malbec in the blend. Owner Marcel Gilbert has a well-established vineyard and he is making some excellent wines in a traditional way, with hand picking and low yields. The 83 (tasted in 1987) showed a rich, almost overwhelming fruit character, with bags of cassis and mint flavours;

the lighter 84 was still filled with tannin and fruit. All the wines need long bottle ageing.

SIMON WHITLAM ** →

Wollombi Brook Vineyard, Broke Road, Pokolbin, Hunter Valley, New South Wales

---

Total v'yds owned: 8ha (20 acres)

A partnership between Andrew Simon and Nicholas Whitlam, Simon Whitlam has made a name for itself with its Chardonnays which, like all its wines, are produced at the Arrowfield Winery in the Upper Hunter. But they also make a Cabernet, the first release of which was with the 85 vintage.

WIRRA WIRRA → ***

McMurtrie Road, McLaren Vale, South Australia

Total v'yds owned: 2.4ha (6 acres)

The Trott's modern, high-tech winery, designed on the lines of a miniature Petaluma is behind a magnificent old brick barn which houses the ageing wine. The Church Block vineyard supplies their best known red, a Cabernet/Shiraz/Merlot blend, with 65 percent Cabernet, the 86 (tasted in 1988) peppery and stalky, softened by the 15 percent Merlot, very perfumed. The 87 Church Block (tasted in 1990) showed excellent dry, but cherry fruit and good acid balance. There is also a straight Cabernet, the 85 (tasted in 1988) with intense fruit colour, restrained acidity and, in youth, a bitter finish.

WOLF BLASS ** →

Bilyara Vineyards, 97 Sturt Highway, Nuriootpa, Barossa Valley, South Australia

---

Total v'yds owned: 283ha (699 acres)

Wolf Blass, known for his bow ties and formidable marketing, makes wines using fruit from newly acquired and planted vineyards in Clare Valley, including the former Quelltaler Winery, and from grapes bought from growers in Clare, Eden Valley, Langhorne Creek and McLaren Vale. He makes a range of wine distinguished by the colour of the label. The basic range is a Red Label Shiraz/Cabernet blend, but there are better wines in the Yellow Label Cabernet/Shiraz blend and the Grey Label Cabernet/Shiraz, both with rich, forward tastes, very oaky and smoky. The top range, the President's Selection Black Label, is a Cabernet/Merlot blend, very big and brassy, but with some restraint from the juicy Merlot tastes.

WOODSTOCK **

Douglas Gully Road, McLaren Flat, McLaren Vale, South Australia

---

Total v'yds owned: 24ha (59 acres)
Cabernet area: 6ha (15 acres)

The Collett family started selling wine under their own label in 1982, and now make a wide range of wines, including a port-style and a botrytis wine. Their Cabernet is based on fruit from their own McLaren Vale vineyard, and 30 percent of the final blend sees three to six months in new oak. The style is light, the 86 (tasted in 1990) having good acidity and structure, pleasant fruit and a forward, light aftertaste.

WYNDHAM ESTATE   **→
Government Road, Dalwood, via Branxton, Hunter Valley, New South Wales

Total v'yds owned: 104ha (257 acres)

Wyndham is the largest producer in the Hunter Valley, owning Hollydene, Saxonvale, Richmond Grove and Hunter Estate, as well as the Mudgee estates of Montrose, Craigmoor and Amberton. In turn, Wyndham is part of the South Australian Orlando group, although Wyndham's previous owner Brian McGuigan remains firmly in charge. The style of wines is consistent and designed for early drinking once released, a policy which must largely account for the rapid increase in the size of the company. Wines such as the Bin 444 Cabernet are soft, ripe, minty, the 80 (tasted in 1988) showing excellent maturity, even though there was some acidity. The Bin 888 Cabernet/Merlot blend is better, ripe and fruity, a good jammy fruit from the Merlot, with a green-pepper flavour from the Cabernet.

WYNNS   ***
Memorial Drive, Coonawarra, South Australia

Total v'yds owned: 535ha (1321 acres)

Wynns, now part of Penfolds, still operates independently as the largest producer in Coonawarra, and the largest owner of land on the terra rosa soil. They make a number of reds in their Coonawarra winery, shown on the label for all their wines. The straight Cabernet is a splendid wine; the 82 (tasted in 1988) maturing well into a rich, tarry, peppery offering, with strong green-pepper and eucalyptus tastes; the 85 (tasted in 1990) full, soft and bursting with fruit. They also make a Wynns Coonawarra Cabernet/Shiraz. Under the John Riddoch Limited Release label they make what some consider their best Cabernet, with its cassis fruit and excellent wood balance.

YALUMBA   **→
Eden Valley Road, Angaston, Barossa Valley, South Australia

Total v'yds owned: 400ha (988 acres)

There are a number of labels under the general ownership of S Smith & Son whose main winery is called Yalumba: there are estate wines such as Pewsey Vale, Heggies and Hill Smith Estate, there is a Yalumba Signature Series wines (classic releases of wines which have been specially held back) and there are the less expensive cask wines. The estate wines are the best: the Pewsey Vale Cabernet, the Hill-Smith Estate Cabernet, the 85 (tasted in 1989) firm and rich, if a little bitter at the end. The Yalumba Signature Cabernets can include releases from bought-in Coonawarra fruit as well as from estate wines.

YARRA BURN   **
Settlement Road, Yarra Junction, Yarra Valley, Victoria

Total v'yds owned: 10ha (25 acres)
Cabernet area: 3ha (7.5 acres)

The Fyffes run this small winery and restaurant at the beautiful eastern end of Yarra Valley where the mountains suddenly rise up as a backdrop. They buy in grapes to supplement their own crop including fruit for the light style Lilydale Cabernet: the 86 (tasted in 1990) tending towards a vegetal taste, light and fruity in style, and herbaceously mature.

YARRA YERING

**

Briarty Road, Gruyere, Yarra Valley, Victoria

Total v'yds owned: 16ha (39.5 acres)
Cabernet area: 6ha (15 acres)

Research scientist Dr Bailey Carrodus was one of the pioneers of the revival of Yarra Valley, founding his winery and vineyard in 1969 as a part-time venture. He now has two vineyards in the valley from which come two reds, numbered precisely as Dry Red Number 1 and Dry Red Number 2. The Number 1 blend is of Cabernet with Malbec and Merlot, light in style, with pleasant cigar-box, cedar tastes.

New Zealand

New Zealand's international reputation has depended more on white wines than reds. It was probably inevitable that the comparatively cool climate of New Zealand (compared, that is, with much of Australia) should immediately lend itself to white wines. But parts of the New Zealand vineyard, certainly in North Island, are really no cooler than parts of South Australia, Victoria and Tasmania, all of which are producing excellent red wines, especially those based on Cabernet Sauvignon.

The reason for New Zealand's late development of its reds is more likely to lie in the fact that while the climate is not cooler than Australia, it is wetter. Summer and autumn rains are common, especially in the humid conditions of Auckland and the Gisborne vineyards in North Island: conditions which encourage vigorous growth and cause plants to shoot out in all directions with leaves covering ripening fruit. Until recently the result was that the grapes did not ripen sufficiently giving the wines an often stalky, herbaceous quality which some found unattractive and which certainly kept the wines out of the top league. Coupled with the fact that most plantings of Cabernet are only now beginning to reach maturity (and hence give their best fruit) it is hardly surprising that the New Zealand Cabernets never received the enthusiastic reviews of the whites.

Things are changing: one of the most significant has been in viticultural practice. The development of canopy management pioneered in New Zealand to cope specifically with the problem of over-vigorous growth has has been of immense importance in improving the quality of the red wines. Canopy management covers many things. It means thinning out the leaves during ripening to allow the grapes to get the full benefit of the sun. But it also means developing different ways of training and pruning the vines so that their vigour is controlled, and they are able to give reliable quantities of good quality fruit.

Vintages of New Zealand Cabernet from the mid-1980s onwards have benefited from canopy management; and, as the vines have matured, from the fruit of older plants. Another reason for the improvement is attributable to better clonal selection. Imports, mainly of California clones, have resulted in virus-free vines with better quality, and more regular, crops. This explains why the quality of current New Zealand Cabernets is so much improved.

The appearance of Merlot and Cabernet Franc and the resultant

Bordeaux blends are also enhancing the quality of many of these wines. New Zealand's climate lends itself to the austerer side of Cabernet, and there are always going to be vegetal hints in 100 percent Cabernet wines: the lusher taste, especially of Merlot, is able to flesh the wines out, and give them a roundness and softness and greater complexity which is most attractive.

Not that even 100 percent Cabernets need anything like the ageing of French Bordeaux wines. They tend to mature at around three to four years, and reach their peak around five. How long they hold that level is still difficult to say – although some examples of ten-year old wines are showing very well.

THE CABERNET ARRIVES

According to Michael Cooper in *The Wines and Vineyards of New Zealand*, the first vines were probably brought in by James Busby in 1833 and by French missionaries in 1838. The Cabernet was sufficiently well established for Romeo Bragato, the first government viticulturalist, to describe it in 1906 as "one of the best varieties grown here." From that point, though, plantings of Cabernet declined. It was not suitable for making the sweet, fortified wines or the cheap table wines that were the staple products of the New Zealand wine industry right up to the 1960s.

It was not until the revival in interest in making premium table wines that Cabernet made a return. Michael Cooper comments that "in 1975 nearly 80 percent of all Cabernet Sauvignon vines in New Zealand were less than five years old." Plantings have rapidly increased since then. There were 290 hectares (717 acres) in 1980, which had increased – to 396 hectares (979 acres) by 1990. That puts it fourth in New Zealand in terms of area after Müller Thurgau, Chardonnay and Sauvignon Blanc, and first in red varieties.

CABERNET VINEYARDS

Cabernet is planted in most of the major and some of the smaller vineyard areas of New Zealand. It is found as far south as Canterbury and as far north as West Auckland. But certain areas are inevitably proving better than others for the vine. Auckland can suffer from too much humidity and is considered as less satisfactory than other areas for growing. However, red varieties do better than white, and Cabernet is found in a number of vineyards in the area.

Of the other main North Island regions, Gisborne/Poverty Bay is the bulk wineproducing area of the country, and its high yields tend not to suit the production of top quality Cabernet. Its humidity and rainfall also act against it. But just further south, in the Hawke's Bay area, we find what is now seen as the best Cabernet area in the country, one which is certainly producing the best wines, and which is now attracting producers. The only other wineproducing area of consequence in North Island – Martinborough – has some Cabernet, but its reputation is being developed on the quality of its Chardonnays and Pinot Noirs.

On the South Island there are considerable plantings of Cabernet in Marlborough, which is the second most widely planted Cabernet region in the country. Here the vine is much less successful than in Hawke's Bay. The climate may be drier than North Island, but it is also cooler – too cool for reliable ripening – and leads to wines which exhibit too much cool-climate, herbaceous quality. The plantings in Canterbury, further south than Marlborough, are even less successful, and it is likely they will be replaced.

MAKING CABERNET

Cabernet production has changed much less rapidly than white-wine production. There are fewer technological breakthroughs for producers of red wines, and the pattern in New Zealand seems to have been well- established by the mid-1980s.

Colour is extracted from the skins of the grapes by macerating the grape must before fermentation. There are experiments with longer skin contact to increase colour, but this also increases tannin levels (not a desirable thing in an age when consumers want wine to drink now) so a balance has to be struck.

A variety of fermentation methods are used for Cabernet: open cement-lined tanks, stainless steel tanks or, increasingly for the better quality wines, French or American oak barrels. Fermentation temperatures of around 20°-25° C (68°-77° F) are normal.

After the first alcoholic fermentation, most New Zealand Cabernets go through the second, malolactic fermentation in order to reduce the acid levels which are a natural by-product of New Zealand's temperate climate.

The only real change in Cabernet production has been the greater use of oak barrels for maturing the wine. These will often be second-year barrels (after a first year with Chardonnay has reduced the oak tastes to a better level for red wines) but new barrels are also used. There is a mix of French and American oak, with French predominating. Ageing can be over a period of anything from nine months to two years depending on the wine producer's preferred style.

PRODUCERS

ATA RANGI   ** → ***

PO Box 43, Martinborough, North Island

Total v'yds owned: 4ha (10 acres)

While Clive Paton's Ata Rangi ("new beginnings") winery is concentrating on the Martinborough speciality of Pinot Noir, its other red is the unusual blend of Cabernet and Merlot with Shiraz. Called Celebre, it has 70 percent Cabernet, and 15 percent each of the other two varieties. The 88 (tasted in 1989) shows more Rhône than Bordeaux character, earthy, meaty and ripe. The winery is still small – a total of 3,000 cases – and the wines have an attractive hand-made quality feel to them.

BABICH   ***

Babich Road, Henderson, Auckland, North Island

Total v'yds owned: 42ha (104 acres)
Cabernet area: 13ha (32 acres)

Babich is one of a handful of wineries which have vineyards in the Auckland area. Some of the Cabernet for its wines comes from these vineyards, but the best comes from the Irongate vineyard in Hawke's Bay, of which the winery owns half. Their blended Irongate red, with Cabernet Sauvignon plus Cabernet Franc and Merlot is a deliciously fruity wine, the 87 (tasted in 1989) quite soft with excellent ripeness and cedary, fruity flavours. The three varieties in this blend are picked and fermented together. The straight Cabernet is somewhat more vegetal, the 87 (tasted in 1989) having good perfumed fruit, and very direct Cabernet taste.

BROOKFIELD   **→

RD3 Meanee, Napier, Hawke's Bay, North Island

Total v'yds owned: 3ha (7.5 acres)
Cabernet area: None

Although Peter Robertson owns no Cabernet vineyards, he buys from local growers to make what is certainly the best of the Brookfield wines, a blend of 70 percent Cabernet Sauvignon with 20 percent Merlot and 10 percent Cabernet Franc. The 88 (tasted in 1989) showed excellent intense character, a good ripe centre and smoky, tobacco flavours. The 87 (also tasted in 1989) was softer, more perfumed, less for ageing than for drinking. A straight Cabernet 89, tasted from cask, showed enormous colour, derived from three weeks skin contact, and super chewy perfumed fruit.

COOPERS CREEK   →**

PO Box 140, Kumeu, North Island

Total v'yds owned: 11ha (27 acres)
Cabernet area: 3ha (7.5 acres)
Cabernet production: 18,000 bottles

Coopers Creek, named after a local stream that runs by the winery, has vineyard land in Huapai and in Hawke's Bay. The grapes for the top red in their range, the Cabernet Sauvignon and Merlot blend (with 70 percent Cabernet), come from Huapai. The 86 vintage of this wine had the classic New Zealand green-pepper taste, and is in the dry, full-bodied style of wines produced by this winery.

CORBANS/COOKS   *→**

PO Box 21-183, Henderson, Auckland

Total v'yds owned: 323ha (798 acres)

Second largest NZ wine producer, Corbans took over Cooks and the the NZ operations of the Australian McWilliams company in the 1980s. Vineyards in Te Kauwhata, south of Auckland, in Hawke's Bay and in Marlborough provide 25 percent of their needs. Cabernet Sauvignon comes from Hawke's Bay and Marlborough. There are two major brands from the company: the Cooks range and the Corbans range of which the Stoneleigh Marlborough wines are the best. Cooks produce two Cabernets: Longridge of Hawke's Bay is a new label, generally blended with Merlot, the 87 (tasted in 1989) a straightforward, pleasantly fruity wine without much complexity. The other is the more serious Cooks Winemakers Reserve, with good depth of fruit, if sometimes an herbaceous edge to it. Corbans also have two Cabernets: one from the Stoneleigh vineyard in Marlborough, the 87 (tasted in 1989) soft, a little stalky, with cassis flavours; and the Private Bin Merlot/Cabernet, ripe fruit, mulberry flavour, but the 87 spoilt by some astringency and too much spicy wood.

DELEGAT'S WINE ESTATE   **

Hepburn Road, Henderson, Auckland, North Island

Total v'yds owned: 40ha (99 acres)

Most of Delegat's vineyards, which are either owned or managed, are in Hawke's Bay, which is where the grapes for their Cabernet come from. The winery, still run by the Delegat family, makes mainly white wines, with only 12 percent of production in reds. Their top

Proprietor's Reserve Cabernet is a blended wine, the 87 with 88 percent Cabernet Sauvignon, plus Cabernet Franc and Merlot, all Hawke's Bay fruit. It received a long skin contact, and fast, high temperature fermentation, then 18 months in cask, to give wine that matures quite fast, with green-pepper tastes, a warm style and some acidity, but also pleasing elegance.

ESK VALLEY → ***
Main Road, Bayview, Napier, Hawke's Bay, North Island

Total v'yds owned: 3ha (7.5 acres)

Known as the Glenvale winery until its purchase by the Villa Maria group three years ago, Esk Valley makes some excellent red wines, using traditional open fermenters in a winery that is now undergoing extensive renovation. The bulk of grapes is purchased from local growers, all in the Hawke's Bay area. They make a Cabernet (60 percent) and Merlot (40 percent) blend, the 87 (tasted in 1989) stalky, firm, dry, with excellent colour and a firm, ripe flavour; a straight Cabernet, the 87 (tasted in 1989) very rich and avoiding any hint of herbaceousness, with again, good colour from long skin contact; and a Reserve Cabernet/Merlot blend, with only 15 percent Merlot, fermented on the skins, aged in 100 percent new wood *barriques* for 19 months, producing in 87 a big, deep, rich wine, smoky, meaty and intense, almost sweet in its concentration.

ESKDALE WINEGROWERS → **
Main Road, Eskdale, Napier, Hawke's Bay, North Island

Total v'yds owned: 4ha (10 acres)

Canadian-born Kim Salonius produces wines only from his small home vineyard, in the remote Esk valley, away from the main centres of Hawke's Bay. In his hand-built winery, he makes a big, chewy cassis-tasting Cabernet Sauvignon, which has wood maturation and is obviously built to last.

GOLDWATER → **
Putiki Bay, Waiheke Island, Auckland, North Island

One of the larger islands in Auckland Harbour is now home to a small group of wineries producing Cabernet Sauvignon, in the good ripening conditions and drier, brisker air away from the mainland. Goldwater is one of these estates, a small estate, established with the help of viticulturalist Richard Smart, who suggested training the vines in a U-shape rather than the usual method. The top red, a blend of Cabernet Sauvignon, Cabernet Franc and Merlot, is fermented in stainless steel and then matured in French oak for up to two years. The results, in a wine like 87 (tasted in 1989) are very firm having an astringency when young and needing time to mature.

KUMEU RIVER → ***
2 Highway 16, Kumeu, Auckland, North Island

Total v'yds owned: 20ha (49 acres)
Cabernet area: 4ha (10 acres)

One of the few producers to use exclusively Auckland fruit, Kumeu River, owned by the Brajkovich family, has made a speciality of a Merlot/Cabernet Sauvignon blend, in which Merlot dominates with 70 percent. However, it is possible this may change with the increased plantings of Cabernet Sauvignon, and the 85 wine (80 percent Cabernet, 20 percent Merlot after the Merlot was damaged by hail) gives an indication of how things might go. This was fermented at high temperatures and has excellent colour extract, 12 months ageing in French wood, and a light egg white fining before bottling, to give an elegant rather than overwhelming wine, which needs time in bottle to enable the fruit to come through.

LIMEBURNERS BAY   **→

112 Hobsonville Road, Hobsonville, Auckland, North Island

Total v'yds owned: 2ha (5 acres)
Cabernet area: 1.7ha (4.2 acres)

Limeburners Bay is just to the east of Kumeu and Huapai, on Waitemata Harbour north of Auckland. The produce of the small home vineyard, entirely planted with red-wine varieties, is supplemented for white wines with Gisborne fruit. The top red, an 85 percent Cabernet Sauvignon blend with Merlot and Cabernet Franc, is a wine that needs time, as do so many of the Auckland Bordeaux blend wines: the 87 (tasted in 1989) was still dominated by wood, but there were obvious signs in the toasty, coffee-bean tastes, that fruit was there to come through. Certainly, the original 84 is now a balanced, mature, very elegant and fragrant wine.

MATUA VALLEY   →***

PO Box 100, Kumeu, Auckland, North Island

Total v'yds owned: 64ha (158 acres)

Fruit from both Auckland vineyards and from Hawke's Bay come to the Spence's winery near Huapai north of Auckland. For their Cabernets, they use fruit from the Dartmoor-Smith Estate in Hawke's Bay, which is sometimes blended with other Hawke's Bay fruit to give what winemaker Ross Spence believes is extra bouquet. The 85 was their best vintage to that date, giving, as do all the Matua Valley wines, the most direct fruit tastes, with good flavour and a pleasing fresh taste. The 87 (tasted in 1990) had good dusty fruit, with slight herbaceousness, but was beginning to open out from its earlier chewy character. Fifteen percent Cabernet is used in the Merlot also produced from the Dartmoor-Smith estate.

MONTANA   *→**

Glen Innes, Auckland, North Island

Total v'yds owned: 808ha (1987 acres)

Cabernet Sauvignon – indeed, red wines in general – form a comparatively small part of the output of New Zealand's largest and most successful wine company. This partly reflects their major interests in Marlborough in South Island, which Montana pioneered and whose cool climate is suited more to white grapes such as Sauvignon Blanc and Chardonnay than to red varieties. However, the Montana Marlborough Cabernet Sauvignon is a widely available wine, showing traditional New Zealand Cabernet herbaceous, asparagus character, somewhat vegetal. Since Montana's purchase of Penfolds' New Zealand operation, they now have access to Hawke's Bay and Gisborne fruit. Other reds in the range include Fairhall, a blend of Pinotage, Pinot Noir and Cabernet and Mount Richmond "Claret", a blend of Pinotage and Cabernet.

MORTON ESTATE ** →
RD2 Katikati, Bay of Plenty, North Island

Total v'yds owned: 105ha (259 acres)
Cabernet area: 8ha (20 acres)

White wines have made Morton Estate's reputation. But the last couple of vintages have seen a definite revitalization of the Cabernets, using Hawke's Bay fruit. New vineyard plantings in Hawke's Bay are also likely to add to this interest. The 88 Cabernet Sauvignon/Merlot blend, tasted from cask, was showing quite a bit of wood, but was developing good ripe fruit tastes and a rewarding fragrance.

NGATARAWA ***
Ngatarawa Road, Bridge Pa, Hastings, Hawke's Bay, North Island

---

Total v'yds owned: 12ha (30 acres)

Alwyn Corban's winery and vineyard occupies a century-old stable block in the heart of the Hastings dry belt, an area noted for its low rainfall. Only at the back of this quiet country structure do you find the modern equipment necessary for making the range of wines under the Ngatarawa label. His flagship red is named after his partners and owners of the vineyard, the Glazebrook Cabernet/ Merlot blend, the 89, tasted in cask, full of intense colour and perfumed fruit, and a splendid sweet tobacco flavour. Corban also makes an unoaked red, called Stables Red, which is designed for easy, early drinking and works perfectly at that. The fruit needed for these two wines comes partly from the surrounding vineyard and partly from grapes bought in from other Hawke's Bay growers.

NOBILO VINTNERS *** →
Station Road, Huapai, West Auckland, North Island

Total v'yds owned: 20ha (49 acres)
Cabernet area: 7ha (17 acres)
Cabernet production: 120,000 bottles

Nobilo's origins in the Huapai region of Auckland has meant that they have a traditional reliance on red wines, and these still form a major part of this surprisingly large family company's output. Vineyards in Hawke's Bay, Gisborne and Marlborough supply their needs for whites, and Marlborough and Hawke's Bay also supply Cabernet Sauvignon. Undoubtedly their most interesting red is Concept, a blend of Pinotage (in which Nobilo has a rare interest for New Zealand) and Cabernet. Numbered sequentially, Concept One made with the 84 vintage, when tasted in 1989 was a rich mature wine, with Pinotage acidity smelling of truffles and tasting of rich mushrooms. The straight 86 Cabernet Reserve, made from Huapai fruit, has distinct smoky, tobacco fruit, and in 89 was drily chewy, obviously needing time.

C J PASK **
Korokipo Road, Hastings, Hawke's Bay, North Island

Total v'yds owned: 32ha (79 acres)

Chris Pask both supplies grapes to other wineries and makes wine on his own account at his Hawke's Bay winery. His Cabernet Sauvignon is a good straightforward wine, the 87 with flavoursome cassis fruit and some oak balance, even if without great subtlety. He also makes a more interesting Cabernet/Merlot blend which has high alcohol and plenty of jammy fruit, and Roy's Hill, which includes Cabernet Sauvignon along with Cabernet Franc and Merlot.

ST GEORGE   ** →
St George's Road South, Hastings, Hawke's Bay, North Island

Total v'yds owned: 6ha (15 acres)

You really need to come to St George's to drink the wines, because producers Michael Bennett and Martin Elliot sell most of it in their winery restaurant. However, it is possible to find the Cabernet/ Merlot blend beyond Hawke's Bay, and the 87, stalky, minty, with American oak flavours and with a dense chewy texture and good ripe perfumed flavours, is a good example of their style.

ST NESBIT   *** →
Hingaia Road, Papakura, Auckland, North Island

Total v'yds owned: 7ha (17 acres)
Cabernet production: 12,000 bottles

Dr Tony Molloy, a lawyer, has established a rarity among New Zealand wine estates, a single-wine winery. His sole production is aimed at a Cabernet Sauvignon/Cabernet Franc/Merlot blend, which is called simply St Nesbit. If his aim is a very French style of wine, he has succeeded, certainly with recent vintages (the first was in 1984). To compound the deliberate Bordeaux imagery, Petit Verdot has been planted and will be added as it comes on stream. Output is planned to peak at 48,000 bottles in the mid-1990s, so this is going to remain the collector's item it already is.

SELAKS WINES   **
Highway 16, Kumeu, Auckland, North Island

Total v'yds owned: 62ha (153 acres)
Cabernet area: 8ha (20 acres)

While white wines take 70 percent of production at this North Auckland winery, a number of reds are made, using fruit from Gisborne and Marlborough. The Cabernet Sauvignon comes in two styles, a standard wine and a reserve, called Founders. The 87 of the latter (tasted in 1989) showed heavy porty qualities, very jammy, and a sweet ripe finish, which leaves a curiously unbalanced wine. Other vintages have been better, and the standard wine has a clearer, more direct taste.

STONYRIDGE   → ****
Onetangi Road, Ostend, Waiheke Island, Auckland, North Island

Total v'yds owned: 2ha (5 acres)
Cabernet area: 1.5ha (4 acres)

The second vineyard to be established on Waiheke Island in Auckland Harbour is also producing one of New Zealand's best Cabernet Sauvignon blends. From Stephen and Jane White's tiny vineyard, comes Stonyridge Larose, made from vines treated in a very Bordeaux fashion, and matured in French oak. The components of the blend – Cabernet Sauvignon and Franc as well as Merlot and Malbec – are vinified separately and are blended to make two wines, the flagship Larose and the more immediately accessible Airfield. The 87 Larose (tasted in 1989) was certainly a star wine, dense and purple in colour, with meaty, tangy rich fruit, balancing wood, and tannins, obviously set for a long haul.

TE MATA   ***
PO Box 355, Havelock North, Hawke's Bay, North Island

Total v'yds owned: 25ha (62 acres)
Cabernet area: 13ha (32 acres)
Cabernet production: 108,000 bottles

One of New Zealand's most famous Cabernets comes from this winery, the home of John Buck, perched spectacularly on a hill overlooking Hawke's Bay vineyards. The home vineyard, Coleraine, also lends its name to the main Cabernet/Merlot blend. Early vintages of this wine, such as 82 and 83, established a fine reputation, but more recent wines, such as 87 and 88, have shown a leaner, more herbaceous quality that is less pleasing. The other Cabernet comes from the Awatea vineyard, and the 87 of this wine (tasted in 1989) showed fuller fruit, even though it had some astringency. Wood dominates, and they need ageing time.

VAVASOUR   **→
Awatere Valley, Marlborough, South Island

It is very early days for this winery and vineyard which has pioneered planting in the Awatere Valley, east of the main vineyard area of Marlborough. The aim of owner Peter Vavasour and viticulturalist Richard Bowling is to show that the region's reds can rival those of North Island – something still waiting to be proved. Both Cabernets and Merlot have been planted for a Bordeaux blend.

VIDAL   ****
913 St Aubyns Street East, Hastings, Hawke's Bay, North Island

Total v'yds owned: None

Part of the Villa Maria group since 1976, Vidal shares its parent winery's reputation for top New Zealand reds. Indeed, as a range they are even more impressive than the Villa Maria wines, with the Private Bin label exhibiting excellent fruit character and a very approachable style for earlier drinking than the Reserve wines. There is also a Cabernet/Merlot blend in the Private Bin range, a wine which in its youth tends to show weight rather than finesse. Of the two Reserve wines, the straight Cabernet is the more elegant wine, the 87 peppery and spicy, but with excellent purple fruit, and a lovely wood and acid balance; the Cabernet/Merlot has warm, country tastes, with piles of wood sustained by the rich fruit. Both wines need a good period of ageing. All four wines are 100 percent Hawke's Bay fruit and show very well the quality of this area.

VILLA MARIA   **→****
5 Kirkbridge Road, Mangere, Auckland, North Island

Total v'yds owned: None

Under the ownership of George Fistonich, another of the many New Zealand wine producers of Dalmatian descent, Villa Maria was built up to be the third largest New Zealand winery, taking over Vidal 1976 and Esk Valley in 1987. After a series of financial upsets, caused by a price cutting war in 1985-86, production at Villa Maria has been switched from bulk lines to premium wines, with spectacular results. The Cabernet Sauvignon range follows the pattern for other varieties: a Private Bin label and a top quality, pricier Reserve wine. In the Reserve range, two wines are produced: a Cabernet/Merlot blend, using Hawke's Bay fruit and 20 percent Merlot, the 87 minty, gamey, with piles of ripe cassis fruit, when tasted in 1989 still showing youth, but obviously one of New Zealand's best reds from that vintage. The 100 percent Cabernet Reserve has the same fruit quality, but the 87 tended to be a little dominated by oak. Private Bin wines, as expected, are less impressive: the 87 rather too vegetal, too herbaceous for real pleasure.

Chile

There is one main reason why Chilean Cabernet Sauvignon should be among the world's best: the vines are planted on ungrafted roots, and are derived from cuttings made in Bordeaux in the last century. While that may not be impressive to the consumer, the wine industry gets terribly excited when they come across a place which can make wine from European *vitis vinifera* vines that are unaffected by the phylloxera beetle, and which can exist, without risk, on their natural roots, rather than on grafted American *vitis labrusca* roots. While few alive today have tasted pre-phylloxera wines made in Europe in the nineteenth century, there is a general belief that ungrafted vines can produce wines with greater depth of flavour, greater concentration and greater ageing ability.

If the example of Chile is anything to go by, little of the above is true. Because while Chile makes some very attractive Cabernets, none can claim world class yet. Ungrafted vines are no substitute for top-quality fruit selection, low yields and a local market appreciative of the more expensive products which would result from aiming for the top. Chile has long been isolated from the mainstream of the wine world by geography and politics, and only in the past decade have producers opened their eyes to what is going on beyond the Andes and the horizon of the Pacific Ocean. There has been new influence from both the Old World and the New. From the Old World have come the innovative ideas of Spaniard Miguel Torres who introduced Chile to the idea of stainless steel, new wood for maturing wine and cool temperature fermentation. From both California and France has come investment in new bodegas and new equipment as well as replanted vineyards. Together these are setting new directions for Chilean wines, but it is early days, and much has to happen.

The style of Chilean Cabernet which seems to be most common is of good fruit tastes, very direct flavours, with sometimes hints of wood and ripe fruit. But the general impression is of softness, lack of firm tannins or real concentration. The wines can more often be described as easy-to-drink rather than top-quality.

THE CABERNET ARRIVES

The 1850s and 1860s were a time of great change in the already long-established Chilean vineyards. The traditional grape was the black Pais, making rough red wine (it is still the most widely planted grape in Chile). But new men, rich with the wealth of the silver mines, came into the industry and wanted to make wines in a French manner. They went to France and brought back cuttings of the noble varieties, including Cabernet Sauvignon. Luckily for them, this was just a few years before the arrival of phylloxera devastated the European vineyards. Why the same predator never reached Chile is a mystery – the geographical isolation, the sands of the northern deserts, the high Andes are all cited as reasons, but neither the Atlantic nor the Indian Oceans proved a barrier to the beetle's move from America to Europe and then to Australia. Whatever the reason, Chile's Cabernet remains ungrafted; and it has been recognized as the major noble red variety since its arrival 130 years ago.

CABERNET VINEYARDS

The Chilean vineyards stretch from north of the capital, Santiago, almost to the borders with the southern region of Patagonia, a distance of nearly 1,000 km (620 miles). Within this vast reach of land, it is the central area, just south of Santiago, which provides the best home for Cabernet Sauvignon. The main vineyards are in an irrigated area lying in valleys between the Andes to the east and the coastal mountain range to the west. Irrigation in a largely rainless area comes from the waters and snows of the Andes. The finest Cabernet vineyards are in the Maipo Valley and in Lontue and Molina south of the town of Curico. Further south, some plantings of Cabernet have taken place in the Maule River valley. The climate here is Mediterranean, with long, dry summers and mild winters.

MAKING CABERNET

Traditional winemaking techniques in Chile have relied on keeping wines for a long period in old wooden casks, and this is still the practice in many smaller wineries and cooperatives. However, the last decade has seen the arrival in Chile of more modern techniques, the use of stainless steel being the most important. For Cabernet wines, there is a gradual growth in the use of small wooden barrels, either of French or American wood, for maturation, in place of the large casks made from the native raule, a type of beech tree, which is a neutral wood. The amount of time spent in cask is decreasing.

Blending of Cabernets is also less uncommon than it was, with Malbec the preferred grape. However, most Cabernets are still virtually 100 percent single-variety wines.

There is now greater emphasis on making more of Chile's great asset – the direct, powerful fruit tastes of its wines. Whether these come from the ungrafted vines, the splendid luminosity of the clear skies that ripen the fruit, or the almost complete lack of any serious vine diseases due to the dry climate, is a matter for debate.

PRODUCERS

CONCHA Y TORO   → ✻✻✻
Fernando Lazcano 1220, San Miguel, Santiago

Total v'yds owned: 1,120ha (2768 acres)

One of the oldest bodegas in Chile, Concha y Toro was founded on money from silver mining. The firm owns extensive vineyards in Maipo, Rancagua, San Fernando and Curico, with new plantings further south for cooler climate wines. Stainless steel fermentation equipment was installed for the 82 vintage, and there has been a gradual movement away from large American oak casks to smaller French oak, certainly for the better wines. Concha y Toro makes a number of Cabernets: a regular bottling, the 85 (tasted in 1990) with intense cassis fruit if spoilt by the smell of dirty barrels, the 84 (tasted in 1988) elegant and intense; the Casillero del Diablo, the 84 (tasted in 1990) smooth, soft, peppery and mellow; the Marques de Casa Concha, which seems designed for early drinking, the 86 (tasted in 1989) showing soft, minty fruit; and top of the range Don Melchor, the 87 (tasted in 1990) spicy, smooth, elegant, but not with the intense fruit of some of the other wines.

COUSINO MACUL   ** → ***
Av Tobalaba Quilin, Santiago

Total v'yds owned: 267ha (660 acres)

The vineyard surrounding the Cousino Macul bodega is almost certainly the oldest in the New World; it was established in 1554. The present firm was established in 1856 and was another of the bodegas to be founded on the strength of a silver fortune. It is still a family winery, only using grapes from its own estates in the Maipo area. As with other Chilean bodegas, small oak barrels are now replacing the traditional large American oak casks. Of the two Cabernet styles they make, the Don Luis, named after the son of the founder, is the more forward: the 84 (tasted in 1988) showing excellent cassis flavours and a warm, ripe taste. The Antiguas Reservas is bigger, the 81 (tasted in 1988) soft and smooth, with charming dusty elegance and some acidity. This wine ages well over about 10-12 years.

ERRAZURIZ PANQUEHUE   ** → ***
PO Box 2346, Santiago

Total v'yds owned: 168ha (415 acres)

This firm, with its – to non-Basque speakers – almost unpronounce-able name, was first established in the unlikely surroundings of the barren Aconcagua Valley, in the desert north of Santiago. While this area is better at producing grapes for rough table wine, the bodega still has 18ha (44 acres) of Cabernet planted there, although most is now further south in the lusher (and cooler) Mataquito Valley. The family-owned firm, produces two Cabernets: the regular bottling is matured in American oak for two years, a very easy-to-drink wine with direct fruit character. The Don Maximiano estate wine, named after the company's founder, is more serious: the 86 (tasted in 1989) has piles of ripe, elegant, intense fruit, with minty and smoky wood tastes, as a result of being aged for two years in French oak.

LOS VASCOS   ** →
Isidora Goyenechea 3156, Santiago

Total v'yds owned: 200ha (494 acres)

The Los Vascos estate, in the Colchagua region 150 km (93 miles) south of Santiago, was in the same family from 1750 to 1988, when 50 percent of the firm was purchased by Domaines Rothschild, of Château Lafite-Rothschild in Bordeaux. Now, it is Rothschild knowledge which is at work in the vineyards and in the new winery. However, wines available when tasting in 1989 and 1990 were from before this era: the 87 Cabernet (tasted in 1990) lightly purple in colour, with a fairly strong load of acidity and plenty of tannin, a wine that needs some French polish!

LINDEROS ★★
Vinedos Ortiz, Alamadea 1370, Off 502, Santiago

Total v'yds owned: 81ha (200 acres)
Cabernet area: 37ha (91 acres)

The Linderos estate dates back to 1865, and until the 1960s most of the 500ha (1236 acres) estate was devoted to wine grapes. Now only 81ha remain, from which the bodega produces a small range of wines, of which Cabernet is the largest. The 85 Cabernet (tasted in 1990) shows good purple, fresh colour, soft, ripe flavours, with some tannins, and a youthful forward, ripe taste.

MONTES ★★
Americo Vespuci 1001, Quillicura, Santiago

Total v'yds owned: 85ha (210 acres)
Cabernet area: 50ha (124 acres)

A new venture consisting of a partnership between four leading figures in the Chilean wine trade, and aimed at the export market. They make two Cabernets, a youthful fresh style under the Montes label, and a fuller, riper style, with greater ageing potential, under the name Villa Montes. Both are clean and well-made.

SANTA RITA ★★★
Gertrudis Echenique 49, Santiago

Total v'yds owned: 225ha (556 acres)
Cabernet area: 152ha (376 acres)

One of the largest of the quality bodegas, Santa Rita uses a mix of grapes from its own land and from long-term contracted growers. Fermentation takes place in cement tanks or stainless steel, with ageing in a mix of American and French small oak barrels. The winery has a high reputation, spoilt in 1990 by the discovery of sorbitol in some of its wines (added to aid smoothness in a wine – surely unnecessary in any Chilean Cabernet). They make four different Cabernets, and a Cabernet Rosé, called Dona Paula, dry and tangy if somewhat unexciting. The red Cabernets start with the 120 Cabernet, named after the party of 120 independence fighters at the beginning of the nineteenth century, who took refuge in the house of the then owner of Santa Rita in 1814. It does not receive long oak maturation, and is designed to be drunk young and fresh. The Reserva Cabernet is still a wine to be drunk relatively young, the 87 (tasted in 1989) herbaceous and fresh. More serious are the Medalla Real, the 86 (tasted in 1989) rich, ripe and spicy, with excellent new wood tastes; and the Proprietary Reserva, rich, smooth and designed for a 10 to 12 year maturation.

MIGUEL TORRES →★★★
Panamerica Sur Km 195, Curico

Total v'yds owned: 150ha (371 acres)

Well known as a leading figure on the wine scene in Penedés, Spain, Miguel Torres Jnr opened a southern hemisphere branch of his family company in Curico in 1979. He bought an existing winery and vineyard, but both have been transformed: the winery by the installation of what were then the first stainless steel tanks in Chile and the importation of small American and French oak barrels for maturing wine (the first for 40 years), new presses and the use of chilled fermentation for white wines. However, there is still a link with the past, in the 80-year old vines whose fruit goes into the top of the range Manso de Velasco Cabernet, the 87 (tasted in 1989) tannic and firm, with blackcurrant and mint flavours, quite austere for a Chilean wine, and built to last. The regular Cabernet is lighter, the 87 (tasted in 1990) rather green and stalky, with crisp juicy fruit and very direct flavours.

VINA CALITERRA $* \rightarrow **$
PO Box 2346, Santiago

Total v'yds owned: 150ha (371 acres)
Cabernet area: 52ha (128 acres)

A joint venture between Franciscan Winery of California and Errazuriz Panquehue, inspired by the fact that one of the partners in Franciscan, Agustin Huneuus, is Chilean by birth. The vineyards are in the southerly Maule Valley outside Curico, and a new winery has been built there.

They make one Cabernet, the 87, their second vintage, a soft wine, with slight hints of wood, and delicate blackcurrant fruit, a wine that suggests it is early days at this bodega.

VINA SAN PEDRO $*$
Aysen 115, Santiago

Total v'yds owned: 420ha (1038 acres)
Cabernet area: 160ha (395 acres)

The first wine to be produced on a San Pedro vineyard was in 1701, but the bodega can more properly trace its origins to 1865 when cuttings of noble French grapes, including Cabernet, were first planted at the estate at Curico.

Now San Pedro has three farms: the original estate, San Miguel and La Huerta, all in the Lontue region. One of the largest Chilean firms, it has been modernizing with the installation of stainless steel fermenters. It was hit by the sorbitol affair of 1990. The main Cabernet production is Castillo de Molina, the 85 (tasted in 1990) is a very soft, easy-to-drink wine without much character or excitement.

UNDURRAGA $* \rightarrow **$
Lota 2305, Santiago

Total v'yds owned: 150ha (371 acres)

One of the most traditional bodegas, still using Bosnian wood (from Yugoslavia) for maturing its wine, a tradition that goes back to the firm's founder Don Francisco Undurraga in 1882. They make two Cabernets, a regular bottling, spoilt by a slight vegetal, herbaceous taste; the 87 (tasted in 1989) compensating with a smooth, easy-to-drink taste. The more serious Reserva Selecion has good oak flavours; the 85 (tasted in 1989) showing ripe, cassis flavours, but again slightly spoilt by a vegetal edge which may be due to the use of old wood.

South Africa

The reputation of South African wines has rested more on its reds than its whites. The hot climatic conditions in much of the viticultural areas of the Cape alone would dictate this. While local red-grape varieties such as the Pinotage have achieved a certain reputation, it is the Cabernet Sauvignon which has revealed the high quality of which South African reds are capable.

That revelation is quite recent. Over the past ten years, a range of Cabernets has been made which match anything the rest of the New World producers can offer. And, at the same time, South African producers have gone further and faster down the road of using Cabernet as the major constituent of a blend with Cabernet Franc and Merlot – much as in Bordeaux – to produce some fine, elegant, top-quality red wines.

The reason for this development lies, of course, with the producers themselves. The younger generation of winemakers is an open, adventurous group. They travel – to France, to California – and they see what is going on there.

There has been a change of emphasis in training as well: traditionally, Cape winemakers went to German schools and learnt to make wines in a German style; clean, precise and using large wooden barrels for maturation. The younger generation goes to Burgundy, Bordeaux or the Napa Valley, and has seen the way small, new oak barrels enhance the character and style of red wines as much as white.

Almost without exception, the best Bordeaux-blend reds are made using small barrels for maturation. The time spent in wood has shortened as well, to one year rather than the two-and-a-half with the large barrels; and producers are making use of a combination of bottle maturation as well as barrel so that they can retain the fruit character as well as giving wood tastes.

THE CABERNET ARRIVES

Records of the original arrival of Cabernet Sauvignon in South Africa are non-existent. The turn of the century is the probable time. Certainly of all the classic varieties which are now producing the best Cape wines – Pinot Noir, Chardonnay, Shiraz and Sauvignon Blanc – it is the one that has been in the vineyards longest. In the early days it was often blended with Cinsaut (as it still is with good effect at Rustenberg) to produce a warm, soft wine, certainly more reminiscent of hot country wines than of Bordeaux.

The arrival of Merlot and Cabernet Franc in quantity, which meant that Bordeaux blends could be developed, took place in the late 1970s. The insistence of the authorities on placing imported vine cuttings in long quarantine has meant that developments such as Bordeaux blends have been more recent in South Africa than in some other New World countries, but Cape producers are now moving ahead fast.

Quarantine has also posed problems for the introduction of new clones of Cabernet Sauvignon, but these higher-yielding clones are now being planted. They tend to make wines which mature faster, and which have a lighter character, and it is to be hoped that producers will not allow the style of their Cabernet-based wines to change too much.

CABERNET VINEYARDS

The hotter, northern and eastern vineyards of the Cape can prove too much for Cabernet which prefers a slightly cooler climate than the local Pinotage, so most plantings of Cabernet are in the Stellenbosch area, or in Constantia, both of which are cooled by ocean breezes. However, producers in the Franshhoek valley, and in parts of Paarl, especially on the mountain slopes, are quite capable of producing fine Cabernet – and do.

In the vineyards the Cabernet is planted on conventional trellising, normally a three-wire cordon system. It is treated for the usual diseases that affect the variety – oidium and downy mildew. New clones of the American rootstocks on to which the vine is grafted to prevent phylloxera are now arriving in South Africa, and vineyards are being replanted. As elsewhere, the Cabernet is a late ripener in South Africa. It is generally one of the last varieties to ripen. However, it is rarely a problem to get ripe grapes from the Cabernet, as it is in some cooler growing-areas of the world. Yields are low, a typical characteristic of the vine.

MAKING CABERNET

The ripeness of most red-wine grapes in South Africa means that colour is rarely a problem. Certainly the must from the Cabernet grapes that I have seen there has the classic intense purple colour which is translated into dark coloured wines. The problem is with tannins, which can sometimes be too intense. So destalking and light pressing, or even the use of free-run juice, are preferred to heavy pressings. A few producers still use open fermenters, but most now ferment either in tanks or, for their top wines, in wood.

Blending for the Bordeaux style blends normally takes place in the spring after the harvest. The wines are then aged in wood for anything up to 12 months – occasionally more – before bottling. Some producers release their wines soon after bottling, but many give them a few years bottle maturation before release.

South African Cabernets tend towards quite a hard, tough character when young. The good ripeness of the grapes in all but a few bad years ensures high tannin levels and considerable extract. However, they soften faster than most Bordeaux wines, for example, because they have lower acidity. An average development period before maturity for a Cape Cabernet would be five to seven years, maybe ten, and a slightly shorter period for the Bordeaux blends.

PRODUCERS

ALLESVERLOREN   ** → ***
Swartland

Total v'yds owned: 180ha (445 acres)

In the hot dry Swartland, Allesverloren is the only wine estate. Its initial claim to fame comes from its ports, made using Portuguese grape varieties, but more recently owner Fanie Malan has concentrated more on red table wines, from Shiraz and Tinta Barocca as well as Cabernet. There has been a change of style, too, away from big, robust wines. This was certainly true of the 82 (tasted in 1990) which despite its complexity is still a relatively restrained wine, full of soft fruit and tarry acidity. The 88 (tasted in 1990) was more of a disappointment, rather hard and tough and lacking sufficient fruit.

ALTO ESTATE   ***
Stellenbosch

Total v'yds owned: 100ha (247 acres)

Although now entirely owned by the giant Bergkelder organization, Alto Estate still retains its connections with its previous owners, the du Toit family, through its winemaker Hempies du Toit. The estate has long had a reputation for red wines, going back to the days just after World War I, when a wine called Alto Rouge was launched, and made a rapid international impact. Still one of the top blended reds, it comes mainly from Cabernet Sauvignon, with Cabernet Franc, Merlot and Shiraz (dropping Cinsaut previously included), and is designed as a relatively early-drinking wine. Recently, a 100 percent Cabernet wine has been made, and this has revived the fortunes of the estate, particularly in vintages from the mid-1980s on. So, while the 82 (tasted in 1990) had become too chewy and hard with age, the 88 (tasted in 1990) shows signs of considerable fruit weight, excellent wood balance, and the ability to age well.

ALTYDGEDACHT ESTATE   **→
Box 213, Durbanville

Total v'yds owned: 150ha (371 acres)
Cabernet area: 13.6ha (33.5 acres)

The Parker family estate, in the lee of the Tygerberg Mountain, on the edge of the northern Cape Town suburbs, has been bottling its own wines only since 1985, although wine has been produced here since 1730. The estate's reputation has been made by the high quality of the Cabernet Sauvignon, a 100 percent varietal wine, which matures in large, rather than small oak barrels, allowing fruit rather than wood tastes to predominate. Only small quantities are made, and I have not had the chance to taste the wine, but reports suggest its strength and power mean it needs anything up to ten years to mature in good vintages such as 87 or 85.

BACKSBERG   **→
Box 1, Klapmuts

Total v'yds owned: 180ha (445 acres)
Cabernet area: 40ha (99 acres)

Sydney Back, the highly-regarded owner of this estate, has developed some top range Cabernet-based wines over the past few vintages, using a lot of Californian and Australian knowhow. The star wine in the red range is the Klein Babylonstoren, a blend of Cabernet and Merlot, which has been designed for relatively early drinking, but now, with the 87 and 88 vintages, seems to be getting firmer and tougher. The 100 percent Cabernet has been less exciting, although the 87, seems destined for greater things.

BELLINGHAM   **
Franschhoek and Wellington

Total v'yds owned: 220ha (544 acres)

The Bellingham estate is part of Union Wine, and some of the wines under the estate's label are, in fact, blends of grapes from a wider area. But the Franschhoek farm remains the mainstay of the wines. The Cabernets have a mixture of small barrel maturation and large casks, giving a style that allows fruit to come through for a medium-bodied wine. The wines seem to be getting lighter than in the early 1980s, and are ready for drinking sooner.

BLAAUWKLIPPEN   ***
Stellenbosch

Total v'yds owned: 92ha (227 acres)
Cabernet area: 21ha (52 acres)

In the hands of Walter Finlayson, Blaauwklippen became famous for its reds, especially its Cabernets, and new winemaker Jacques Kruger seems set to continue this. There are two Cabernets made on the estate at the foot of the Stellenbosch Mountains, a Reserve and a regular. The Reserve, which sometimes contains some Cabernet Franc, is a classic wine, with cedary, lead-pencil smells and cassis-flavoured fruit coupled with good wood tannins. The best I have tasted was the 86, still (when tasted in 1990) much too young. The regular is matured in French and Yugoslav wood, and the 86 was firmly structured, with good tannins, a strong dry taste and hints of cigar-box tobacco-y smells.

BLOEMENDAL ESTATE   **→

Total v'yds owned: 145ha (358 acres)

Despite the size of this estate on the northern edge of Cape Town, not much wine is produced here. In fact, although vines were planted 20 years ago, estate bottling only started in 1987. The first Cabernet from that vintage, released in 1990, under the hands of winemaker Jackie Coetzee, shows that this Durbanville estate, cooled by sea breezes, is set for great things. Matured in French and American wood, it has a delicate, complex character, with good cassis flavours, excellent tannins, and a hint of spicy wood.

BOPLAAS   **→
Calitzdorp, Klein Karoo

This estate, on the remote and arid Klein Karoo, about as far east as the Cape vineyards go, has established a fine reputation for its port-style wines, and now is aiming to set standards with a Bordeaux-blend red. The first vintage of Grand Vin Rouge, a blend of 90 percent Cabernet and 10 percent Merlot, was the 87. The second, a blend of 50 percent Cabernet Sauvignon, 25 percent Cabernet Franc and 25 percent Merlot, was produced in 1989. They are being matured in Nevers wood.

BOSCHENDAL ESTATE   **→
Groot Drakenstein, Paarl

Total v'yds owned: 400ha (988 acres)

One of the largest of the Paarl estates, Boschendal is now part of the giant Anglo-American group. Under its previous winemaker and estate manager, Achim von Arnim, a massive replanting scheme took place, and the vineyards are now models of their kind. The estate produces one Bordeaux blend, called Grand Vin, which in the 86 version (the second vintage of this wine, tasted in 1990) was 85 percent Cabernet, 15 percent Merlot. A comparatively lean wine, it still has good fruit, and an attractive minty quality to go with the acidity.

BUITENVERWACHTING   **
Klein Constantia Road, Constantia

Total v'yds owned: 70ha (173 acres)
Cabernet area: 15ha (37 acres)

One of the few organic vineyards in the country, Christine Muller's Buitenverwachting operates on the principle of minimal interference in the vineyard and the use of high technology in the winery. The results are starting to show, after the initial bottlings with the 85 vintage. The first release of the Bordeaux blend, Buitenkur, was with the 86 vintage, and while this came from mainly young vines, it already showed the potential of the vineyard: quite austere, firm, but with good cassis qualities. This wine will mature soon, subsequent vintages will last longer.

DELAIRE VINEYARDS   * → **
Stellenbosch

Total v'yds owned: 22ha (54 acres)
Cabernet area: 5ha (12 acres)

Its spectacular position high on the Helshoogte Pass makes Delaire probably more of a success with whites than reds. But winemaker Mike Dobrovic is producing one red, a Bordeaux blend, called Barrique with 50 percent Cabernet Sauvignon, 50 percent Merlot: the 88 (tasted in 1990) is full of spicy wood, smoky, rather dry and cool. Future reds are more likely to concentrate on Merlot.

DELHEIM   *** →
Koelenhof, Simonsberg, Stellenbosch

Total v'yds owned: 118ha (292 acres)

Out of a huge range of wines produced at Delheim, the Cabernet-based blends stand out as the best, vying with a few others as the best in South Africa. Owner Spatz Sperling and his winemaker Philip Constandius have two main vineyards Driesprongh and the warmer Veracruz, both on the slopes of the Simonsberg Mountain, which supply most of the grapes for red wines. The Grand Reserve is a Bordeaux blend, with anything from 65 to 75 percent Cabernet Sauvignon plus Merlot and Cabernet Franc. The wines are blended before one year's maturation in small French oak barrels. They get better and better, with the 85 and 86 showing ripe, ready tannins and fruit, while the 88 (tasted in 1990) is bigger, bolder, made from a new Cabernet clone which shows great intense, concentrated fruit tastes. The second red was until 85 a straight Cabernet wine, but now has some Cabernet Franc and Merlot. It is generally softer, with less wood tastes, and matures around four years, compared with ten for the Grand Reserve.

FAIRVIEW   ** →
Suider-Paarl, Paarl

Total v'yds owned: 130ha (321 acres)

Both a Reserve and a regular Cabernet are made at this estate, which operates on semi-organic principles. The Reserve is the better wine, and is now aged in small French oak barrels, giving good tarry, cigar-box qualities and greater complexity. The regular Cabernet, which has some wood maturation or none at all, has seemed to become lighter in recent years.

GROOT CONSTANTIA   ** →
Constantia

Total v'yds owned: 150ha (371 acres)

This historic state-owned farm, home of the famed sweet Constantia wines made at the turn of the 19th century, is now regaining its former prestigious reputation. Its position in the cool Constantia Valley in the lee of Table Mountain allows it to produce reds of complexity rather than weight. A new Bordeaux blend of Cabernet Sauvignon and Cabernet Franc from the 86 vintage, released in 1990, spent 18 months in 500-litre French oak barrels. The regular Cabernet is now also benefiting from new oak, and the 86 and subsequent vintages show marked improvements on what went before. Constantia Rood is a blend of the two Cabernets with some Merlot and Shiraz or Pinotage, and is designed for early and enjoyable drinking.

KANONKOP   *** → ****
Muldersvlei, Stellenbosch

Total v'yds owned: 140ha (346 acres)
Cabernet area: 30ha (74 acres)

The name of this estate commemorates the cannon on top of a neighbouring hill which was fired to alert farmers of the arrival of Dutch East India Company ships in Cape Town. Previously part of Uitkyk estate, it is now owned by the Sauer family, with Beyers Truter, and they continue its specialization in red wines, which are still made in traditional open fermenters. There are two principal varieties: the local Pinotage, from which the estate makes some of the best examples in South Africa, and Cabernet. There are three Cabernet styles. Paul Sauer, named after a previous owner, is the top wine, a Bordeaux blend with 70 to 75 percent Cabernet Sauvignon plus Cabernet Franc, Merlot, Malbec and the Portuguese variety, Souzão: the 86 and 89 are best of recent vintages. A special bottling for the Cape Independent Winemakers' Guild is known just as Kanonkop, and is a blend of barrels from the Paul Sauer selection. The regular 100 percent Cabernet wine is big, beefy and tannic, the 83 (tasted in 1990) still needing time, the 84 a superb wine, full of smoky wood, concentrated fruit and plenty of tannin.

KLEIN CONSTANTIA   ** → ***
Constantia

Total v'yds owned: 70ha (173 acres)

Since its first bottling in 1986, Klein Constantia has shot to the top, as a result of the excellent vineyard location, the huge and serious investment by owner Duggie Jooste, the winemaking talents of New Zealand-trained Ross Gower, and the rigorous control of yields (12 tons per hectare for reds). The first red release was a Cabernet Sauvignon 86, which (tasted in 1990), showed full, minty character, still lean and tannic and with plenty of cassis fruit. While the concentration is there, the wines can only improve as the vines get older.

LE BONHEUR   → ***
Klapmuts, Stellenbosch

Total v'yds owned: 70ha (173 acres)

Le Bonheur's owner, Mike Woodhead, only makes three wines: two whites and a Cabernet Sauvignon. From the first vintage in 82, the Cabernet has shown elegance and restraint, rather than overt power, the 84 the best, balancing fruit and new wood flavours and spice, complex and obviously able to age well.

L'ORMARINS
Franshhoek, Suider-Paarl, Paarl

$** \rightarrow ***$

| Total v'yds owned: 167ha (413 acres) |
| Cabernet area: 20ha (49 acres) |

The beautiful setting of the L'Ormarins homestead and winery, has in the past seven years been reflected in the quality of the wines coming from Nico Vermeulen and owner Antonij Rupert, which are made on the estate but bottled by the Bergkelder. The 100 percent Cabernet Sauvignon wine now goes under the name La Maison du Roi: the 84 (tasted in 1990) was the second release, and shows pepper and spice and ripe cherry-flavoured fruit; a Reserve 84 had greater intensity and colour. Wines are not released before five years, after anything up to two years in small wood and bottle maturation.

MEERLUST
Stellenbosch

$** \rightarrow ***$

Total v'yds owned:240ha (593 acres)

The ninth generation of the Myburgh family to own this classic Cape estate (the first Myburgh bought it in 1756) took over in 1988 and, working with winemaker Giorgio dalla Cia, are continuing its reputation for red wines. The flagship red is Rubicon: the 86 with restrained use of wood, still young and tannic when tasted in 1990, very French in style. The blend usually has 65 percent Cabernet Sauvignon, plus Merlot and Cabernet Franc. The straight Cabernet Sauvignon is showing signs of an increased use of new wood, and is becoming much more New World in style.

NEDERBURG
Paarl

$**$

Despite its seemingly independent existence, Nederburg is in fact part of Stellenbosch Farmers' Winery. While part of its grapes do come from the estate vineyards in Paarl, much of this is then blended with bought-in grapes from other farms. There are essentially three ranges of wine produced: the regular commercial range, a series of Limited Release Vintages, and Private Bin wines, many of which are sold at the famous annual auction. The regular Cabernet Sauvignon is a pleasant enough medium-bodied wine. The Private Bin wines are much the most interesting: although there is not always a 100 percent Cabernet Sauvignon, the grape normally features largely in the main blends, along with Cinsaut and Shiraz. These wines, normally matured in large wooden casks, can last well, with a style of generous rich, soft fruit.

NEETHLINGSHOF ESTATE
Stellenbosch

$** \rightarrow$

| Total v'yds owned: 150ha (371 acres) |
| Cabernet area: 7.4ha (18 acres) |

The arrow in the rating says it all: this is an estate which is on the way up, after massive investment in replanting the vineyards and re-equipping the cellars, and the appointment of Gunter Brozel, as new managing director. The current range consists of two Cabernet-based wines: the Lord Neethling Rouge, an unusual blend of Cabernet and the Portuguese Tinta Barocca, and a 100 percent Cabernet, which comes from old vines and has all the intensity these could be expected to provide.

OVERGAAUW   ** → ***
Stellenbosch

Total v'yds owned: 71.5ha (177 acres)
Cabernet area: 9ha (22 acres)

This estate was one of the first in South Africa to produce a Bordeaux blend, and the Tria Corda, matured in French oak, with 60 to 65 percent Cabernet Sauvignon, plus Cabernet Franc and Merlot, is still exhibiting the elegant, soft style that made its initial success. The 86 and 84 have been the best of most recent vintages tasted. The 100 percent Cabernet Sauvignon is matured in a mix of small and large wood for up to 27 months, and vintages like the light but tannic 85 (tasted in 1990) need up to five years for maturity.

ROZENDAL FARM   **
Stellenbosch

Total v'yds owned: 5ha (12 acres)
Cabernet area: none

Until 1989 the major outlet for the wines made by chef and winemaker Kurt Amman was in the nearby Doornbosch restaurant. The Cabernet Sauvignon for this all red-wine production comes from the nearby Lanzerac vineyards, while the Merlot in the Rozendal blend is grown on the farm. Proportions of Cabernet Sauvignon vary from 50 percent to 20 percent, and recent vintages have a ripe, plummy feel that comes from the high proportion of Merlot. The first, 83 vintage, was a blend of Cabernet and Cinsaut. The same wine is exported under the name Konstanz. There is also a lighter 100 percent Cabernet wine, called Doornbosch.

RUSTENBERG   ***
Stellenbosch

Total v'yds owned: 80ha (198 acres)
Cabernet area: 31ha (77 acres)

The beautiful Rustenberg estate in the southern foothills of the Simonsberg Mountains, shares vineyards with sheep, Jersey cows and large fruit orchards. The wines are made in open-top fermenters, without any artifical yeasts, and are then matured both in large vats and French wood. The top red, named simply Rustenberg, is a Bordeaux blend, distinguished by its gold-rimmed label, with 60 percent Cabernet Sauvignon, plus Cabernet Franc and Merlot. A big, weighty, astonishingly fruity wine, the 86 (tasted in 1990) was full of intense fruit and tarry, cedary tastes. Special bottlings are called Reserve, and are kept at the estate for auctions. The regular 100 percent Cabernet Sauvignon exhibits excellent fruit character, even though it is firmer and more tannic than the Rustenberg: the 87 (tasted in 1990) has been matured in more new wood than previous wines, and this shows in the extra spiciness and wood tannins. Rustenberg Dry Red, the standard red from the estate, features Cabernet, normally with Cinsaut, and now with some Cabernet Franc and Merlot as alternatives.

RUST EN VREDE ESTATE →***
Stellenbosch

Total v'yds owned: 40ha (99 acres)

Exclusively devoted to red-wine making, Rust en Vrede Estate has been restored since 1978 by owner Jannie Engelbrecht. The major planting is of Cabernet Sauvignon, which goes into the two best wines from the estate. The top red, called simply Rust en Vrede, was first made with the 86 vintage, which has 75 percent Cabernet plus Merlot, but could, in other vintages, contain other varieties such as Shiraz. Fruit quality is obvious here, and the blackcurrant flavours shine through the oak. The 100 percent Cabernet has improved with vintages of the late 1980s, and can be expected to look even better since the arrival in 1988 of new winemaker Kevin Arnold.

THELEMA MOUNTAIN VINEYARD →***
Dennesig, Stellenbosch

Gyles Webb's stint with the Heitz family in Napa Valley, California, is standing him in good stead, as is shown by the quality of the first Cabernets to come from this steep mountainside vineyard on the slopes of the Simonsberg. Using new French wood, he is making a firmly New-World style of wine, full of heavy fruit and wood flavours, the initial vintage 88 (tasted in 1990) with mint hints on full-bodied fruit, and plenty of tannins to give every sign of long life. Expect even more with the advent of Merlot in 91.

VILLIERA ESTATE **→
Koelenhof, Paarl

Total v'yds owned: 120ha (297 acres)
Cabernet area: 12ha (30 acres)

While sparkling wine is the main production here, the Grier family also make two Cabernet-based reds. Top of the range is Cru Monro, a Bordeaux blend of roughly 60 percent Cabernet and 40 percent Merlot, first produced with the 84 vintage. The 86, matured in French oak for over a year (tasted in 1990), is very spicy and cedary and has a definite New-World jammy character. The straight Cabernet is a light wine, matured in two-year old barrels, and with pleasing fruit flavours.

VRIESENHOF ***→
Stellenbosch

Total v'yds owned: 15ha (37 acres)
Cabernet area: 4ha (10 acres)

Jan Coetzee, owner of Vriesenhof, produces two of the Cape's top Cabernet-based wines on this small estate on the outskirts of Stellenbosch. Top of the range is Kallista, a Bordeaux blend, with up to 25 percent Merlot alongside the Cabernet Sauvignon. Best vintage so far of this wine was 86 (tasted in 1989) with plenty of cassis fruit intensity married with good new wood flavours. The straight Cabernet is harder, and takes longer to mature than the blended wine, needing a good ten years in bottle. The 87 (tasted in 1990) was still very firm, but showed classic varietal character.

WARWICK ESTATE

→ ****

Muldersvlei, Stellenbosch

Total v'yds owned: 60ha (148 acres)

Although this has been a vineyard for many years, it was only with the 85 vintage that any wine was made here in serious quantities. But from this first vintage, Norma and Stan Ratcliffe have set one of the highest standards for red wines in the Cape. Norma makes the wine, Stan runs the vineyards. The Bordeaux blend, Trilogy, with 75 percent Cabernet Sauvignon plus Merlot and Cabernet Franc, shows enormous style as well as fruit character and balance. The 86 is fuller and richer than the 87. The straight Cabernet is full of spicy fruit, and has the same huge colour and concentration of all the Warwick wines, the 86 with delicious spicy overtones, the 87, matured in small wood for two years, full of splendid fruit.

WELGEMEEND ESTATE

*** →

Klapmuts, Paarl

Total v'yds owned: 13.5ha (33 acres)

This was the estate which pioneered the trend to Bordeaux blends in the Cape in 1979, with its Welgemeend Estate Wine, which is still the winery's top wine. A classic Bordeaux blend, now with 50 percent Cabernet Sauvignon, 20 percent Cabernet Franc, 25 percent Merlot and 5 percent Petit Verdot – one of the few producers in South Africa with this variety – it can in the best vintages show remarkable finesse, elegance and complexity. Best vintage of the 1980s latter half was the 86 (tasted in 1990) which had classic poise and balance, with fine fruit, just edging to maturity. Until the 86 vintage, the Hofmeyr family also made a straight Cabernet Sauvignon, suspended in favour of the blend. The wines are only lightly filtered, and yields in the vineyard are low – all of which contributes to the quality of the wines from this outstanding estate.

ZEVENWACHT WINES

** →

Kuilsriver, Stellenbosch

Total v'yds owned: 150ha (371 acres)

Zevenwacht is the conflated name for two estates, Zevenfontein and Langverwacht, which architect owner Gilbert Colyn bought in the late 1970s. The Cabernet Sauvignon is used in two wines from the winery – a straight varietal wine, which tends towards high tannins and rich fruit; and a 50 percent blend with Shiraz called Zevenwacht, made for early drinking, but which can develop well in an old-fashioned Cape red style.

Italy

The Cabernet would seem to be almost redundant in Italy. With its wide variety of red-wine grapes, and its absorbing and fascinating range of wines from these native varieties, why should Cabernet have any place in Italian viticulture?

Cabernet Sauvignon has actually been in Italy for longer than we imagine. It was planted in Piedmont in 1820; it had arrived somewhat earlier in the northeast; and it was in Tuscany by the middle of the last century, and has been planted and been producing there ever since. While it has never – and is quite unlikely to – replace Sangiovese as the quality red grape of Tuscany, its presence in Chianti has considerable tradition behind it.

But it is really since the creation of Sassicaia, a 100 percent Cabernet wine made in western Tuscany, that a craze for planting Cabernet has evolved. It was stimulated by the high prices and critical acclaim that accompanied the introduction of each successive Sassicaia vintage, and, of course, by the common Italian desire to follow a fashion.

Cabernet has emerged in two guises. It has been used to make 100 percent Cabernet wines, or wines which follow the Bordeaux blend formula with Merlot or Cabernet Franc; and it has been added in small proportions to wines made mainly from native varieties – particularly the Sangiovese of Tuscany – to produce wines which have added character and complexity. Despite the success of some of the French-style Cabernets, for me it is the second way of treating Cabernet in Italy which is so much more successful.

The style of the wines varies considerably. Many Cabernets from the northeastern regions of Italy are thin, rather uninteresting offerings. They taste dilute because the yields are too high (this is especially true if there is a high proportion of the more generously yielding Cabernet Franc), are made in stainless steel rather than wood, and are designed for early drinking.

Contrasted with this are wines which aim at either a New-World Cabernet style (as in the Darmagi Cabernet Sauvignon of Angelo Gaja in Piedmont) or at a Bordeaux look-alike (as in La Stoppa from Emilia Romagna).

THE CABERNET VINEYARDS

The main plantings of Cabernet are in the northeast of the country, in Trentino-Alto Adige, in the Veneto and, more particularly in Friuli. Its plantings are often muddled up with those of Cabernet Franc, and very often, in Italian eyes at least, there is little to distinguish between the two. An Italian wine labelled simply Cabernet will have a blend of both Cabernets, in indeterminate proportions, although it is likely that Cabernet Franc will predominate. Only with the growing fashion for Cabernet Sauvignon have producers learned (or bothered) to distinguish between the two.

In Piedmont Cabernet Sauvignon is now grown in small quantities, despite the obvious rival attractions of the local Nebbiolo wines. It is grown perhaps more as a status symbol, but there are a few world-class wines being made. There is an enclave of Cabernets – again, mainly Cabernet Franc – in the Lombardy vineyards of Franciacorta, and another in Emilia near Bologna.

Across the Appenines, in Tuscany, it is Cabernet Sauvignon all the way. It is used for blending with Sangiovese in the Chianti vineyards and in the smaller area of Carmignano. And it is used to make the 100 percent wines which have come to the worlds notice such as Sassicaia and Solaia.

There are plantings of Cabernet Sauvignon elsewhere in Italy. Umbria has a small quantity, as does Lazio, in vineyards around Rome. No doubt it is planted further south, although I have only come across wines made from Cabernet Sauvignon's Bordeaux companions, Merlot, Malbec and Cabernet Franc.

THE LAW AND CABERNET

The Italian equivalent of the French *appellation contrôlée* system is called DOC, Denominazione di Origine Controllata. A few, supposedly top quality zones are designated DOCG, with the wines being Garantita as well as Controllata. The rules for both DOC and DOCG lay down the specific grape varieties which are permitted. Interestingly, no DOC zone in Italy actually specifies the use of Cabernet Sauvignon as against Cabernet Franc. Generally, the law simply says Cabernet, and leaves the choice or proportions up to the producer. The only DOC Cabernet wines are in Trentino Alto Adige, Veneto and Friuli. Other areas which permit Cabernet (either Cabernet) to be used, allow it as part of a blend rather than by itself: thus Franciacorta has the unusual combination of Barbera, Nebbiolo and Merlot in addition to the Cabernets, while the small Valcalepio DOC near Bergamo, specifies a minimum of 55 percent Merlot with the specified Cabernet Sauvignon. Wines made from 100 percent Cabernet Sauvignon outside the three northeastern regions are invariably designated *vino da tavola*. This, the lowest category in Italian wine law can describe anything from the basic village plonk to the most expensive wines in Italy – if their blend of grapes happens to fall outside the local DOC law. Every producer, certainly in Tuscany, wants to make one of these super *vini da tavola*: there are some 100 percent Cabernet Sauvignon wines which fall into this category.

PIEDMONT

Despite the historical links with France, Cabernet Sauvignon has never taken off in Piedmont. The traditional reliance on Nebbiolo and Barbera red wines, which remains very strong in the hills of the Langhe, south of Turin, is quite enough to explain this. With red grapes of this quality, who needs Cabernet Sauvignon. Recently, there has been one fine Cabernet which shows that the grape could be successful here if the will and justification were there.

ANGELO GAJA   →***
Darmagi

Piedmontese superstar Angelo Gaja has proved that fine Cabernet can be made in Piedmont. Darmagi (the word translates as ''what a pity'', the response his father gave when Angelo said he was planting Cabernet) comes from the Bricco vineyard in Barbaresco. The 82 (tasted in 1986) was huge, tough and very unwelcoming at that stage, deeply purple in colour, stalky and quite acid. Given that it came from young vines, things should improve.

TRENTINO/ALTO ADIGE

Foreign and local grape varieties mix happily in the Alpine regions of Italy. While the Alto Adige (or Sudtirol as it is also called) is German in outlook and language, Trentino is Italian. Both areas, however, have long had Cabernet plantings. While Cabernet Franc has been the predominant variety in the Alto Adige, Cabernet Sauvignon is now beginning to replace it. A shorter growing season, coupled with the Cabernet Franc grassiness, has tended to produce rather green, bitter wines, but that it is possible to produce better than this is shown by some of the wines coming from hillside – rather than valley floor – vineyards using a high proportion of Cabernet Sauvignon.

In Trentino we move into the world of the young, fresh, rather dilute Cabernets which spread eastwards to Friuli. Again, a few producers are doing something more.

GIORGIO GRAI ** →
Cabernet

Previously sold under the Herrnhofer label, Giorgio Grai's Alto Adige Cabernet is a blend of both Sauvignon and Franc, made with unusual care and with low-yielding vines to give some intensity, even if in a fresh style.

ALOIS LAGEDER ** → ***
Lowengang

One of the leading producers in the Alto Adige, Alois Lageder makes two wines under the Lowengang label, a *barrique*-fermented Chardonnay and this Cabernet Sauvignon, which only contains 5 percent Cabernet Franc. The 84 (tasted in 1988) had a good Francophone style, with warm fruit flavours and almost a tobacco-y taste.

SCHLOSS SCHWANBURG **
Castel Schwanburg

A blend of Cabernets/Merlot, aged in *barrique*. I have not tasted it.

TENUTA SAN LEONARDO **
Cabernet Sauvignon

A *barrique*-aged Cabernet which has acquired the style and elegance that earlier examples from this estate (owned by the Marchesi Guerrieri Gonzaga) using both Cabernets failed to offer. There is also a Cabernet/Merlot blend, called Campi Sarni.

VALLAROM → **
Cabernet Sauvignon

The family estate of viticulturalist Attilio Scienza produces a Cabernet Sauvignon which has been praised.

VENETO

Here we enter the land of the "Cabernet" with a vengeance. Many of the DOCs of the central hill zones of the Veneto – Breganze, Colli Berici, Colli Euganei – all have provisions for wines labelled simply Cabernet. The same is true for Piave, north of Treviso and its next-door neighbour Lison-Pramaggiore. There are no requirements for the use of either Cabernet, and no regulations setting out percentages. On the whole, assume that most of the Cabernet is Franc, unless told otherwise. However, there are a few producers making mainly Cabernet Sauvignon wines.

CASTELLO DI RONCADE ** →
Villa Giustinian

A Bordeaux-blend wine, containing Merlot as well as the two Cabernets, from the Montello e Colli Asolani DOC area near Treviso. The long-established firm is reviving a tradition with this wine.

MACULAN ***
Fratta

Fausto Maculan has singlehandedly revived the fortunes of the Breganze vineyards in the Alpine foothills north of Vicenza. His Fratta from a 1ha (2.5 acre) vineyard, is a Cabernet Sauvignon/ Franc blend, the 83 (tasted in 1988) a top-rate wine, warm and fruity, with a big undertow of wood and tannins, balanced but with a hint of bitterness. Maculan also makes small quanities of a pure Cabernet Sauvignon wine, Palazzotto.

VENEGAZZÙ-CONTE LOREDAN GASPARINI   **→
Venegazzù della Casa

Wines produced at the former estates of the Loredan Gasparini family at Venegazzù di Volpago. There are two styles, a white label, and a reserve black label, Etichetta Nera. The quality of these wines has declined recently, but the Black Label is still a classic Bordeaux-style wine, full of tarry, cedary fruit.

FRIULI-VENEZIA-GIUILIA

The far northeast of Italy is awash with French varietal wines. By far the largest quantity of red wine comes from the Merlot, but there are also both Cabernets. Cabernet Franc still dominates Cabernet Sauvignon here (the higher yields probably help), but there is an increasing interest in redressing the balance in favour of Cabernet Sauvignon in blended wines, and in making some straight Cabernet Sauvignons. Neither grape variety is a stranger here: they probably arrived at the time of the Napoleonic wars, some 200 years ago.

The Collio Goriziano (Collio) is the only DOC to specify Cabernet Franc to the exclusion of Cabernet Sauvignon. And since many Collio producers also operate in other Friuli DOC zones, they still manage to make a Cabernet Sauvignon wine if they want to. These include some curious blends, such as the Cabernet Sauvignon/Merlot/Pinot Nero Rivarossa of Mario Schiopetto, or the even more exotic Ronco dei Roseti of the Abbazia di Rosazzo.

RONCHI DI MANZANO   **→
This estate in Colli Orientali del Friuli, on the borders with Yugoslavia, makes separate *crus* of Cabernet Sauvignon and Cabernet Franc, rather than blending them.

RONCO DEL GNEMIZ   **
Owner Enzo Natisone has 6ha (15 acres) of vineyards from which he makes the usual bewildering Friuli array of wines, as well as a blend of both Cabernets, also called Ronco del Gnemiz.

EMILIA-ROMAGNA

The Cabernet was planted in Emilia in the last century, and is now undergoing a cautious revival in two of the hill vineyard areas, the Colli Piacentini on the border with Lombardy (adjoining the Oltrepò Pavese vineyards) and the Colli Bolognesi in the east of Emilia.

LA STOPPA   **→
Stoppa

One of the top estates in the Colli Piacentini actually makes very little DOC wine, concentrating instead on super *vini da tavola*. The Cabernet Sauvignon/Cabernet Franc blend is called simply Stoppa, which I find can tend to over-ripeness in some warmer years, although years such as 84 had good fruit character.

TERRE ROSSE   →***
Cabernet Sauvignon

The Vallania family makes all its wines, including this, in stainless steel rather than using wood in order, they say, to preserve the character of the fruit. The philosophy certainly works with the Cabernet Sauvignon, the 83 (tasted in 1988) warm, soft, only slightly tannic with a delicious nutty quality, and excellent direct, mature fruit tastes.

LOMBARDY

The region centred on Milan is home to one DOC which was created in 1976 specifically to allow the blending of Merlot and Cabernet Sauvignon and thus revive a declining viticultural area. Apart from that, all Cabernet Sauvignon wines are *vini da tavola*.

BELLAVISTA **
Solesine

This Franciacorta producer makes a *vino da tavola* Cabernet Sauvignon, blended with Merlot, called Solesine. The 85 (tasted in 1989) was austere, full of tannins with a slightly bitter finish.

CA' DEL BOSCO **→
Maurizio Zanella

The most prestigious estate in Franciacorta has built its reputation on its sparkling wines, which are regarded as some of the best in Italy. Owner Maurizio Zanella makes this Cabernet and Merlot blend, which he has named after himself, specifically in a French way, with small oak *barriques*, but he seems to have a penchant for a richer New World style which creeps into the lush 85, tasted 88.

CAVALLERI **
Tajardino

Another Franciacorta producer who is making a *vino da tavola* Cabernet Sauvignon/Merlot blend, called Tajardino.

TUSCANY AND UMBRIA

Tuscany is the home of the super *vini da tavola*, a phrase whose origin lies as much with wine writers as producers, and which describes highly-priced fantasy wines which do not fit into any DOC or DOCG rules but are created by producers to express their estates' – or their own – personality. Hundred percent Cabernet Sauvignon wines, actually quite few in number even in Tuscany, have stolen the headlines that perhaps should have been accorded to Chianti itself.

But Cabernet is not a total parvenu. It has long been a constituent of the wines of Carmignano, and it was certainly planted in the estates of the Marchese Frescobaldi at Nippozano over a century ago. Its arrival in Chianti also dates back to the 19th century when Barone Ricasoli allowed for some "foreign grapes" to be included in the blend. While these were traditionally grapes (or wine) from the south of Italy just to bolster quantities, more recent times have seen a shift by some quality conscious producers to the use of Cabernet Sauvignon. With the introduction of the DOCG regulations in 1984 for Chianti, Cabernet Sauvignon can now form up to 10 percent of the final blend. But the spread of Cabernet has produced a reaction. Many – perhaps more enlightened – producers are returning to the Sangiovese, the traditional Tuscan red grape, and are refining wines made from this native variety rather than the French import. They are combining it in varying proportions, as in the Alto d'Altesi of Altesino in Montalcino, or the Concerto of Fonterutoli and Ripe delle More of Castello Vicchiomaggio in Chianti, the Grifi of Avignonesi and Le Stanze of Poliziano both in Montepulciano. But for many, the 100 percent Sangiovese *vini da tavola* are more interesting and exciting than the Cabernet wines. Both show the vitality of the Tuscan winemaking scene.

In Umbria the principal producer of Torgiano DOC wines, Lungarotti, also makes a Cabernet wine.

MARCHESI L & P ANTINORI　　　　　　　　***→
Solaia

The Antinori firm was the original distributor of the legendary Sassicaia. The Solaia came originally from the family's Santa Cristina estate, which is now used as a separate brand name. The wine is designed more as a New World wine than a Bordeaux, simply because its rich, concentrated fruit is too heavy to compare with any but the ripest Bordeaux in the warmest years. The 85 (tasted in 1989) is smooth, silky, incredibly rich, full of the most generous fruit, overwhelming to the palate. The other Antinori *vino da tavola*, Tignanello, has some Cabernet in the blend.

VILLA DI CAPEZZANA　　　　　　　　　　→***
Ghiaie della Furba

Made with equal proportions of Cabernet Sauvignon, Cabernet Franc and Merlot, this comes from the leading estate of Carmignano, west of Florence. The owner, Ugo Conti Bonacossi, was instrumental in getting Cabernet Sauvignon included in the blend for the Carmignano DOC wines. The 83 Ghiaie della Furba (tasted in 1987) had one year in new *barriques* and one year in larger barrels: it showed considerable wood at that stage, but had excellent smoky, meaty fruit underneath.

RICCARDO FALCHINI　　　　　　　　　　**→
Campora

Based in the hills around Siena, Falchini produces Chianti Colli Senesi and Vernaccia di San Gimignano. He also makes two wines with Cabernet – the 100 percent Campora and a blend of Cabernet and Sangiovese, called Paretato.

ISOLE E OLENA　　　　　　　　　　　　***
Collezione De Marchi

Paolo De Marchi makes highly regarded Chianti Classico as well as Tuscany's first Syrah wine. Under the Collezione De Marchi label he has introduced a Cabernet Sauvignon.

LUNGAROTTI　　　　　　　　　　　　　**→
Cabernet di Miralduolo / San Giorgio

The virtual creator of the Torgiano DOC zone, with its Rubesco brand, Cantina Lungarotti made a single-vineyard Cabernet, di Miralduolo, starting in the 1970s. More recently, this has been superseded by a blended wine, San Giorgio, which takes in some of the local grape varieties as well as Cabernet.

MONSANTO　　　　　　　　　　　　　**→
Nemo

Another of the top Chianti Classico producers who make small quantities of a 100 percent Cabernet wine, called Nemo, as well as a Sangiovese/Cabernet blend, Tinscvil.

MARCHESE INCISA DELLA ROCHETTA　　***→
Sassicaia

The original 100 percent Cabernet from Tuscany, and still probably the best. It is made in the unlikely surroundings of Bolgheri in the west of Tuscany, close to the sea, in hillside vineyards of gravel and loam soil. The first vintage of this wine was 1958. The blend is 70 percent Cabernet Sauvignon, 30 percent Cabernet Franc. Of recent vintages, the best are the 81 and 82, followed by the 85 and 88. The 82 (tasted in 1989) was just beginning to be drinkable, with medium-weight fruit, very ripe in flavour, not French, more New World, except for the backbone of acidity and mature tannins and dryness that gave it an extra elegance.

TENUTA DELL'ORNELLAIA   **** →**
Ornellaia

Ludovico Antinori, a member of the Antinori wine family, has created an estate near the Sassicaia vineyards in Bolgheri, where he is making Bordeaux style wines, with the first vintage in 1987. The blend of Ornellaia is 65 percent Cabernet Sauvignon, 30 percent Merlot and 5 percent Cabernet Franc. At present the reputation is in the name, rather than the wines, but it is early days yet, and some of his 100 percent Merlot wines show great style.

CASTELLO DEI RAMPOLLA   ***** →**
Sammarco

An essentially Cabernet-based wine, with a small amount of Sangiovese which adds a twist of complexity. For some, this is a rival of (indeed better than) Sassicaia. Alceo Di Napoli makes a huge, ripe, plummy, cigar-box, spicy wine – any adjective for great red Bordeaux fits here. The 85 (tasted in 1989) was amazingly rich and concentrated with layers of complexity. They are not, however, wines for ageing in the same way as great red Bordeaux: drink the 85 in the mid-1990s.

VILLA BANFI   **** →**
Tavernelle

The space-age technology of the Villa Banfi winery in the south of the Montalcino vineyards makes a 100 percent Cabernet wine, Tavernelle, which takes its name from the neighbouring village. There are 160 ha (395 acres) of Cabernet planted, making it the largest planting in Tuscany. The wine is matured in new French wood, and generally tastes correct rather than exciting. However, the 86 (tasted in 1989) with plenty of purple fruit, had good chewy ripeness, some cassis flavour, and was only spoilt by some bitterness at the end.

Spain

The Cabernet Sauvignon has been in Spain for more than a century. It was introduced to form part of the blend for the wine of Vega Sicilia in what is now the region of Ribera del Duero, the vineyards along the banks of the Duero, northwest of Madrid in the province of Burgos. It still forms 25 percent of the blend for this, Spain's foremost and most formidable red wine. As a consequence of this model, other Ribera del Duero producers are allowed to use Cabernet Sauvignon in addition to the local Tinto Fino or Tempranillo.

Elsewhere, though, Cabernet Sauvignon is a relative newcomer. It is most at home in Catalonia, where it is used to make some of that region's best reds, as well as being used in blends to bolster up the local red varieties.

It is probably true to say that it has been planted in most regions on an experimental basis, even though the local regulations often forbid its use in the DO (Denominacion de Origen) wines of an area. That is true of Rioja, where a number of bodegas have planted Cabernet and are using small quantities to flesh out some of the wines. In Rioja, it is the only vine which may be trained on wires in the vineyard, while all other vines have to be left in the typical Spanish bush, trailing along the ground.

In Navarra, to the north of Rioja, the Cabernet is now a recommended variety. Here it makes a fairly tough wine, but one which can be used for blending with local grapes like the Garnacha in order to flesh out the wine. There are experimental plantings in Somontano (Aragon). It is made into fine wines at the Marqués de Griñon's estate near Toledo (see below). It is planted in La Mancha and Valdepenas. It has even been found on the island of Mallorca in the Mediterranean.

Cabernet has to be treated somewhat differently from local Spanish grapes. For a start, it needs to be trained on wires. It also needs to be irrigated in many parts of Spain – the summers are just too dry and hot. Irrigation is forbidden by European regulations for DO wines, but allowed for experimental purposes, so the rules can be neatly circumvented with a grape variety which is still in an experimental stage in many areas. In Catalonia, where it is more widely planted, there is less of a problem with dry summers.

Whether Cabernet Sauvignon plantings will extend much beyond these fairly tentative beginnings is uncertain. There is not the pressure among Spanish producers to produce "fashion" wines as in Italy. However, the paucity of really exciting native red-grape varieties – the only two are Tempranillo and Garnacha under a variety of names – means that, unlike Italy, the Spanish vineyards are more wide open to a "foreign" invasion.

PRODUCERS

JEAN LEÓN   →***
Cabernet were the first vines to be planted by Californian restaurateur Jean León in 1967. He returned to his roots in Catalonia to make Spanish wines his Californian customers would enjoy. Needless to say the wine is in a strongly New World idiom, showing concentrated, almost sweet fruit, coupled with strong wood tastes. Originally 100 percent Cabernet Sauvignon, it is now blended with some Cabernet Franc, which has had the effect of lightening the style slightly. But wood ageing for at least two years does mean the wine is going to be weighty. The 83 (tasted in 1990) was heavy, with dusty perfume and concentrated fruit, beginning to mature, but unlikely to be totally smooth.

MARQUÉS DE GRIÑON   **→***
Carlos Falco, Marqués de Griñon, planted Cabernet Sauvignon with cuttings taken from Bordeaux at his estate in Toledo back in 1973. At the time, he was not even allowed to do it, but he released a wine of 50 percent Cabernet Sauvignon, 50 percent Tinto Fino in 1981. Professor Emile Peynaud acted as consultant to subsequent vintages. The vineyard, which is about 1 percent of the Griñon estate, is planted with Cabernet and Merlot at an altitude of 500 metres (1640 feet). As the vines mature, the wines get better: the early vintages were rather light, if with some good perfume, but the

85 (tasted in 1988) shows considerable complexity and an elegance of style, despite the rather obvious taste of the American oak in which it is matured.

RAIMAT   **→

The Raimat estate, owned by the Raventos family which makes the Codorniú sparkling Cava in Penedés, is in an outlying, semi-desert region to the west of Lérida. The newly-established DO is Costers del Segre, but in effect Raimat is the only producer of note in the area (apart from the estate of Castell del Remey, where there are small plantings of Cabernet Sauvignon). The estate has been planted since 1914, but it is still conveniently regarded as experimental, which means that essential irrigation is possible. Cabernet Sauvignon is used in two wines, the Raimat Abadia, a blend of 50 percent Cabernet with 35 percent Tempranillo and 15 percent Garnacha, recent vintages of which seem to be much too heavily dominated by wood; and a Cabernet Sauvignon (with 10 percent Merlot and 5 percent Tempranillo), the 85 (tasted in 1989) smooth, rich and elegant, but stylishly concentrated.

BODEGAS TORRES   ***

The Torres family has been instrumental in opening up the vineyards of the Penedés, in Catalonia, to the use of imported grape varieties, either in a blend with local varieties or on their own. They have taken advantage of the different climates in the area – very hot on the coast, much cooler inland up the slopes of the hills at 700 metres (2297 feet) – to plant varieties in the climatic region that would suit them. The Cabernet is planted in the central area, between the coast and the hills. Torres make a number of wines using Cabernet. Coronas is based on 14 percent Cabernet with the balance from Tempranillo; Gran Coronas is 70 percent Cabernet, 30 percent Tempranillo, making richly toasty wine with piles of ripe fruit. Gran Coronas Black Label, from the single Mas la Plana vineyard is 100 percent Cabernet, matured half in French and half in American oak: the 83 (tasted in 1990) showed the quality of this wine, with mature, spicy fruit, ripe taste, excellent wood and fruit balance, excellent cassis flavours, and still with some tannins.

Portugal

The spread of Cabernet Sauvignon in Portugal has been slow. There are still only a few plantings spread around the country. In the Douro one estate, that of Pimentel, has some Cabernet which is blended with local grapes in the red Douro table wine to considerable effect. Further south, the Ribatejo region in the Tagus river valley has some Cabernet, but I have yet to find out where the grapes go once picked. In the Setúbal peninsula, the go-ahead winery of João Pires, with its Australian winemaker, produces a Cabernet Sauvignon and Merlot wine from the nearby Quinta da Bacalhoa (**→) which is aged in wood to give a well-balanced perfumed wine, the 87 (tasted in 1990) showing considerable new wood tastes on firm, slightly acid wine, the whole needing ageing for two to three years more.

Bulgaria

The Cabernet Sauvignon has been the catalyst for Bulgaria's enormous success as a wine exporting nation. Bulgarian Cabernet Sauvignon is the biggest selling red wine in the shops in Britain. Its low price, and reliable quality, coupled with the British consumers' familiarity with a winestyle based on Bordeaux grapes, have all ensured its leading place.

The modern wine industry in Bulgaria is a product of the collectivization of farms after the Communist government came to power in 1946. This enabled large-scale vineyards to be planted, and modern processing facilities to be installed. In the early 1960s, a range of non-Bulgarian grape varieties were introduced, including Cabernet Sauvignon, and it is now the dominant red-grape variety in the country. The Bulgarian authorities have delimited certain areas for grape growing, and have specified varieties to be grown. As a further parallel to a French *appellation contrôlée* system, they have also created smaller areas within each larger region which can produce what are called Controliran wines which are regarded as reserve wines.

Cabernet is now planted widely throughout the country, but certain areas are seen as making the best examples. The northern and southern regions are the main Cabernet areas. The Suhindol winery in the north of the country makes the largest quantities of Cabernet, and supplies the most familiar blend for export; the winery further north at Svishtov on the banks of the Danube also makes a delimited Cabernet. In the south of the country, the winery of Assenovgrad in the Plovdiv region is another source, while Cabernet also comes from Melnik and the mountains of Sakar.

Identifying regional characteristics is difficult. The aim is to make wines that suit Western European palates rather than emphasizing origins. But it does seem that Svishtov is the source of some of the most classically French Cabernet, slightly austere, but elegant; while Plovdiv makes a wine that is richer, more New World in style.

The overall quality of the range would put many producers in Italy or France to shame. High production of the Cabernet from Suhindol has had its effect on quality: the 85 (tasted in 1989) showed decent enough varietal character, but did seem somewhat dilute. However, the 84 Cabernet from Plovdiv (tasted in 1989) showed depth of flavour and strong woody tannins, while the 85 Svishtov Cabernet (tasted in 1989) was ripe, soft and elegant, with good clean fruit. The superior 84 Controliran Cabernet from Svishtov (tasted in 1989) had an old, mature taste, rather too acid and woody for the fruit. The 85 Cabernet from Melnik (tasted in 1989) had ripe, dusty, perfumed flavours that showed well against light tannins. The 83 Sakar Mountain Cabernet (tasted in 1989) seemed too light for the amount of wood used.

Argentina

The Argentine wine industry has 346,000ha (855,000 acres) of vineyards, making it the fifth-largest producer in the world. Yet the overall quality of the wine is still so poor that little gets exported. There are large-scale Cabernet plantings in Mendoza province on the eastern slopes of the Andes, and the grape makes the best red wines around. Good producers include: Bodegas Trapiche with their Andean Vineyards label; José Orfila with their Cautivo label; Humberto Canale; Goyenecha, with the strangely-named Aberdeen Angus wine, a blend of Cabernet and Syrah; and Bodegas Esmeralda, who produce a blended Cabernet with Malbec, called St Felicien.

Brazil

Cabernet Sauvignon is planted among the 70,000ha (173,000 acres) of vines in the southernmost province of Brazil, Rio Grande do Sul, bordering Uruguay. I have only tasted one Cabernet from the country, produced by the largest firm, Palomas. On the basis of that tasting, it seems the country has a long way to go.

Israel

The new high-tech winery of Yarden in the Golan Heights is producing a good range of varietal wines, including a Cabernet Sauvignon: the 86 (tasted in 1988) had excellent character, good purple colour, with a slightly sweet, warm flavour and cassis fruit.

Lebanon

Cabernet Sauvignon is one of the elements in the blended Château Musar, grown in the Bekaa Valley of Lebanon and made at winery north of Beirut. Apart from losing crops because of the devastating effect of the Civil War, producer Serge Hochar manages to make remarkable wines of world-class quality, with a blend mainly of Cabernet, with some Syrah and Cinsaut. The wines age remarkably well, and the 80 vintage (tasted in 1989) was vibrantly youthful, with rich, smooth fruit tastes.

Index

Page numbers in **bold type** refer
to main entries.

Adelaide 9
Alexander Valley 8, 78
Alto Adige 10, 147, **148–9**
Anjou 75
Appellation contrôlée 16, 26
Aragon 154
Arcins 34
Argentina **157**
Arsac 57
Auckland 123, 124
Australia 4, 8–9, 14, 15, 16, 17,
    18, 19, 21–2, 26, **103–23**
    autovinification 21–2
    blended wines 5, 103–4
    climate 15, 104, 105
    wine-making process 21–2,
    105–6
Authorised Vineyard Areas
    (AVAs) 78

Barossa Valley 9, 104, 105
Baux-en-Provence, Les **74**
Bekaa Valley 157
Bergerac **71–2**
Blended wines 5, 10, 76, 77,
    101, 103–4, 133, 137, 138,
    147, 148, 153
Bordeaux 4, 14–15, 20–1,
    26–71
    appellations 16, 26, 28
    claret 26
    classification system 26–7
    climate 14, 15
    diseases 16–17
    second wines 27
    soil types 14–15
    vintages 29
    wine-making process **20–1**,
    29–30
Bourgueil 75
Boutique wineries 76
Brazil **157**
Breganze 149
Buena Vista 8
Bulgaria 10, **156**
    Controliran wines 156
Burgundy 4
Buzet **72**

Cabardès 73
California 4, 8, 14, 15–16, 17,
    18, 22, 26, **75–100**
    Authorised Vineyard Areas
    (AVAs) 78
    autovinification 22
    blended wines 76, 77
    boutique wineries 76
    climate 8, 15, 78
    Reserve Cabernets 77, 79
    single vineyard wines 76
    wine-making process 22, 76–7,
    79
Canopy management 123

Cantenac 57
Canterbury 124
Carmignano 147
Catalonia 153
Chaptalization 20
Charentes 15
Chianti 10, 147, 151
Chile 9, 15, 16, 17, 18, **132–6**
    climate 133
    ungrafted vines 9, 132
    wine-making process **133**
Chinon 75
Cissac-Médoc 34
Clare 9, 105
Claret **4**, 26
Climate 5, 7, **15–16**, 26, 28–9,
    78, 104, 123, 124, 154
    Australia 15
    Bordeaux 14, 15
    California 15
    diseases 17
    New Zealand 15
Colli Berici 149
Colli Bolognesi 150
Colli Euganei 149
Colli Piacentini 150
Collio Goriziano (Collio) 150
Columbia River 101
Constantina 138
Controliran wines 156
Coonawarra 14, 15, 18, 104, 105
Corsica **75**
Coteaux d'Aix en Provence **74–5**
Côtes de Bergerac 71
Côtes de Duras **72**
Côtes du Lubéron 73
Côtes de la Malapère 73
Côtes du Marmandais **73**
Côtes de Provence 74, **75**
Couquèques 14
Cru bourgeois 27
Cru Bourgeois Supérieur 27
Cru classé 27
Cru Grand Bourgeois 27
Cru Grand Bourgeois Exceptionnel 27
Curico 133
Cussac-Fort-Médoc 34

Denominacion de Origen (DO)
    154
Denominazione di Origine
    Controllata (DOC) 148
Denominazione di Origine
    Controllata Garantita (DOCG) 148

Emilia-Romagna 147, **150**
Entre-deux-Mers 6, 7, 18
Eutypiose 17

Fermentation **19–22**, 29, 79,
    105–6, 138
    autovinification 21–2
    chaptalization 20
    malolactic **21**, 29, 79, 106, 125
    Potter fermenters 19–20, 21–2,
    105

rotofermentation 22, 79
stalks and pips 105
wood, fermenting and ageing in
  20–1, **22–3**, 29–30, 76, 79,
  101, 106, 125
Fernhill 15
Food and Cabernet Sauvignon
  11
France 14–15, **26–75**
Franciacorta 147, 148
Franshhoek Valley 138
Friuli 10, 147, 148, **150**

Geelong 105
Gisborne 123, 124
Giulia **150**
Golan Heights 157
Goulburn River 9
Graves 4, 5, 6–9, 14, 16, 18, 28,
  66–71
  classification system 27
Grey rot 16–17
Growing Cabernet Sauvignon
  14–19
  Australia 104, **105**
  Bordeaux **28–9**
  California **78–9**
  canopy management 123
  climate 5, 7, **15–16**, 26, 28–9,
    78, 104, 123, 124, 154
  clonal selection 18–19, 123
  diseases 7, 16–17, 78–9, 133
  growing season 17
  harvesting 18
  history **5–10**
  Italy **147**
  New Zealand **124**
  quality management 17–18
  ripening techniques 17–18
  soil types **14–16**, 26, 28, 40,
    45, 52, 57, 64, 67, 78
  South Africa **138**
  trellising 18
  ungrafted vines 9, 132
  yields 16, 79
Guyot trellising 18

Haut-Brion 27
Haut-Médoc 27, 28, **34–40**
Hawke's Bay 14, 15, 124
Heretaunga Plain 15
Hunter Valley 9, 104, 105

Israel **157**
Italy 10, 16, 18, **146–53**
  blended wines 10, 147, 148
  Chianti 147, 151
  Denominazione di Origine
    Controllata (DOC) 148
  Denominazione di Origine
    Controllata Garantita (DOCG)
    148
  Sassicaia 16, 147
  Solaia 147
  vino da tavola 148, 151

Labarde 57
Lamarque 34
Langhe 148

Languedoc **73**
Lazio 147
Lebanon **157**
Léognan 67
Lison-Pramaggiore 149
Listrac 28, 34, **64–6**
Loire **75**
Lombardy 147, **151**
Lontue 133

McLaren Vale 105
Maipo Valley 16, 133
Mallorca 154
Mancha, La 154
Margaret River 18, 105
Margaux 28, 34, **57–64**
Marlborough 124
Martillac 67
Martinborough 124
Maturation 10, 20, 23, 29, 30,
  76
Maule River Valley 133
Médoc 4, 5, 6–9, 14, 16, 18, 28,
  30–4
  classification system 26–7
  crus bourgeois 27
Melnik 156
Mendocino 78
Mendoza 157
Midi 73
Milawa 105
Mildew 16
Molina 133
Montalcino 151
Montepulciano 151
Monterey 8, 17, 78
Moulis 28, 34, **64–6**

Napa Valley 4, 8, 14, 15–16, 18,
  76, 77, 78
Navarra 154
New South Wales 105
New Zealand 4, 9, 14, 15, 17, 18,
  104, **123–32**
  canopy management 123
  climate 15, 123, 124
  wine-making process **125**
Ngaruroro River 15

Oak, fermenting and ageing in 5,
  20–1, **22–3**, 29–30, 76, 79,
  101, 106, 125, 133, 137, 138,
  155
  new wood 22–3
  toasted casks 23
Oakville 78
Oidium 7, 16
Opus One 77
Oregon 8, 17

Paarl 138
Padthaway 105
Patagonia 133
Pauillac 28, 34, **45–51**
Pécharmant **71–2**
Pessac 67
Pessac-Léognan 27, 28, **66–7**
Phylloxera beetle 7, 9, 77, 78–9,
  132, 133

Piave 149
Piedmont 10, 147, **148**
Plovdiv 156
Pomerol 7, 14, 26, 28
Portugal 19, **155**
Poverty Bay 124
Premières Côtes de Bordeaux 6,
  18
Provence **74**
Pyrenees (Australian) 105

Reserve Cabernets 77, 79, 156
Ribatejo 155
Ribera del Duero 153
Rio Grande do Sul 157
Rioja 154
Roussillon **73–4**
Rutherford 78
Rutherford Bench 15–16

St-Emilion 7, 14, 26, 28
  classification system 27
St-Estèphe 14, 28, 34, **40–4**
St Helena 78
St-Julien 28, 34, **51–7**
St-Laurent-et-Benon 34
St-Sauveur 34
St-Seurin-de-Cadourne 34
St-Yzans de Médoc 14
Sakar 156
Santa Barbara 78
Santa Clara Valley 8
Santa Cruz mountains 8
Santiago 16, 133
Sassicaia 16, 147
Saumur-Champigny 75
Sauternes
  classification system 27
Second wines 27
Setùbal peninsula 155
Soil types **14–16**, 26, 28, 40, 45,
  52, 57, 64, 67, 78
  Bordeaux 14–15
Solaia 147
Somontano 154
Sonoma 8, 15, 77, 78
Soussans 57
South Africa 9–10, 17, 18,
  137–46
  blended wines 138
  climate 137
  wine-making process **138**
South Australia 9
Spain 10, **153–5**
  blended wines 153
  Denominacion de Origen (DO)
    154
Stag's Leap 78
Stellenbosch 10, 138
Sudtirol **148**
Suhindol 156
Svishtov 156

Tasmania 9

Touraine 75
Trentino 147, **148–9**
Tuki Tuki River 15
Tuscany 10, 16, 147, 148,
  151–3

Umbria 147, **151–3**
United States 4, 8, 14, 15–16,
  17, 18, 22, 26, **75–103**
  Authorised Vineyard Areas
    (AVAs) 78

Valcalepio 148
Valdepenas 154
Value for money **25**
Veneto, The 10, 147, 148,
  149–50
Venezia **150**
Victoria 9, 105
Vin de Pays de l'Hérault 73–4
Vin de Pays de l'Isle de Beauté
  75
Vino da tavola 148, 151
Vintages 29

Walla Walla Valley 101
Washington State 8, **100–3**
Wine-making process **19–23**
  Australia 21–2, **105–6**
  autovinification 21–2
  blended wines 5, 10, 76, 77,
    101, 103–4, 133, 137, 138,
    147, 148, 153
  Bordeaux **20–1**, **29–30**
  bottle-maturation 23
  bottling 30
  California 22, 76–7, **79**
  chaptalization 20
  Chile **133**
  fermentation **19–22**, 29, 79,
    105–6, 138
  filtering 30
  fining 30
  malolactic fermentation **21**, 29,
    79, 106, 125
  maturation 10, 20, 23, 29, 30, 76
  modern techniques 19–20, 21–
    2, 29, 79
  New Zealand **125**
  Potter fermenters 19–20, 21–2,
    105
  remontage 20
  rotofermentation 22, 79
  South Africa **138**
  tannin levels 105, 125
  toasting barrels 23
  traditional 20–1
  wood, fermenting and ageing in
    5, 20–1, **22–3**, 29–30, 76, 79,
    101, 106, 125, 133, 137, 138,
    155

Yakima Valley 101
Yarra Valley 105